Show Me the Place

Show me the Place
ESSAYS

HEDLEY TWIDLE

JONATHAN BALL PUBLISHERS
JOHANNESBURG & CAPE TOWN

All rights reserved.
No part of this publication may be reproduced or transmitted, in any form or by any means, without prior permission from the publisher or copyright holder.

© Text: Hedley Twidle (2024)
© Published edition: Jonathan Ball Publishers (2024)

Originally published in South Africa in 2024 by
JONATHAN BALL PUBLISHERS
A division of Media24 (Pty) Ltd
PO Box 33977
Jeppestown
2043

ISBN 978-1-77619-320-2
ebook ISBN 978-1-77619-321-9

Every effort has been made to trace the copyright holders and to obtain their permission for the use of copyright material. The publishers apologise for any errors or omissions and would be grateful to be notified of any corrections that should be incorporated in future editions of this book.

jonathanball.co.za
x.com/JonathanBallPub
facebook.com/JonathanBallPublishers

Cover by Gretchen van der Byl
Design and typesetting by Johan Koortzen
Set in Adobe Garamond Pro 11.5 pt on 15 pt

The troubles came, I saved what I could save
A thread of light, a particle, a wave
Leonard Cohen, 'Show Me the Place'

A journey is a gesture inscribed in space, it vanishes even as it's made. You go from one place to another place, and on to somewhere else again, and already behind you there is no trace that you were ever there. The roads you went down yesterday are full of different people now, none of them knows who you are. In the room you slept in last night a stranger lies in the bed. Dust covers over your footprints, the marks of your fingers are wiped off the door, from the floor and table the bits and pieces of evidence that you might have dropped are swept up and thrown away and they never come back again. The very air closes behind you like water and soon your presence, which felt so weighty and permanent, has completely gone. Things happen once only and are never repeated, never return. Except in memory.
Damon Galgut, *In a Strange Room*

Contents

Offshore	1
To spite his face	17
The transformation workshop	39
A line of light	53
The utopia project	79
The lonely planet	101
Otro mundo	125
Monsoon raag	143
Five by three	179
Notes and sources	225
Acknowledgements	229

Offshore

Thirty-six is no longer young, promising or even emerging. It's one year too late to join the Youth League and twenty years too late to start surfing, especially in the wild, cold waters at the southern tip of Africa.

All that lost time weighs on us, Alex and me. We watch teenagers or outright children paddle onto some heaving Atlantic swell, make the drop, carve some shapes along the moving, blue-green wall then kick out like it was the easiest thing in the world.

'Poets,' he would say, beard in hand, as we watched from a car park in the depths of winter, when the swells come in. 'There are poets among us.'

Alex and I both have beards that are beginning to go silver, but I'm average height and skinny while he is tall and rangy, muscular. We are both only children, sort of, both loners who like having someone to play with, now and then. We both have odd surnames that nobody can spell or pronounce.

After sessions that had gone more than usually badly – when we had fluffed a take-off in front of Coach, or our boards had gone vaulting over the white water, or (worst of all) we had pretended to paddle and miss a wave when in fact we were too chicken to take it – Alex could be less philosophical:

'All those years, doing what? Jerking off in the suburbs. When I could've been at Long Beach in fifteen minutes.'

His new cold-water hood made him look somehow Nordic. Hooded, bearded, grizzled: he looked, I guess, better than he was. Out in the back line he seemed to get the kind of respect I never do. He looked like the kind of Kommetjie big wave surfer who might get towed onto a moving hillside of ocean out by Dungeons, then keep it monosyllabic in the post-sesh debrief: 'It's a team effort out there, I rely on my guys.'

But the fact is we were struggling to deal with a dirty two-foot shorebreak off the Milnerton lighthouse carpark, where the water tasted of phosphates and Alex had at one point emerged trailing a nappy from his leash. And this gap was getting to him, to us: the gap between our surfing aspirations and abilities. Between the utter sublimity of what we were seeing – up close at the Gat or the Hoek; online in YouTube clips from Portugal, Ireland, Bali, the endlessly spooling barrels of Namibia's Skeleton Bay – and the prolonged humbling that the middle-aged kook (beginner) must endure.

When we were younger, Alex did a school exchange and as a result still holds the Scottish under-16 record for high jump. Many of us remember how he would sail over that bar in a state of grace. That strange, floating, corkscrewing motion – I didn't have the vaguest notion of how it might or could feel in the body: it was literally unimaginable. He played club football in Cape Town for many years with great focus, forbidding anyone he knew to come and watch him. He venerates the one-time midfielder Zinedine Zidane and in fact looks a bit like him: craggy and intense. His mother has dementia, as mine once did: something we have discussed far out to sea in a world of grey glass and mist, or in a howling offshore that whips our words away as soon as they are spoken. The only memory that his mother has left of me is school sports days, when all those who didn't qualify for anything else were placed in a 1 500-metre race at the end of the day, a sort of hold-all charity event.

'And I remember how he used to *wa-a-a-a-a-ve* when he went past!' This is what she would say, and he liked to bring it out. 'With a big grin on his face, so happy! *W-a-a-a-a-ving* to the crowd.'

My only claim to sporting prowess was a brief period when my tennis was good enough, or infuriating enough, to earn me the nickname 'The Wall'. And this difference between Alex and me – not just in athletic ability, but also sporting philosophy – has played out in various ways during our surf career to date. He wants grandeur, the Romantic sublime, feats of perfection and beauty. He has known them in his youth, and so expects them, hopes for them again. Any success for me would come, if at all, via attrition and doggedness. But mostly it was undiluted humiliation out there: being whistled off a wave by a seven-year-old, or chucking your board and diving for the bottom as the next set rumbles in near the Koeberg nuclear plant, on a day when no one else is in the water and your car window's already been smashed, when you start hyperventilating to get enough air into your system ahead of what you know is coming: the underwater somersaults of a long, glorious Atlantic hold-down.

'Five years,' said Alex, who had been googling, 'Five years to get to a decent level. If—,' and this was the kicker, 'you surf every day.'

Coach believed there was still time for us. He grew up near Vic Bay, one of the most reliable point breaks in the country: endless afternoons of peeling rights. What one needed to learn, he said, was a consistent wave without too many changing variables. One needed the closest natural equivalent to Kelly Slater's wave pool in California, recently constructed and consistently delivering identical, mud-coloured inland tubes in front of all the Budweiser stalls and corporate boxes. Working with chaos mathematicians, the ex-world champion had engineered the surf equivalent of cracking the human genome: truly we were living in the end times.

Coach's build was compact and muscular. He had that mystical quantum of extra time afforded the athlete. When catching a wave (seemingly without paddling – he was always at the right peak at the right time) he would do a sort of mini cobra pose, a half-press-up, looking left and right before deciding whether to pop up. If yes, it was already done, and he was now moving along the face, describing thoughtful curves, his gaze far ahead and down the line.

Though ten years younger than us, Coach brought great emotional intelligence to bear in the role of surf mentor. Never too quick to praise nor to blame, he was a master of understatement (to Alex's annoyance he would never specify how big a swell was in figures), and a paragon of back line etiquette. On his own time he mainly surfed the feral, kelpy breaks near Cape Point. Snorkelling once in those parts had been enough for me. As I dropped from a rock ledge down through water so planktonic and full of nutrients that it was almost soupy, I had a strong bodily sense that something was near, was aware of me.

Coach downplayed such dangers and said these breaks were the only places left where surfers had any manners. But for a year or so, right at the start, he graciously accompanied us to wherever the wind was offshore.

The on/offshore question is the fundamental binary of surfing; it determines everything. Onshore winds (blowing from sea to land) are pure evil: they mangle the swell, breaking ranks, knocking waves on the back of the head, spilling them over themselves into a grey-brown mush. Offshore winds (blowing from land to sea) are godly: they comb the swell into stately lines, with spray pluming behind, walls going green and barrels hollow.

Offshore winds 'wreathe waves in glory', writes William Finnegan in *Barbarian Days*: 'They groom them, hold them up and prevent them from breaking for a crucial extra beat ... On a good day, their sculptor's blade, meticulous and invisible, seems to drench whole coastlines in grace.' His epic memoir of a surfing life ranges from the warm-water tubes of Hawaii and Bali to the cold-water bombs of San Francisco and Madeira. And since the author spent some time teaching at a 'Coloured' school in Cape Town's Grassy Park during the 1980s, the book even touches on Surfers' Corner, the nursery at nearby Muizenberg. Vaguely embarrassed even to be thinking about waves at the height of the anti-apartheid struggle, Finnegan quickly dispenses with it as 'a wide, shapeless beach break' that he surfed when not too busy grading papers or planning lessons. It stung a little, seeing a patch of ocean where I'd spent so much time reduced to those four words.

Because Cape Town is at the head of a coastal peninsula, you can, in theory, always find a break where the wind is offshore. If the summer southeaster is turning False Bay into a foaming algal mess, it will be producing crystalline A-frames on the other side at Dunes. If the winter northwester has reduced Glen Beach to a disgusting slop of stormwater and sewage blowback, then Muizenberg might finally be coming into its own. Pulled over near the Shark Spotters booth uphill, you will see dark-blue lines queuing up from far out to sea.

There is, however, a problem with learning to surf in this city, or at least with advancing beyond beginner. Yes, there is the broad, sheltered, multidenominational church of Surfers' Corner. Here, young and old, short-boarders and long-boarders, stand-up paddlers and surf tourists, can all have a grand old time getting in each other's way and being very decent about it.

'Too happy clappy,' said Alex. 'It's like Sunday school out there'.

But as soon as you want to move out and up a step, there is no intermediate stage. The remaining options are the icy, bone-crunching breaks of the west coast, where waves are fast, steep, hollow and (like the local crews who dominate them) unforgiving.

'The close, painstaking study of a tiny patch of coast,' writes Finnegan, 'every eddy and angle, even down to individual rocks, and in every combination of tide and wind and swell – a longitudinal study, through season after season, is the basic occupation of surfers at their local break. Getting a spot wired – truly understanding it – can take years. At very complex breaks, it's a lifetime's work.'

My local break is Glen, just five minutes up and over the hill from the city apartment where I live. I have been conducting a longitudinal study of it for ten years now – first as bodysurfer, then surfer – but the results remain inconclusive. It is so fickle, changeable, powerful – by turns sucky, wedgy, peaky, slabby – and full of the city's best surfers. During one session, I tried to duck-dive under a set and failed; or at least the wave somehow took and pushed me about fifty metres backwards, all of this underwater, like a cold relentless hand against my forehead, pushing me until I was almost back on the beach. I bobbed up near a local who was just beginning his paddle. 'Fuck,' he said, looking straight at me. Not 'fuck you' or 'fucking hell,' just 'fuck' – as if the disbelief, or maybe just the cold, was so intense that he couldn't bring himself to go any further. Having witnessed this, Alex had to go back to shore and lean on his knees, he was laughing that hard.

Over beers afterwards, I was tempted to broach the issue of the 'poo stance': a derisive term for beginners who do a bent-kneed squat on the board, and which is more prominent (and hilarious) in a taller 'poo man' like Alex. With typical ambition, he would crouch down on a narrow, five-foot-something, high-performance board that I christened the Toothpick; whereas I (five ten) went for a seven-footer: longer boards are more buoyant and easier to paddle. But this kind of teasing was against the advice of Coach, who had said that the question of poo-manning was 'a sensitive issue that needed to be delicately handled'.

Alex, not making as much sporting progress as he was used to, was trapped inside on a biggish day soon after. He stormed out of the ocean and began a six-month, anti-surfing sulk during which I was left to plough the choppy furrows of False Bay alone. There were tantalising moments that winter, glimpses of greater things: there always are. One day the ragged lines resolved into a long, grey wall that delivered me all the way from back line to shallows, a full minute's worth it felt like, until I dived ecstatically off the board way out beyond the old pavilion.

But a surf session often proceeds according to the law of diminishing returns: as your arms tire out, you are less and less able to paddle onto waves, or under them. Sometimes I would reach a kind of disorientated fugue state out there in the grey wash cycle, towed along the coast by strange rips, far from shore, not knowing quite where I was or what I was hoping to achieve. Where were the outputs, the deliverables, the take-homes? What was there to show for this outrageous amount of time devoted to sitting on a seven-foot fibreglass raft while the world burned? You should have called it after that last decent ride; but you don't, and then there is the ultimate humiliation of paddling back to shore. At certain points that winter, I remember being almost too exhausted to pull off my wetsuit. There I would be, towel round my knees in a car park near the railway line, freezing, thinking: What are you *doing*?

Alex was focusing on his job as the headmaster of a primary school in Philippi, one of the poorest and most violent parts of the city. He had been the founding teacher and was growing the school year by year: each January another intake of Grade Ones. I had gone out there a few times to give the kids ukulele lessons. Alex stalked around in his skinny jeans and long coat, six foot plus and mock serious amid all the kids who would mob his car when he arrived each day, shouting his unpronounceable name with delight. I put it to Principal that

Muizenberg was actually very close, for an after-work session, I meant. But he spoke disdainfully about all the tourists clogging up the water now that summer was coming, and bent his head back over Singapore maths, saying maybe we could try Derdesteen, if traffic wasn't too bad.

As I slowly improved, I also began trying out a bit of surf lingo and surf hauteur, which is full of mockery poked at beginners and complaints about crowds and tourists. But to disparage tourists while being a tourist, or traffic when you were traffic, or crowded breaks when you were part of the crowd – this was, Coach had once pronounced, 'the way of the barbarian'.

The remark was not related to Finnegan's book but somehow got tangled up in my reading of it. The title *Barbarian Days* comes from an epigraph by Edward St Aubyn: 'He had become so caught up in building sentences that he had almost forgotten the barbaric days when thinking was like a splash of colour landing on a page.'

Throughout his life, Finnegan chases some of the world's greatest waves as antidote to his job as foreign correspondent and *New Yorker* staff writer: the sea as a respite from tinkering with sentences. But when he turns to writing about waves in late career (and becomes famous for it), he must reckon with a paradox at the heart of surf culture: that the search for the perfect, uncrowded wave inevitably contains (when photographed or written or bragged about) the seeds of its own downfall: surf tourism. As a young man, Finnegan is one of the first to surf a paradisal reef break on a remote island off Fiji. Towards the end of the book he returns to the place, now a surf lodge full of social media streams and spectator boats.

Barbarian Days is wonderfully ambivalent about the world it describes. Finnegan doesn't even seem sure if he likes surfers, or surf culture. Living and paddling out along San Francisco's forbidding Ocean Beach, he is steadily writing about other things: finishing his books on 1980s Cape Town and travels with black reporters in Soweto, still feeling 'mentally flayed' by his time in the country. To write about surfing was something different, and closer to home: it risked losing the 'sizable tract of unconsciousness' near the centre of his life, the self-enclosed, non-verbal quality which means that most surf line-ups are quiet, with everyone cocooned in their own space and silence, not places for the loud or garrulous.

Stacked five deep in my local surf shop, *Barbarian Days* must be responsible for unleashing droves of bookish, middle-aged groms like me on the already crowded line-ups of the English-speaking world. And it is in the surf shop that such contradictions reach a particular intensity, since they are run by locals who are often kitting out kooks (from the Hawaiian *kuk*, meaning shit). The proprietor didn't seem amped to be selling me a wetsuit, given that it might enable me to ruin his wave later that day at Llandudno.

'Your arms are thin all the way up to the shoulders, so this one isn't tight enough.'

I soon realised that it was a broad-based misanthropy though: nothing personal. When another customer walked in, they soon established they were both from Durban, where all you needed was boardies and at worst a rashie. The shop owner began a litany of complaints:

'It's shit in Cape Town. First it's kak cold, then you have to drive everywhere, it's always a mission. In summer it's the wind, in winter it's too big. I've got ear infections bru – three operations now. In Durbs you just stroll on over.'

'But Glen?' said the punter. 'That's nearby?'

'It's a kak wave. Those sandbars move around, then there's all that churned up kelp, all those little bits. And the stream running in there – disgusting. All the shit they pump out there. No man, it's a kak wave, literally.'

Drone footage shot by concerned ratepayers had shown plumes of raw sewage being released just off the city's most expensive beaches, a few hundred metres away from the bungalow mansions and anchored party boats. According to a recent scientific study, Kalk Bay snoek were full of ibuprofen and Hout Bay anemones showed traces of antiretrovirals. High levels of anti-anxiety and heart meds in the urchins off Sea Point – just some of the many drugs that filtered daily through bladders and pipes and then out to sea. Every sea creature was full of caffeine, apparently, and probably cocaine too: what must that be like? And several of the desalination plants meant to rescue us from drought couldn't run. On the Atlantic coast the water in the docks was too polluted; on the Indian ocean side the problem was algal blooms and red tides.

Despite knowing all this, I somehow still retained my idea of seawater as a healthy, bracing, salty tonic – right up until the session when Alex brushed his foot against a rock in Glen and walked out with an inflamed toe 'so angry that it was squeaking'. Only swift medical action saved the digit, or even the foot. The staph infection required hospitalisation, and he was on crutches for a while.

After 'Glen Toe', he was more ready to dial things down a little, and we began leading surf outings for the kids from Philippi and Marcus Garvey. I was feeling good about this: taking kids to the ocean, suiting up, combining surfing with social outreach – what was not to like? And they were hugely excited as we guided them across the car park and into the hire shop. The man behind the counter looked up at me and said:

'Your wetsuit's on backwards.'

I ran out and back to the car to rip off this burning shirt of humiliation: how could it have happened, a wetsuit I had put on a hundred times before?

Alex wisely didn't refer to this moment ever again, but he and the owner would exchange a knowing smile every time we arrived with the kids. Then we would wade out into the shallows with two or three shrieking, terrified, delighted children attached to us and try to stand them on a foam board, while also scanning obsessively to make sure that none of the others were being dragged out or under. Often we had to cut our sessions short because one of the assistant teachers would find us and say that people were throwing stones at Golden Arrow buses on Eisleben Road, or that tyres were burning near the school gate, and it looked like it might get worse, so we should go now. I half suspected they were just bored waiting on the shore, but we would then drag everyone out of the water and the wetsuits and back onto the bus. Then we might paddle out to the back line for our own session, and the quiet and self-enclosure would return. Thinking back to that melee with the kids in the white water – touch and go at times – I realised I had never been clutched so hard by anyone.

After the trials of summer – crowds, traffic, wind, days of flat seas – winter is here again. Monster storms detonate somewhere between Africa and Antarctica, aftershocks of swell hit the southern peninsula days later, and these break in turn into our social media feeds. Suddenly there are galleries of old warriors and young chargers dropping unimaginably deep into hollows that – just from the wind-scoured, bottle-green of them – you know to be utterly, skull-achingly frigid: the kind of cold that sews ear bones closed. At this point Alex will start getting excited and sending messages, wanting us to hit up Llandudno or Thermopylae, a menacing spot named for an old wreck off the Sea Point promenade, one only roused by the chunkiest westerly swell. Here we will (if we even manage to make it out) sit on our boards and let wave after wave pass underneath us, spray whipping back into our faces and the boom of it reaching us a second later.

After several sessions of this, when there was no more pride left to swallow, I had to give a pep talk:

'We're ten years away from those waves, at least. Not five, *ten*. We're Chopsticks level, and this is Rachmaninov. We're ukulele, this is Stradivarius.'

And when he started complaining again about the crowds and evangelists at the surf-industrial complex of Muizenberg, I reminded him that we were socialists. Or at least that he had a poster of Jeremy Corbyn on the wall, and that on our surf trip to Vic Bay he had talked my ear off about the British Labour leader and the unwarranted attacks on him by the corporate media. All the way from Riviersonderend to the PetroSA refinery, Alex raged against the anti-Corbynite smear campaign, which was destroying one of the last hopes for a progressive government in the West, which hid its nefarious agenda under the patently ridiculous accusation of anti-Semitism. Which got him started on Israel and Palestine, and then the Christian Zionist lobby, then Modi, Bolsonaro and Trump, who was building sea walls for his Scottish golf courses even while denying climate change – the sheer anti-human cynicism, the flagrancy of these people, like being forced to eat a turd! Every day, another turd like the one we'd seen floating off Milnerton being gradually forced into your mouth.

It was such a long and impassioned performance, continuing along the backroads as we were diverted off the highway, first due to protests and then smoke from bushfires, that I eventually asked him, over some lasagne in Wilderness, what was actually on his mind. And he confessed that he had just learnt, just before getting in the car, that he was going to be a father.

And so our trip became both the peak of our surf career so far and the beginning of its end, or at least the end of its beginning. The barbarian phase was over. The scandalous stretches of open time and space needed for the pastime would soon be radically reduced, at least for one of us. We needed, Alex said, to make it count.

Vic Bay is V-shaped and compact with steep walls, more of a cove, really. On its right-hand shore, cottages line a track almost all the way to the point, which means that instead of paddling from the beach you can walk right up to the take-off zone, then pick your way across a few rocks, jump out and you're in position. Schooled on the wide, shapeless beach breaks of Cape Town, where sometimes the backline moves hundreds of metres out to sea and a stepladder of rumbling white water bars entry, Alex and I could hardly believe this set-up. We found a room in the guesthouse closest to the point, where, from our romantic and well-appointed flatlet, the wave was just metres away.

For that first afternoon we hung back off the shoulder, sussing it out and catching a few scraps left behind by the locals; but in fact there were no leftovers – every wave got ridden, every set picked clean. So, the next morning we woke before dawn and picked our way down the rocks in the dark. One of us watched for a lull between sets and gave the signal, the other launched across the white water and into position.

For half an hour in the pre-dawn light, we were alone in the water. Great things were accomplished, apparently. Alex says it was my finest hour, but it's curiously hard to remember.

What I do remember is that after a while we were joined by another party, who paddled in from the beach: one woman and three men. From the first instant that she pulled into a wave, it was clear that this was a superb surfer. Her power, control and room for manoeuvre within the tight space of the break was awesome. At one point she came pumping down the line towards me, less with aggression than supreme confidence, then cut back mere centimetres from my face, so that I was drenched by the torque and spray of her board.

'I've been baptised!' I said to the other guys in the line-up, who seemed to be her entourage, maybe one of them was her husband. He laughed.

'I know the feeling.'

A month or so after our trip, Alex emailed me with the subject heading: 'CHECK OUT 5mins47!' and a YouTube clip titled 'Pop Up Like the Pros'. After segments on Kelly and Jordy, there she was, hunkering down at Pipeline doing sick bottom turns. The three-time world champion Carissa Moore, resident of Honolulu! Yes, undoubtedly, I recognised the open face and the powerful stance. We had indeed been baptised by greatness, sprinkled with holy water.

As we sat there, pensive in the dawn, trying to hold our place and maintain our dignity, Alex's board suddenly popped out from between his legs like a piece of soap. Entirely unprovoked, and from a resting position, the Toothpick shot skywards like a surface to air missile, and he capsized backwards into the water right next to Carissa and her husband, her coach, maybe her dietician, the whole crew obviously on the way up the coast to the J-Bay Open, where she would go on to lose ('probably the lowest I've ever felt', according to her Instagram), but then stage a triumphant return the following year. 'My journey is imperfect but I am laughing, loving and learning every step of the way. Thanks for sharing it with me.'

After the birth of his son, Alex began travelling out of the country with his partner, who is French, so that young Marcus (named half after Marcus Aurelius, and half Marcus Garvey) could spend time with his grandparents. I began getting swell updates from the coast of Brittany, and pictures of mussels cooked in cider. Then he would come back alone for stretches, resuming his duties at the school. Though I had the sense that he was winding things up there, and would soon break it to me, somewhere beyond the back line, that they were leaving South Africa for good.

After work and on weekends he would surf obsessively as a means of coping with the sudden separations and was now clearly better than me: a strong paddler who could power through the impact zone. But our attitudes had shifted slightly, switched around a little. He had less to prove, and seemed more at peace with the Anthropocene shore, no matter how scruffy or unromantic. We met more often in the lumpy swell of Milnerton, where the beach was slowly washing away and plastic bags brushed against your feet like delicate seaweed. When conditions were glassy, a brown haze hung over the docks at the foot of Table Mountain.

Whereas I was now more open to the moments of sublimity that surfing reliably delivers, if not in person, then at least via the feats of others. After all, doesn't the world need people who love music without adolescently wanting to be in a band? Yes, absolutely, said Alex, whose decks and vinyl had been in storage for years. And doesn't the world need people who love reading without needing to write books? Who know that there are enough books in the world already, great and unrepeatable masterworks, to be read and enjoyed without childishly comparing every sentence with your own paltry efforts? Yes, all true, he agreed – to act otherwise was the way of the barbarian.

A kind of middle-aged enlightenment was dawning, I told him as we pulled off our wetsuits in the car park, keeping an eye on the twerking video being filmed next to us. A woman in a mini skirt bent over the bonnet and did her thing as the latest gqom banger throbbed from inside a BMW. 'Stop it I like it!' said the car guard who had been trying to sell us fossilised shark teeth. I began shouting it after a pummelling out to sea: 'Stop it I like it!' Now we made a noise out there at the back line, crying to heaven with mock anguish if we fell off a two-foot wave, shaking our fists at the gods. Hamming it up, puncturing the macho solemnity of it all.

Then one day all the breaks suddenly emptied. The COVID pandemic was keeping everyone at home. Our strict lockdown was a special kind of anguish for the surf community, since as the winter swells came in you knew that conditions would never be this perfect and uncrowded again. After a month or so, news spread that surfers had begun violating the regulations: mass paddle-outs, beach trespasses.

Footage went around of police staring helplessly out to sea.

But I was happy to stay home and dry, and to pursue my car park argument to its final logic. The world needed people who loved surfing without feeling the need to surf themselves. Or even further still (I was reinventing the wheel here): who loved watching waves with *nobody on them*. Alex sent me Kookslams compilations of appalling drop-ins and rookies getting dashed onto rocks. I replied with a brooding short called 'Empties': drone footage of Portugal's Nazaré on days just too big and unruly to be rideable. Sixty-foot swells detonated in high definition slo-mo; whole fogbanks of spray blew back across the water in their aftermaths, skittering across the sea surface in the lulls between sets. Now this, I said, was enlightenment: the camera lingering in the emptiness, the stillness between two waves of the sea.

He messaged back that I should pull myself together, do push-ups and be ready to get back in the water.

To spite his face

The nose disappeared from Cecil Rhodes's face in September 2015. It was sliced off the bronze bust in the Rhodes Memorial on the slopes of Table Mountain. The plinth below was spray-painted: THE MASTER'S NOSE BETRAYS HIM.

Since then, it has been at large. Was it stashed at the back of some cupboard or put to use as a paperweight? Did it go underground at a safe house, or was it ironically mounted on the wall by student comrades? Maybe it fled to New Zealand, trying to shuck off its colonial past and live in peace.

I work at the university just downslope from the memorial, and around the time of the disappearance, I was teaching Nikolai Gogol's 1836 story 'The Nose'. In it, the nose of a St Petersburg bureaucrat, Major Kovalyov, vanishes under mysterious circumstances. He wakes up to find a blankness, 'quite flat, just like a freshly cooked pancake', in the middle of his face. We follow this hapless and petty man as he tries to find and confront his nose, which has taken on a life of its own. It is gallivanting round town, wearing a uniform of higher rank than the major, disowning him at every opportunity.

'Imagine what it's like being without such a conspicuous part of your anatomy!' says Kovalyov as he tries to place an advertisement for his missing organ in the papers. When he finds it at Kazan Cathedral, we read: 'The nose's face was completely hidden by the high collar and it was praying with an expression of profound piety.' Censors forced Gogol to change the cathedral to a shopping arcade, on grounds of blasphemy – an example of how the story can co-opt any reader into its ridiculous universe. 'Whatever you may say, these things do happen in this world,' the narrator reflects. 'Rarely, I admit, but they do happen.'

So, when Rhodes's nose vanished, I felt intrigued and somehow implicated. I admired the gesture. Each year as I taught the Gogol again, I was reminded of the unsolved mystery, and would ask for information at the end of lectures, promising to protect my sources. I dreamed of holding that bronze nodule in the palm of my hand. I wondered where it had been and what its adventures might reveal.

In South Africa, the first semester starts in February: high summer, the dry season, fire season. I would be standing up in front of Literature 101 on the hottest day of the year, which often coincided with the opening of Parliament. Rhodes left his Cape Dutch mansion just downslope to future heads of state and the highway below campus would be sealed off so the president could make his way into town to deliver the State of the Nation address, causing mayhem during Cape Town's already chronic rush hour. With the heat, the traffic, the army, the helicopters rattling overhead, the evidence of presidential corruption stacking up, the Rhodes Must Fall student protests brewing – things had a manic feel, as if the city, the country, the whole world was fraying at the edges.

The wind worked on your nerves, kicking up dust on the dry slopes and turning small mountain fires into epic blazes. I often worried that a fire would sweep down from the slopes above the Rhodes Memorial and engulf the university – and then one day it did, just about. I'm writing up this investigation – which is a convoluted one – opposite a charred library, with a view of blackened cypresses outside my office window. They went up like Roman candles, ignited by flying embers.

After several years of asking, I finally got a tip from a student. She said she knew someone who knew someone who had removed Rhodes's nose. Not only that: this person kept on removing it whenever a replacement was stuck on by an organisation called the Friends of Rhodes Memorial. There was a kind of arms race in progress.

'So apparently he has a whole collection of noses,' she told me. 'His name is Josh.'

He'd been at a homeless shelter – that's all she knew. There was a police docket open and her source was nervous, wouldn't say more. But apparently some of the noses were just lying around in the shelter, next to the toaster.

Josh. It didn't sound particularly pan-African, Azanian, or decolonial.

But then again, you never could tell. So much had been written about Rhodes – his statues, his crimes, his legacy. But in the world of the nose, I came to realise, things were never quite what they seemed.

The bust in the Memorial is one of several Rhodes statues in Cape Town. There was a bronze in the middle of the university campus (Rhodes sitting, like Rodin's Thinker) until it was removed during the Rhodes Must Fall protests of 2015. There is another in the city centre (Rhodes striding) amid the trees, museums and pigeons. He raises a vaguely Fascist arm, more Mussolini than Hitler – 'Your hinterland is there!' – and points (as the writer Alex La Guma liked to remark) towards what were once the 'segregated lavatories' of the Company's Garden.

Then there is Rhodes Avenue, Rhodes Drive, Mount Rhodes, not to mention Mandela Rhodes Place – you can't move a metre without running into him. A Rhodesia Road still survives somewhere. There is also Cecilia Forest, which I'd always associated with Simon and Garfunkel and making love to Cecilia in the afternoon, so it came as a shock that I was actually making love to … Cecil John Rhodes.

Who was very likely a closeted gay man. Who kept a collection of stone phalluses from Great Zimbabwe and other ancient African sites in his mansion at Groote Schuur. And surrounded himself with adoring young men who were known as 'Rhodes's lambs'. And had a big granite bathtub of Roman stature – but such a big hunk of stone that it was impossible to have a hot bath: the granite drained out all the heat. No matter: Rhodes the mining magnate, prime minister, financier, fruit farmer, empire builder, white supremacist and warmonger preferred cold, manly baths – of course he did.

Why do I know all this? Because while doing a PhD on the literary history of Cape Town, I got sidetracked by the cautionary tale of Rudyard Kipling, who spent many summers on these slopes as Rhodes's pet writer-in-residence and imperial PR man.

Along with the Roman lion cages, Mediterranean pines, English songbirds, summer houses and zebra paddocks that make the landscape around the University of Cape Town such a bizarre imperial pick 'n mix, Rhodes also installed a cottage in the woods for poets and artists so that they could draw inspiration from the mountain. In this cottage, Kipling read the *Just So Stories* to his kids, but his writing for grown-ups took a drastic downturn. He became a fervid champion of the South African War, putting Rhodes on a pedestal as a British hero with an almost divine right to oversee the development of southern Africa (even referring to Him with the capital usually reserved for deities). This is why statues of Rhodes in Cape Town tend to come paired with lines of bad verse by Kipling.

All the statues have long histories of alteration, both authorised and not. On Heritage Day in 1999, contemporary artists were allowed to creatively deface public memorials. The Rhodes Memorial lions found themselves caged under a banner that read FROM RAPE TO CURIO (a riff on Rhodes's obsession with building a railway that might run from Cape to Cairo). The statue in the Company's Garden was strung with brick-weighted ropes: a kind of ghost image, the artist explained, of the mine riggings in Kimberley where Rhodes founded his De Beers company.

The Rhodes Memorial bust has been repeatedly daubed, spattered, bludgeoned and even necklaced. This is when a tyre full of petrol is placed round someone's neck and set alight (a way of rooting out suspected informers during the 1980s, when the anti-apartheid struggle reached its climax). Over the years on campus, I had seen the sitting Rhodes wearing traffic cone hats, wrapped in black bin bags and swaddled in green fabric. This last reference was to Mgcineni Noki, also known as The Man in the Green Blanket. Thirty-year-old Noki was the leader of the striking rock drillers who were shot down by police at Lonmin's Marikana platinum mine in August 2012.

In March 2015, the statue was pelted with shit that had been brought in from Khayelitsha, where thousands of residents were still using bucket toilets. When the Rhodes Must Fall movement began making international headlines, the statue was removed from its prime position in the centre of campus.

Felling that Rhodes, up there on his plinth like a sitting duck, was a fairly simple process, technically speaking. He was unbolted from the platform and hoisted up with a crane, not so much falling as ascending or levitating. It was an uncanny thing to see: something that had been so still, such a fixture for so long, suddenly beginning to move, wobbling in the harness of a crane. There is an iconic image of the moment, in which the performance artist Sethembile Msezane seems to be lifting him up with her wings. She turns her back on History while everyone else is saluting it with their smartphones. NEXT THE INVISIBLE STATUES read one of the placards; LEGALIZE WEED! read another. Rhodes was lowered onto a flatbed truck and then raced down the highway to a secret location, the empire builder now in the position of day labourer. A grey box was placed over the plinth and that was that.

But the Rhodes Memorial further up the slopes is a different proposition for the aspiring Fallist. It's a big, hulking acropolis: part-Greek, part-Roman, part-Egyptian, with a touch of Nuremberg. You approach the inner sanctum via granite steps (one for each year of Rhodes's life), flanked by bronze lions with shiny rumps from all the kids riding on them. The steps and pillars make it a popular backdrop for wedding and birthday pictures. On any given Sunday, people will be queueing between the columns with foil balloons.

And there he sits, the arch-imperialist. Or rather slouches, leaning on his arm, with a masklike face and cleft chin. 'The immense and brooding spirit still shall quicken and control', reads the inscription by Kipling, 'Living he was the land and dead his soul shall be her soul'. Perhaps there's a little sneer of cold command, but mainly he looks bored and slightly bloated, gazing out 'across the lands he'd won', the poem continues, 'the granite of the Ancient North, great spaces washed with sun'. Some two thousand kilometres to the north are the granitic domes of the Matobo Hills in Zimbabwe, where Rhodes is buried – and where ZANU-PF loyalists periodically threaten to dig up his bones, whenever some distraction is needed from the tanking economy or electoral gains by the opposition.

Rhodes died of a bad heart in 1902, murmuring his famous last words: 'So little done, so much to do.' It was said to be heart trouble that made him come to southern Africa in the first place. A sense that he didn't have long to live urged on his feverish imperial dreaming, his obsession with legacy, secret societies, scholarships – a desire to keep shaping the world from beyond the grave. 'In its own way, Rhodes's heart was almost as significant an organ as Cleopatra's nose,' wrote one biographer (not realising that one day the reverse would also be true): 'Had it been weaker – or stronger – the whole aspect of Africa would have been altered.'

The Rhodes Memorial, in other words, is not of the cheapskate, Soviet variety. It's not like the Lenins and Stalins put out to pasture in Budapest's Memento Park, or the heroic, quota-exceeding steelworkers whose legs go *dong* when you rap them. Nor is this a Saddam Hussein or a Confederate general who can be hooked up to a truck and bent to the ground like a cheap toy. This is the British Empire in the final flush of its power and, like Ozymandias, the granite temple will probably be the last thing standing around here. Removing that nose must have required a serious power tool. It was sliced clean off, leaving a patch of bright, untarnished metal.

Five years later, during the hard pandemic lockdown, the memorial bust was beheaded. Someone had accessed the padlocked Rhodes Estate at night, during a huge winter storm – perhaps to disguise the sound of a portable angle grinder. That's what had been used in 2016 on the striding Rhodes in the city centre. Operating in broad daylight, a group in orange vests had posed as construction workers. They put caution tape around the statue and got a quarter of the way through its lower right leg, leaving a serious gash in the heel.

But portable angle grinding technology continues to improve. In the lockdown operation, about 70 per cent of Rhodes's head was ground off (starting just above the jawline), then rolled across the plinth and dropped to the ground, where it left a dent in the pine needles, evidently too heavy to move any further.

It was found 'in low scrub', according to press reports. A picture showed a noseless severed head resting in the fynbos, so presumably the grinder got away with that keepsake at least. This was the difference between Gogol's nineteenth-century tale and my more postmodern predicament: here, the nose was continually respawning.

After some tense diplomatic negotiations between South African National Parks, Heritage Western Cape and the city government, the head was handed over to the Friends of Rhodes Memorial, which stated that they wanted to prevent it from falling into the hands of some sort of government-sponsored 'theme park'. The Friends then repaired, reaffixed and fortified the head. This involved filling it with industrial cement, making 3D-scanned replicas for future reference, and (so they claimed) installing a GPS tracker inside.

This cat-and-mouse game had become, by then, part of a much larger phenomenon. In Pretoria's Church Square, a top-hatted Paul Kruger (once seen by some as a hero for standing up to Rhodes and the British Empire) had been spattered with paint by Economic Freedom Fighters (EFF) – and then surrounded by khaki-wearing defenders; black steel fencing was later installed. 'It is a shame that these dark figures of our ugly past continue to haunt us as we walk and drive on our roads,' said the EFF councillor Moafrika Mabogwana. The party called for Kruger to be replaced with Winnie Mandela.

In 2014, a nine-metre statue of Nelson Mandela throwing his arms wide in front of Pretoria's Union Buildings was found to have a tiny bronze rabbit in its ear. It was a secret sign-off from the sculptors that did not go over well with the Department of Arts and Culture. 'We don't think it's appropriate,' said spokesman Mogomotsi Mogodiri, 'because Nelson Mandela never had a rabbit in his ear.'

The sculptors apologised, pointing out that it could only be seen with binoculars; they had only put it there because the Department had denied their request to engrave signatures 'onto the sculpture's trouser'. The rabbit was removed and given to Dali Tambo, son of Oliver Tambo, leader of the African National Congress in exile. Tambo the younger led the company that built the statue, and he had also been the driving force behind the Long March to Freedom, a massive installation of one hundred figures from southern African history, all walking towards liberation, that was first exhibited on the outskirts of Pretoria. Billed as 'The World's Greatest Exhibition in Bronze', the Long March had recently arrived in Cape Town, installed on a strip of Astroturf between a shopping mall and the N1 highway.

Nelson and Winnie Mandela are at the front, where you enter, with Oliver and Adelaide Tambo close by. Both couples raise their hands, striding into a future that is fast receding. The march ends with

Mandela walking out of prison in 1990, poised to lead the country to democracy four years later. Behind him, a parade of activists, organisers and freedom fighters stretch back into history. There are Cuban and Communist fatigues (Chris Hani, Samora Machel), lawyerly suits (Govan Mbeki, Bram Fischer), Nehru jackets (Chief Albert Luthuli), then the waistcoats of the early twentieth century (John Dube, Walter Rubusana). There was Miriam Makeba with a microphone and Solomon Mahlangu with a machine gun. There was Solomon Plaatje on his bicycle, collecting testimony from those displaced by the Natives Land Act of 1913, and another writer, Olive Schreiner. She has a little dog and is carrying a letter addressed to Rhodes, who so fascinated and then disgusted her. 'The perception of what his character really was in its inmost depths', she wrote, 'was one of the most terrible revelations of my life'.

Critics had said that the Long March was kitsch, triumphalist, or just plain weird. But I found it quite affecting, walking backwards through the spaced figures, feeling that huge historical tide running. Further back came the kings: Cetshwayo, Sekhukhune, Maqoma, Moshoeshoe, Mzilikazi, Faku, Dingane, Hintsa, Shaka, Makhanda the Left-Handed. Until finally you reach Autshumato, the interpreter who outwitted the Dutch colonists of 1652 and was the first political prisoner sent to Robben Island. There he was: grey-moustached and grizzled, looking exhausted at the five centuries of struggle to come. The logo of a Mercedes dealership revolved slowly in the background.

The Long March, presumably, was the ANC-aligned 'theme park' that the Friends of Rhodes Memorial wanted to keep his severed head away from. But who were these Friends exactly? Their website had photos of regular 'flash mops' that were held whenever the memorial's central alcove was spray-painted or set on fire. On Heritage Day they would be out in force, mopping away. Elsewhere on the website was a photo of a chameleon: a beautiful blue-green creature with sad eyes and a curly tail. The accompanying post read: RHODES STATUE PROTEST— IS TO SAVE THE CAPE DWARF CHAMELEON NOT RMF AS IMAGINED.

The Friends, that is, claimed the defacements were not political, but stemmed from a campaign on behalf of Cape dwarf chameleons. These creatures had been threatened by the introduction of a mechanised, shaker-type harvester on fruit farms. The man believed to be behind the vandalism, the Friends claimed, had a record of mental illness and was a patient at Valkenberg Psychiatric Hospital.

It sounded ridiculous, like pure conspiracy. But it was stirring a memory.

Kabelo Sello Duiker was a beloved post-apartheid novelist who took his own life at the age of thirty. In his 2001 magnum opus, *The Quiet Violence of Dreams*, the narrator, Tshepo, spends time in Valkenberg – for 'cannabis induced psychosis', say the doctors, but maybe just for absorbing some of the trauma and madness of the society around him. This is what the novel suggests, a wild and haunted book that is something of a cult favourite among younger South Africans.

In Valkenberg, Tshepo befriends a man named Matthew who is obsessed with: chameleons, with saving chameleons from the machines used to harvest grapes on vineyards. 'Went on a rampage,' Tshepo tells his friend Mmabatho, 'saying that these farmers should destroy the wine because it's got chameleon blood in it and that terrible things would happen because it was bad muti. Ntho tsa boloyi.' Occult doings, bewitchment.

The character in Duiker's novel is based on a real person, Matthew Louwrens, the same person whom the Friends of Rhodes Memorial suspected of defacing the bust. Matt's chameleon campaign had appeared in the papers at the turn of the millennium, and had even been the subject of a televised investigation. MENTAL ASYLUM IS FULL OF PROPHETS, COURT TOLD, read a local headline from the time:

> The man accused of setting the chapel at Rhodes Memorial in Cape Town alight and vandalising the monument earlier this year has told the Wynberg magistrate's court that there were many prophets in Valkenberg Hospital – a psychiatric institution. William Matthew Lourens [sic] said two men at the hospital believed they were Jesus Christ. He added: 'In fact if Jesus were to grace us with his presence he would immediately be sent to a psychiatric institution.'

There were pictures of Matt in a magazine article about Valkenberg, bare-chested in one of the outdoor yards, flanked by guys in low-slung pants and gang tattoos. The pictures were, I noticed, taken by a friend of mine. I called him up, and he arranged a meeting with Matt at a bar in the Observatory, a neighbourhood that everyone calls Obs.

How to describe Obs? 'Oh, that's easy,' said a visiting American friend as soon as he saw it. 'This is the Bob Marley neighbourhood. Every city has one.' The main drag is filled with Rasta murals, herbalists and health food shops. But on the other side of the Liesbeek River, the suburb becomes something else, something starker. Amid wetlands and wind-bent trees are the nineteenth-century telescopes that gave the suburb its name. On one side of the old observatory is a driving range; on the other is Valkenberg. Most wards look like nondescript houses or classrooms, painted mustard yellow. But set apart across the water is a building surrounded by high walls and coils of razor wire.

Matt had done time in the mythic Ward 20, a maximum-security portion of the hospital for patients with criminal records. He'd then lived nearby at Oude Molen, an unkempt urban parkland where he'd established a gardening programme to help patients reintegrate into daily life. You can reach it if you carry on past the wards, away from the mountain, through a patchwork of small organic farms, scrapyards and squat buildings. I used to wander there when I lived in Obs. There was something exhilaratingly unresolved about the place: derelict wards and runner beans barely holding on against the wind, the scrap collectors in their horse-drawn carts, Devil's Peak in the distance. The peak would split the sun's rays like a huge dark prism looming over the city.

On the phone Matt had seemed a bit wary: Was this some academic bullshit? He'd had university types bugging him before. Absolutely not, I assured him. And then I reminisced, when we met, about my years of walking around Obs in Guatemalan shirts and no shoes, lodging with a self-described white sangoma (traditional healer) named Edna.

She specialised in doing 'geoharmonic clearings' of public spaces and healing events, and had done psychic clearances on car parks built over cemeteries and boutique hotels built over slave burials. But she'd turned down Rhodes's old zoo – an eerie, overgrown place on the edge of campus where students go to smoke spliffs among the lion cages. The energy there, she said, was just too heavy.

'That zoo is Masonic shit,' said Matt, nodding and smoking vigorously. 'Runes, Freemason symbols. Demonic.' That was partly why he torched the chapel: 'It was an exorcism.'

If you had to pick someone out of a line-up for anti-imperial arson, Matt may not be your first choice. He was a tough-looking farm boy from Kokstad with plenty of laughter in his eyes. Back in the Eastern Cape, he'd also begun training to become a traditional healer. This was a calling where hearing voices in your head – or your stomach – didn't necessarily mean you had schizophrenia. It might be *amafufunyana*, as the people in Xhosaland said, or *ukuthwasa*: the ancestors talking to you, calling to you, asking you to take action.

'I shook that vine,' Matt said, pulling hard on his cigarette. 'I shook that beanstalk and all kinds of things came down on me. Heavy things, hectic things.'

He opened a folder and began taking out well-thumbed letters, court documents, press clippings. A front-page picture in the *Cape Times* documented his handiwork: Rhodes daubed in bloody enamel. There was MM at the top (for mass murderer, he said) and VIVA below one of the lions. There were pictures of him wearing a tweed flat cap and holding up dead chameleons, handfuls of them, in front of vineyards.

'Good looking, hey?'

This was a man in the prime of his life: photogenic, charismatic and fired up by a moral crusade. It was the late nineties and he'd been working in the Stellenbosch area, living on a vineyard on an island in a lake. Mechanical harvesters were being introduced for the first time, partly, he explained, as a way to break strike action in the wine region. The same industry responsible for creating an alcoholic society via the 'dop' system (paying wages partly in alcohol) was now reducing its labour requirements. And doing nothing, Matt said, flushing red, to remedy the fact that South Africa had the highest rate of foetal alcohol syndrome in the world.

Our table was now covered with handwritten letters, pages and pages of them. 'These machines use vibration to harvest grapes and can harvest up to ten tons an hour,' he wrote to South Africa's congress of trade unions: 'Unfortunately the machine does not have eyes and cannot see that the grapes are not alone.' Not only chameleons were affected, he'd pointed out to the South African Broadcasting Corporation, 'but also skinks, snails, snakes, locusts, ladybirds, and mice'. The Cape dwarf chameleon was, he reminded the director of public prosecutions, an endangered species that was illegal to transport without a permit. All parties were referred to Phillip Kubukeli, president of the Western Cape Traditional Doctors, Herbalists and Spiritual Healers Association, Macassar Location, who had ruled that 'Wine which contains chameleons is poisonous. Tel: 021 3627024 (call box nearby)'.

Was his Rhodes protest related to the chameleon campaign? Not really, Matt said. So then why were they linked in the press? I pointed to a clipping: SOUR GRAPES LED MAN TO PAINT RHODES RED.

'I probably told them that,' Matt said, smiling his trickster smile. 'It was a hectic time in my life. Things were linking, overlapping. My wife divorced me, my family had me committed. To tell you the truth, I was also smoking a lot of dagga.'

His family put him in a hospital in Pietermaritzburg, where he was diagnosed with schizophrenia – a diagnosis that he later contested in court. This was where he had got to know Sello Duiker.

'Different mental institution. Fuck, I know them all,' Matt said. 'Anyway, Stellenbosch University got big agri and its scientists to refute me. They said the machines only shake at 2.5 newtons, or whatever it was, and the chameleons can hold on for 3.5 newtons. There was a *Carte Blanche* episode on it. They said I was sensationalist.'

He held up a picture of himself looking into the eyes of a shrivelled chameleon. I had the sense that he had been carrying this folder around for years, its petitions and court documents the mementos of a blazingly vivid youth. As we emptied it out, there were also nude photographs of old girlfriends and – this took even him by surprise – a close-up of a penis being gripped in braai tongs. 'These photos haven't been properly sorted,' he admitted.

Because of Matt's direct action – chaining himself to harvesters, smashing bottles of offending vintages in pubs – he had been arrested and roughed up by the police. But then he was deemed unfit to stand trial. Nonetheless, even as the case was being thrown out, he had conducted his own defence and delivered a denunciation of Rhodes – his trickery of Lobengula, his brutality in Mashonaland, his disgusting labour compounds in Kimberley – while dressed in a leopard-print suit. 'And I got a standing ovation,' he said.

Matt messaged me often after our meeting, sometimes up to thirty times a day. He was, by his own admission, having an episode. But new things had come to light, new intel on political assassinations and other conspiracies – it was never who you thought it was. To catch a nose I should keep my mind open, he said, open to things beyond the rational.

In South African mythology, the tokoloshe is a lusty imp that preys on its victims at night. Tabloids are always claiming to have caught one on camera, making someone its sex slave or wreaking havoc among churchgoers.

In Cape Town, an anonymous cabal of graffiti artists had taken its name from this anarchic creature. The Tokolos Stencil Collective went around spraying NON-POOR ONLY in trendy Woodstock and DESIGNATED MUGGING AREA on the Sea Point promenade. On the edge of the old District Six they stencilled GENTRINAAIERS, which means either 'fucking gentrifiers', 'gentrifucks', or 'gentrifuckers' (but it's hard to translate that delicious insult from Kaaps Afrikaans). Their stencil of Mgcineni Noki in his green blanket was everywhere: REMEMBER MARIKANA.

In September 2015, the collective announced that it had received a pseudonymous email from someone called The Nose, alerting them that something had happened at the Rhodes Memorial. Was this a copycat artist wanting some affirmation? The email made a literary allusion: 'We have stolen the nose of Rhodes at the memorial on the hill dedicated to this racist, thief, murderer and of course philanthropist,' it read. 'The nose of Rhodes (Gogol) has left his face and developed a life of its own. It now goes on a journey. Where will the nose show up next? Time will tell.'

I added this new lead to the detective corkboard I had made, like the ones in serial-killer movies. The Rhodes bust with 'that ridiculous blank space' at the centre, strings and arrows radiating outward. To Kipling's drawing for his kids of a crocodile pulling an elephant's nose from the Limpopo River. To Rhodes's bath and ancestral dildo collection. To chameleons and a dreadlocked K Sello Duiker. Around the border danced various other noses: stage designs by the artist William Kentridge for a production of Shostakovich's 1928 opera based on Gogol's tale. Kentridge had gone for a Socialist International aesthetic, so there were drawings and cut-outs of Soviet noses riding horses and ascending monumental pedestals. They got around on Constructivist stilts, and even (in one etching) performed cunnilingus. Next to that I placed an article from the *Daily Sun*: TOKOLOSHE BLOW JOB TERROR.

It was this new Gogol/Tokolos lead, I think, that proved crucial in my email courtship of the chairman of the Friends of Rhodes Memorial, which had been going on for months. If this was the man who had been methodically replacing Rhodes's noses, I needed to speak to him. The chairman was clearly on the opposite end of the ideological spectrum from Matt and the Tokolos Stencil Collective. He was suspicious at first, wondering what my politics were, but I persevered, changing my colours as needed. Did I agree, the chairman asked, that the defacements were probably not linked to RMF or BLM – and were more likely a prank inspired by Gogol? When I emailed him about the allusion I had unearthed via the anonymous message to the collective, the chairman finally agreed to a meeting, and a handover.

'Drinks on me,' I emailed.

'Nose on me,' he shot back.

We met at a hotel bar in the no-man's land between Valkenberg and the N2 highway. Gabriel Brown is a tall, shambling man with an expressive face that would suit a comic actor. 'First things first,' he said, removing a blue-green nose from his breast pocket and putting it on the table. 'I'm not happy with the colour, actually.'

I picked it up with a warm glow of achievement. My inquiries had finally yielded something concrete, something real: a fake plastic nose. Gabriel had arrived with several Shoprite bags full of models and replicas, which he laid out on the table between the bar snacks. There were the lions, the bust – meticulous 3D-printed plastic figurines – and then a much bigger nose, a massive hunk of cast resin that had been treated to look like weathered bronze.

'But nothing is lasting in this world', as Gogol reminds us when Kovalyov's Nose is intercepted at the border and returned to him by the authorities: 'Even joy begins to fade after only one minute'. My sense of achievement soon gave way to nose envy.

This, Gabriel explained, was the master nose. What he had given me was a smaller, cheaper replica: the offcut that corresponded to the tip of the nose that had been repeatedly sliced off and replaced. The tip that I held in my hand was about human-size (if you were generously endowed). The master nose, which he kept on his side of the table, was superhuman.

When the nose first vanished in 2015, Gabriel said, it plunged him into a terrible depression. 'I had to do something,' he said. 'No one else was going to.'

He experimented with green Plasticine, then resin. But making it stick was the real challenge. He tried double-sided tape, various glues – but the nose kept falling off. Eventually he drilled a hole into the flat space to insert a stabilising dowel.

'A black dust came out of the statue,' he said. 'I thought: I'm the first person to inhale this for a hundred years, like Tutankhamun's tomb. It was the greatest moment of my life.'

As Gabriel spoke, I realised I'd seen him before. He was the person who used to heckle Rhodes Must Fall rallies back in 2015. I'd seen people throw food at him, pull him out of venues, try to rough him up. When student cadres chanted 'Rhodes must fall!' he would shout back, 'Rhodes will rise again, Mugabe said so!' At one point he'd been dragged away to a waiting car, thinking it was all over, that his body would be found dumped in the Liesbeek. But it turned out they were undercover police officers.

'I think they saved my life,' he told me. 'I was stupid, trying to go against that mob mentality. After that, I thought about how I could actually make a difference. I decided to look after the memorial instead, so that all kinds of people can enjoy it.'

The Friends of Rhodes Memorial was founded as a nonpartisan body, meant to break the post-decapitation deadlock between South African National Parks, controlled by the ANC, and the city authorities, which were in the hands of the Democratic Alliance, the opposition. The ANC and the DA were, as usual, playing political football with Rhodes's eighty-kilogram head.

'I was the one who found it, actually,' Gabriel said. 'It was there in the bushes, hollow like a big soup tureen. There was a trail across the flagstones, then a dent in the grass, and then a track into the bushes. He was lying there, like something out of classical mythology. I mean: What do you do when confronted with the head of a god?'

He paused for effect.

'I faltered. I'm a mere mortal. I should have taken it then, but I decided to come back with help the next day. But it was gone, dragged to the car park. Then it was weeks before Table Mountain National Park admitted to having it, even longer before they handed it over.'

He leaned closer.

'But I'll tell you a secret: *It's not the real head.* It's also a copy. They wouldn't give up the original. It's still in some apparatchik's filing cabinet. But who cares – authenticity doesn't matter so much any more.'

When I asked him whether there were any other Rhodes statues I didn't know about, he bristled, suddenly suspicious. Why was I asking that? 'I don't know who you are,' he said. 'I might be speaking to the enemy here.'

To calm his nerves I brought out my dissertation and showed him the picture of Rhodes's tub.

'I simply *must* have a bath in that!' he said.

Rhodes left his Groote Schuur (Big Barn) mansion to future prime ministers, so I wondered who else had sat in it. Generals Botha, Smuts and Herzog, farmers and soldiers who felt ill at ease here in the wet Cape winters and left little trace. After 1948 the double-initialled architects of apartheid: DF Malan, HF Verwoerd, BJ Vorster, PW Botha, FW de Klerk – alone with themselves in the bath. When I visited Groote Schuur in 2007, a cat followed behind the Iziko Museums tour party, very white and suffering from hair loss. It had been a pet of the De

Klerks in the 1990s, our guide said. In a democratic South Africa, Groote Schuur had become the deputy presidential residence; but Jacob Zuma (then deputy to Thabo Mbeki) had asked to move out, since his kids didn't like playing amid all the colonial relics. And so Mimi the albino cat was the last resident of Rhodes's mansion.

Gabriel seemed reassured. The Friends of Rhodes Memorial, he admitted, attracted some strange bedfellows via their Facebook page. Some conceptual art student emailed about wanting to make an installation. He couldn't remember the name: some breast-beating liberal, a white-guilt type. And then there were the evangelical Christians who helped with the flash mops, but who also liked to preach from the steps.

'Charismatic,' he said, looking into his beer. 'But not very gay-friendly. American money, I think, with links to Trump and all that, Zionists, the Rapture. Once they even sprayed graffiti on the walls: Mount Sinai.'

So, he was getting it from both sides, the radical left and the religious right?

'Yes, it does seem to attract oddballs. Like me.'

He finished his beer, smiled.

'And you.'

A few weeks later Gabriel sent an email saying that he was making another nose for me, a better one. Oh, and he'd remembered the name of that annoying art student – it was Josh.

Had the nose been hiding in plain sight all along? On Josh's Instagram was a Greek statue, rotating in digital space. On his website was a short film of the bust growing a shiny new nose, which hung there for a minute, pregnant with significance, then fell off. There was also a project in which the artist had made a virtual 3D model of his own flaccid penis. If I were an art critic, I might suggest that Josh's work operated on a continuum, or dialectic, between hard and soft: an unresolved tension between (public) noselike rigidity and (private) penile slackness. 'Dick pics are about ego and power', he had written on his website. 'How hard can you get? What's your capacity to penetrate?' Hard penises lent themselves to crude doodles and sculpture; soft penises were embarrassing, and lacked representation: 'No one wants to speak about them. When shown on film, they're shyly glanced at for only a second.'

I made contact, and he suggested that we meet in Paradise, a little urban parklet along the Liesbeek River. On the drive over, I felt anxious that he was going to be too cool for me, smarmy and supercilious. But Josh was nothing like that. The long-haired man who emerged from the dappled shade was gentle, soft-spoken, earnest. I got straight to the point and took out the blue-green nose. He smiled and nodded, as if he'd been expecting this: 'I see he's changed the colour scheme a little.'

Josh said he had about seven or eight noses in his possession. But not the original, not the ur-Nose – he confessed that straight away – and he had no idea who might have removed it. The Rhodes he'd first encountered was noseless, but when he returned to make a scan of the head for a 3D model, one of Gabriel's replacements was attached. He'd felt upset. He thought the bust looked really interesting without a nose, beautiful even. Replacing the nose was like defacing an artwork, one that he wanted to restore to its original state. So, he'd entered into a kind of – he paused for the right word – conversation with the person who'd been replacing it.

At first they were hard to remove, Josh went on, but now it was easier. He'd knocked one off the other day with a garden trowel. But it bothered him, how long the whole thing had dragged on for, how determined the nose replacer was. That's why he'd taken it further and got involved in the decapitation. This was a major operation involving three people, a cold chisel, a hacksaw, a crowbar and an angle grinder. And the noise!

Telling the story in his soft voice, he sounded a little mystified at how he'd got himself into all this, even a little rueful. He'd arrived at Cape Town's art school from Grahamstown, or Makhanda, rather, as an evangelical Christian, wanting to 'make art for Jesus'. But doubts crept in. He'd since left the church, but still tried to serve in homeless shelters.

When I asked how he had found himself knocking off noses with trowels, Josh didn't have a direct answer. He didn't know all that much about Rhodes, to be honest. But he'd never seen such extremes of rich and poor before – there just wasn't that much wealth back home. He felt he had to do something, and Rhodes was the focus, was all anyone talked about.

When they beheaded him on that stormy winter night, they noticed there was already a deep cut in the neck from a previous attempt. The original nose removal, Josh reckoned, was unpremeditated, opportunistic: 'I think they just cut off what they could.'

Two days after I met Josh, the Rhodes Memorial exploded. Matt sent me a clip of fire sweeping down off the mountain and igniting the gas canisters of the tearoom: 'Wasn't me!'

Some blamed vagrants, others arson. Or the colonialist pine trees Rhodes had planted, the alien invasives that burned so fiercely. Some cheered the fire on as it came down the slopes towards the university, fanned by a dry wind: Rhodes and his legacy would finally be cleansed. Of course, that granite temple couldn't burn down, but the most beautiful reading room of the library could, and did. Blood-red flames, the African Studies collection reduced to ash, students in terror or heroically putting out burning palm trees – I followed it all online, right down to the meals abandoned in the tearoom, pictures of pickled fish left on plates.

It wasn't really the time for this, he knew, but Josh sent me the longer edit of his film. On the bust of Rhodes, the nose slowly grows back, holds still, drops to the floor. Then another one grows, drops down the steps, and then another, faster and faster, becoming a torrent of shiny new noses, cascading down the steps, like you'd pulled some monumental slot machine and hit the jackpot.

'But the strangest, most incredible thing of all is that authors should write about such things,' says Gogol's narrator towards the end of the story, admitting that his account doesn't really add up:

> That, I confess, is beyond my comprehension. It's just … no, no, I don't understand it at all! Firstly, it's no use to the country whatsoever; secondly – but even then it's no use either … I simply don't know *what* one can make of it.

All I'd really uncovered, in the course of a five-year investigation, was a succession of charming oddballs. Josh, a lapsed evangelical with interesting things to say about slack penises. Matt and Gabriel, with their radically opposed ideas of how to go about being a white man in Africa. One who wanted to be a sangoma, travelled all over the continent, tried so passionately to indigenise himself. The other content to keep living in a Rhodesian fever dream, making the memorial nice for the procession of Muslim wedding parties that queued up there on weekends.

I had found a lot of noses, but not the original. I was disappointed but also relieved. Disappointed that I hadn't found the ur-Nose, but relieved that the true perpetrator was still out there. That he might still be a prophet or madman, a homeless savant, a radicalised rough sleeper or whatever else I needed him to be. That he wasn't an art student. That he, or she, might perhaps be reading this, and might one day provide me with an answer.

The transformation workshop

I found myself drawing up to the gateposts of a guest farm after a long drive through the summer heat. East along the highway, then south down one of the roads that leads to Cape Agulhas. It wasn't an area I knew well. The highway kinked north, the coastline bent south; between them was a region of dusty farms and vast, lonely bays. These were dotted with a few hardscrabble towns that I dimly associated with shark cage diving, perlemoen poaching and yellow face-brick beach houses.

This was the venue for the inaugural Transformation Workshop of the Agulhas Futures Research Initiative for Climate Resilience (AFRICR). Someone I knew, Jo, was trying to start a career as a workshop facilitator with her partner Kev, a laid-back American guy who was into powerlifting. And she wanted me to be part of their first gig.

I was reluctant. I told Jo that I knew nothing about this part of the world. She said that was precisely it. My non-specialist perspective would help everyone get beyond the silos (she used that word a lot) that they normally worked in. A humanities person would be crucial among all the scientists, planners and practitioners. 'Practitioners' was their term for the locals who got drawn into this affair, which was something to do with climate change, land, race, the ocean, poverty, conservation, renewable energy, gender, justice and how entangled they all were. Even now, I'm not entirely sure what AFRICR was all about – one of those acronyms where, you felt, the tail was wagging the dog a little.

As it happened, the turnoff to the guest farm was opposite a cluster of massive canola oil silos. They served as a landmark in a flat brown landscape that gradually crept up to some low hills in the distance, where the rotors of a windfarm stood dead still. It was terribly hot.

Here, you crossed a river and drove up to the old gateposts of the guest farm, which stuck in my mind somehow, whitewashed and arbitrary in the dusty landscape: Brandfontein 1744. And so this is what I mentioned during the check-in session when we gathered on the farmhouse stoep. We were asked to introduce ourselves by saying something that we had noticed on the way here today.

Excellent noticing, said Jo with grateful eyes.

Sometimes in Japanese temples there's a raised ledge at the entrance.

This was Busi, a sociologist whom I knew a little from faculty meetings: very kind, a little esoteric.

You step over, cross into another kind of space.

I admired the calm way she dealt with her twins, Miso and Yoko, who were chasing an Egyptian goose through the walled vegetable garden. This was a workshop that welcomed the whole family, Jo and Kev had stressed. Significant others could go birdwatching or see the flowers; there would be a parallel activity programme for children, with its own sub-facilitator. Over the next days I would look out the window and see them covered in mud, leaves and feathers, playing their games in the appalling heat.

You noticed the National Monument plaque as you drove in?

This from a bald man wearing aviator sunglasses and a chunky, Xhosa-patterned knit. As the owner of Brandfontein, Tom Faulk explained that the property was historic for its well-preserved and unusually long werf: the bluegum-lined avenue in which our dusty vehicles were parked.

At its one end was the farmhouse, at the other, a pigpen and the stables. Then sheep paddocks and a mud pan where a windsock lay still. Lining the avenue were thatched cottages that had once been for farm workers but were now guest accommodation. Full of porcupine quills and pressed flowers, paintings of the Anglo-Zulu War, the Zambezi, Dr Livingstone I presume – that kind of thing. Heavy curtains and drapes, mosquito nets hanging over the four-poster beds.

The mosquito nets, said Chalwyn, the manager of a local cement works. I feel like the Queen Mother!

We laughed energetically, because along with Tom and Chalwyn, the only other practitioners were Desree (local tourism) and Pontsho (local municipality), and we wanted them to stay on board and think the best of us and the whole transformation process. Though I was beginning to wonder if Jo and Kev knew what transformation was – its local meaning, I mean. And if they did, why were we sitting on a kind of Cape Dutch theme farm, being facilitated by a Minneapolitan bodybuilder, with roast boar on the dinner menu?

Andreas mentioned the windfarms and his interest in the region as a possible heartland of renewable energy. He was from the Global Futures Institute in Malmö, which I sensed was the major funder of this gathering (the Scandinavian approach to childcare, for example).

Desree said the peacocks. They stalked around the terraces between the farmhouse and the river, letting out *heh-keh-keh-keh* sounds that set the nerves on edge.

Thanks so much, said Kev. I think we've now heard from everyone?

No.

Serge spoke for the first time. He was an agronomist from Uganda who'd been sipping water continuously since the beginning of the session, filling and refilling his glass. We were sharing a porch in the African Twin Double.

I'm sorry Serge. What did you notice?

Nothing.

Nothing at all?

I'm trying …

There was a long pause.

Not to.

The workshop venue was a converted barn on the adjoining farm, owned by Tom's brother. More of an absentee landlord, one had to say, Tom told us next morning as we drove over in his old Merc. His brother lived in a clifftop mansion on the coast and phoned in contract labour: those buildings near the dam were dormitories for grape and tomato pickers, seasonal work. But now look, they were mid-drought, the road was thick with dust, and the Merc skidded to and fro through the powder. There were several gates to be opened and closed; I launched out before the car had come to a halt, determined not to leave it to Serge. He was sitting in the front passenger seat, staring out at the landscape. Not saying anything but (you got the feeling) absorbing a lot.

Over the next few days, his behaviour got steadily stranger. But this was hard to admit at the time. We were, after all, being asked to undiscipline ourselves, to be intellectually disobedient. This was a space in which any kind of intervention or provocation was welcomed and deemed significant. No box required, as Kev liked to say (going one better than thinking outside it). The tone of Zen-like acceptance was set by the words written on a flipchart where we gathered for the first session:

Whoever comes are the right people.
Whatever happens is the only thing that could have happened.
Whenever it starts is the right time.
When it's over, it's over.

I want to go back to what Busi said yesterday, Jo began. About gateways and crossings, portals. Because the prefix 'trans' means to cross over.

Kev flipped the chart and there was a list of words beginning with 'trans': transform, translate, transplant, transport, transpose, transmute, transition …

This was the problem, I felt: everything became a thing. You couldn't just leave chance observations and insights alone. You had to milk them, input them into some output, make them squeal. But I told myself to stow the scepticism and be supportive of Jo and Kev in their facilitation debut. To just (as they asked us) listen without judgement – which seemed like a wise way of being in the world.

Kev explained that over the coming days we would be walking in each other's shoes and going on Learning Journeys together. We would listen to each other's stories to create a storied landscape (Tom gave a little snort). The idea, said Jo, sharing a sisterly glance with Busi, was to become a Learning Clan. Busi tipped her headwrapped head down on its long neck and pointed at Jo. Together they explained that Learning Clan was a play on Burning Man, the desert festival based on self-reliance, radical inclusion and a non-capitalist gift economy. A local version was held in the Karoo each year and Busi (I knew from Instagram) attended religiously. A well-respected sociologist and mother of two who loved stomping along to desert trance, which was possibly the worst (and surely the whitest) genre of music in existence – this total departure from cultural norms gave me a weird kind of hope.

Chalwyn cut in and asked how all this was going to benefit the local community. This caused Pontsho to lift her head from municipal spreadsheets for the first time and nod. Kev said it was a great question and began flipping through lots of diagrams in the shape of a U-bend, explaining how we would be moving down and then up again through a collaborative project of co-initiating and co-sensing (on the descent), then co-creating and co-evolving (heading up again). At the base of the diagram was a crucial stage in the process – the bottom of the U – where things could, and would, get messy and confused. We shouldn't be scared of that; in fact, we should welcome it.

By day two, the tension between what Chalwyn and Pontsho liked to call 'the facts on the ground' and what Jo and Kev termed 'reflecting on process' only became more acute. We kept reflecting on process without any real process having started. The watercooler belched as Serge filled and refilled his cup.

Jo and Kev were over-facilitating, which (unlike, say, over-catering) is not really facilitating at all. Perhaps through nervousness and wanting to do a good job on the Swedish krona, they were taking up all the space, filling up silence like rookie teachers, putting all sorts of conceptual carts before horses. And whenever participants did say anything interesting – when Andreas talked about scientifically modelling past climates, for example: a reverse weather forecast that was called a 'hindcast'; or when Pontsho explained the economics of marine poaching in the area – you were just bracing for the moment when Jo or Kev would interrupt and try to convert it into a 'take home' that could be written on the flipchart. The result, in the dust and the heat, was something dreamlike and slightly infernal. As if we were building fantastical structures – mind maps, storyscapes, transitional economies – on no actual basis, on something as powdery as the dust heaped like ash at the edge of the farm roads.

After lunch we were asked to go outside, find a shady tree and journal. To put down our thoughts and feelings about how to 'dream things forward'. But I found myself going backwards, into reverie. 'I've seen things you people wouldn't believe' – I thought of the famous speech from *Blade Runner*. But instead of attack ships on fire off the shoulder of Orion, I was thinking back over years of attending academic workshops and conferences.

Near the ring road in Leeds, I'd seen a man, a white British man, act out his paper on African occultism using three soft toys: a green snake, a Madiba doll and the third something so politically incorrect that it can't even be named. At different points in the presentation, he made the soft toys interact: now Mandela was coiled up in the snake, now he was being pinned down by the unnameable toy – poor Madiba. But no one batted an eyelid.

At a Berlin–Nairobi exchange on post-postcoloniality, I'd watched the Kenyan contingent come later and later to the venue each day, shuffling in with bigger and bigger shopping bags. The German hosts were too impeccably polite to say anything. And so by the final day, we sat all morning and afternoon in the venue, waiting for a workshop that never came.

Then there was the residency where a beautiful half-Lebanese, half-Swedish woman spoke for days, in the knottiest art theoretical jargon, about her work, its relation to the crisis in the Middle East, and how profoundly her hybrid heritage had informed her practice. On the final evening, she finally showed a picture of the art she had been talking about: a cartoonish sculpture of a 'camel-moose' built in a Stockholm playground. The audience nodded gravely.

What linked all these events? A kind of all-embracing acceptance, perhaps. A well-meaning desire to honour all kinds of human truth, approach, idea. Everything was as valid as everything else; or at least, no one wanted to take the risk of saying otherwise. Also an assumption that any kind of mix-and-mash-up of human culture was to be encouraged, all in the name of border crossing, transgression, inter-disciplinarity. Not staying within the usual, boring containers and structures of knowledge was key. But then, the risk was (as when wedding officiators did away with religion) that things could easily become a free-for-all.

That afternoon we went on a Learning Journey through the surrounding area – which was a relief. We were actually doing something (but I was already worried about how much we would have to reflect on it afterwards: there would be hell to pay). Chalywn guided us around Soetwater, the Moravian mission town where he was a church elder. With Pontsho we inspected the municipal offices in nearby Klavier, a town famous for its sour fig relish. Then we convoyed down to the most southerly tip of Africa: just some low rocks leading a bit further out to sea than the surrounding rocks. Standing in the wind near the lighthouse, Desree pointed out the old military zone to the east, the longest unbroken stretch of beach in the southern hemisphere.

The coastline here I found unsettling. It was wild and always windy, and the wind was always cold, even in summer. Odd things washed up on the sand: weird sea tubers that looked like soldered metal and stank terribly.

Redbait, said Chalwyn. He took out a pen knife and cut one open to reveal the innards: fleshy like lungs or gills, a lurid Day-Glo orange. Great for fishing, said Tom. Serge looked uneasy.

We arrived back at Brandfontein to find Andreas's wife upset. Her three kids were sunburnt: something the children's sub-facilitator should have prevented. Miso and Yoko hid behind Busi's skirt, perhaps feeling a little responsible for their Scandinavian playmates' discomfort. Andreas escorted his family back to their thatched bungalow, but Tom played down the tension and urged the rest of us towards the stables. The men were rounded up and put on horses – everyone except Serge, who began running away every time Tom approached him with a bridle. Eventually he allowed himself to be talked onto the trailer that had been hitched behind a tractor. This would now drag him and the women through the fields.

The horse riding was unbearable, requiring core, thigh and back muscles that obviously neither I nor Kev engaged in daily life. We sidestepped and zigzagged behind Tom and Chalwyn, who were both confident horsemen. The horse party and the tractor party each stirred up a huge amount of dust. When we intersected at the far end of the property, the orange cloud blotted out the sun – it felt unreal, apocalyptic. That was where we transitioned, I felt. That dusty farm tour was where the whole affair began tipping from just a very odd experience into the more rarefied category of fiasco.

Serge didn't want to attend the banquet that night in the farmhouse, but I eventually found him in the walled garden and said we could walk over together, couldn't we, the African Twins? Going through the farmhouse he slowed down and down, eventually coming to a dead halt at the entrance to the dining room. Inside were chandeliers, candles, bottles of wine, the sound of plates and cutlery – but he wouldn't cross the threshold.

Serge, come with me, said Tom, strolling over. I've seated you at the high table.

Serge wouldn't budge. He only said: I don't use the language of the high table. I don't use the language of the high table. I don't use the language of the high table.

He went to sit in the kitchen instead. It was full of warped Formica from the 1970s and formed a surprisingly small and grotty back end to the banqueting hall. I wondered how the kitchen staff managed to prepare such large meals in here, while also having to serve and clear as Tom rang little bells.

The centrepiece of the meal was what he called wild boar, but was most likely just the little bushpigs that I had seen scurrying into the bushes ahead of the tractor. By now there were mutinous feelings coursing through the dining room. Sunburnt children wailed with exhaustion and their parents chafed at having to sit through a five-course meal, let alone the Chopin preludes that Tom insisted on playing for us afterwards in the parlour. On Andreas's face, I could see deep concerns beginning to form about whether all this was funding well spent.

On the third and final day, the army arrived. I woke up to find men in camo pants setting up tents on the riverbank, unloading tarps and Portaloos from the back of military trucks. Tom was striding around the werf, giving instructions, very much in his element. The commanding officer sauntered over in boardshorts and asked if the female medic in the camp could have a shower in the farmhouse.

Yes sergeant, if your men move that in there for me, said Tom, pointing at a gas cylinder with a sjambok. Come on now. *Aandag, aandag!*

Yes my sir, said the officer, squatting and sticking out his rump. Give it to me!

Tom made some whipping motions, to the great amusement of the troops, then took me down to feed the pigs, explaining that the soldiers were here to practise river crossings. He allowed them to come each year, on one condition. That when they drilled in the morning, they had to do it outside his bedroom window, like so. He crouched down and did a little toyi-toyi war dance, rocking from one leg to the other.

I-hate-the *white* man! I-hate-the *white* man!

I could see he was searching my face for traces of liberal outrage, but I kept it blank.

Though as you well know, he went on, many of these soldiers have not grown up in the privileged spaces that we have, with access to water, rivers, swimming pools and so forth. Swimming is not a given. And so I try, in my own small way, to do my little bit.

He could pivot his discourse like this, I'd noticed. Now reactionary, now socially sensitive, sounding whatever notes were needed according to his changing guest roster, while his eyes, when not behind the aviators, stayed twinkling and ironic – the eyes of a sensualist.

The sight of men in combat fatigues did not have a good effect on Serge. He sat rigid with tension as we drove over to the final session, which was about how to navigate different spaces. He seemed desperate to make an intervention – kept putting up his hand, could barely sit in his chair – but Jo and Kev had a lot of interdisciplinary diagrams and flowcharts to get through. There would, they assured us, be time for questions later.

It's not a question, said Serge, when the time finally came. It's a statement.

It was a statement about the Nile: angry, garbled and hard to follow, but he kept going on about the source of the Nile – which was in his country, his father's and mother's and everybody's country, so why weren't we swimming up that stream? – until he was standing right in front of Jo, shouting into her face. If we were supposed to be navigating all these different spaces, Serge shouted, then why weren't we navigating the Nile? It went on like this, his interventions partly entangled in the facilitator speak, which seemed to be causing him even more anguish, as if some truth he had glimpsed could not shake itself free of Jo and Kev's optimistic lingo.

Things had now reached a crux: were we all finally going to admit that something was not right here? Were we going to concede that here was a man in the throes of something? Or was all the talk about the Nile and the high table once again going to be – with a quiet, well-meaning violence – folded back into some overarching process?

I could see Jo's mouth opening and closing. I sensed that she was looking for the words to honour this important contribution, but they weren't coming.

It was true that Serge had, in his cryptic non sequiturs, somehow made the most sense of this whole gathering. But Kev must have been concerned, as we all were, that Serge was about to headbutt Jo. With his big arms outstretched in a T-shape, Kev slowly began edging his body into the gap between the two of them, forming a human shield in front of his co-facilitator. At this point Busi stood up and talked to Serge in a language which I guessed must be Swahili – she really did contain multitudes. Kev and Busi triangulated their serene energies towards Serge, until eventually he calmed down and allowed himself to be talked into Desree's car. She drove him to the nearest clinic, where he was put onto antipsychotics.

For a while, we milled around outside, looking at the dust of the vehicle as it sped over the river, past the silos and away. It was hard to know what to say. Nothing was probably best.

But Jo and Kev felt that they needed to do something to decompress the space. She brought out a Tibetan singing bowl and Kev picked a flower. The flower went round to each of us as we sat in a circle. When you held it, Jo would gong the bowl. And then for a minute, the rest of the group was asked to throw out positive, single-word descriptions of you. Thoughtful. Articulate. Incisive. Which felt absurd, doubly absurd considering what we had just gone through, but also quite nice when the flower came your way. Then the bowl gonged, the flower passed on and it was all ridiculous again: Chalwyn holding a wilted Namaqualand daisy with a look of total disbelief on his face. You could see him just waiting to tell all this to his colleagues back at Boland Cement.

We've gone through something here, said Kev, trying to draw it all to a close. And it's not uncommon. It can be very unsettling when you reach …

He looked at Jo, who gave the go ahead, a tiny nod.

The bottom of the U.

We were given explanations after the fact: that Serge drank so much water in the heat that his potassium levels were thrown out. That he was stressed ahead of a big funding deadline, that he'd forgotten his meds at home. But I wondered if there wasn't some deeper reason running underneath it all, between the banqueting bells and the grey, greasy river, the heavy drapes and the dusty farmyard – how hot and oppressive it all was, even to me.

In AFRICR we had co-evolved something bizarre and eye-wateringly awkward. But maybe the people who had come were, after all, the right people. And maybe whatever had happened *was* the only thing that could have happened. Though as for it being over when it was over, there I wasn't so sure. Something unresolved seemed to be hovering back there in the dust of Brandfontein, something I couldn't put my finger on.

Years later I bumped into Desree and Pontsho at the start of a trail-running event. They were kitted out with matching gear, ready to run for charity. As we warmed up, I asked if they remembered the Transformation Workshop. The heat, the horses in the dust, that final showdown between Serge and the facilitators. Oh yes, they said, who could forget. What was the meaning of it all, I wondered, what was the moral of the story? Desree paused for a while, mid-hamstring stretch, then said:

That nothing like that should ever happen again.

It was a valid conclusion to draw. But as time went on, I thought that maybe the workshop had done its work after all. Ordeals were getting rarer in a world where you could opt out of anything difficult or awkward. Nobody went through anything together any more.

Desree and Pontsho now worked together for a legal aid charity in the NGO sector. Tom and Chalwyn were fishing buddies who walked the lonely beaches together. Serge spent six months of each year in Sweden, running a PhD programme with Andreas at the Global Futures institute. His breakdown had been followed by a series of hugely cited papers on soil science and low-carbon agriculture – a total reimagination of African farming for the future.

For Jo the Transformation Workshop had also been a turning point. She left the facilitation sector for preschool teaching in Johannesburg, where I bumped into her at a book launch. It was a surprise, she said, how quickly one's old life receded in the mirror.

Busi asked me to dinner a few times (until she was headhunted by an American university and left the country). It wasn't a date – she thought she should make that clear. I think she just sensed how lonely I was, kind woman. We would hang out with the twins and watch classic British romcoms. It was her way of decompressing from the stresses of campus life, she said, and her work with the victims of domestic violence.

It's not like this! I would object as cosy images of Notting Hill or country weddings came up on the screen. That place is a dump.

She still wanted to visit, she said. The English, the Japanese – she loved these repressed cultures. As part of her obsession with Japan, she was learning shiatsu, which involved pressing hard into pressure points all over the body. She could demonstrate if I was okay with it. You had to press right into those points of discomfort. Which is painful at first, but you bear with it. And after a while, you'll see, it releases.

A line of light

I.

When I finished school, my parents moved from a mining town outside Johannesburg to the coast where we had gone for family holidays, over a thousand kilometres away. My father wanted to leave his old life behind. He got rid of almost all our possessions and bought a flat – the unit, he would always call it – in a new housing complex. He and my mother made the long drive down in separate vehicles. She had once owned a mustard-yellow Fort Escort, but that had gone too. They convoyed south in two company cars that my father had lovingly cared for and then bought from the mine, two grey Audis.

They drove across the Highveld and the Free State, across the Karoos great and small, through the Swartberg and over the Outeniquas. South to a new life, caught up in the transitions of the 1990s. Except that, several times towards the end of the journey, they became separated on the roads. My father looked in the rear-view mirror and my mother was no longer there. Or maybe it was dark and he assumed that the headlights behind him were those of his wife when in fact she was lost. She had taken a wrong turn somewhere in the winding poorts and passes that deliver you from the interior to the coast. My father backtracked and found her eventually, disorientated and tearful in the George traffic department, or maybe it was Wilderness.

She put it down to the stress of the move, the long drive. But looking back, it must have been – like the muddling of names and the missing of finer points – a sign of the Alzheimer's disease she was diagnosed with not long afterwards. At 59 years old, she suffered an early-onset, aggressive form of this dementia. Soon she could no longer drive at all. She spent most of her days in the sparse rooms of the unit and the grounds of the complex. She died eight years later.

Sometimes during those eight years I wondered if she should rather have vanished on those dark roads, and so been spared what came after. There are many things that I wish I had read, known and thought before the forgetting came upon her. These are some of them.

2.

My mother could no longer drive and I was not yet able to. I mean I could drive, but I kept failing the test. For years I took and failed it each time I came home. This meant that my mother and I were stuck in the complex.

The complex was known as a regional eyesore, especially in those days when the gardens were not yet established. It sat on a ridge above town, its boom-gated entrance just off the N2 highway. At the turnoff was a place where men would wait every morning for casual work, hoping to be picked up in a bakkie. The municipality eventually formalised it as a waiting area, paving it and putting in some bus shelter awnings. From there a pedestrian bridge led across the highway to an informal settlement, where a double-storey shack flew Rasta colours. Beyond that was light industria: windscreen repair and calamari wholesalers. The units of the complex all looked the other way, towards the sea, but the coast was distant, kilometres away. As soon as you walked out the gates you were on busy roads, on verges of broken glass and blown-out tyres.

This was a worry since several times my mother had been found wandering along the highway. Once, my father said, she'd been about to climb into a car with some unsavoury types, gangsters really. Another time she had seen a man covered in blood out there. 'Such a beautiful man,' she said dreamily. 'In such a beautiful suit.' From the patio of the unit she looked across the valley at the highway. She watched the vehicles blinking in the distance and asked what they were.

The complex security, which was mainly to keep people out, also worked to keep my mother in. The lawns, driveways and carports ticking in the sun, the faux-Tuscan blocks of timeshare – all were patrolled on foot. The guards were required to tap a fob at various places, as proof that they were physically doing their rounds. There was a keypad just outside our unit, so several times a day we would hear the *bloop* as the guard tapped in, and maybe waved at us through the window.

Or it was Tyler, a young guy from across the road in his groundsman's uniform. Sometimes Tyler and I drove around the complex together (he was trying to help me get a licence). We did tortoise-like 20 km/h laps, easing over speed bumps in the complex bakkie. 'One time!' he would say when I got a gear change smooth.

What were my mother and I doing? There was not much to do. Maybe we were sitting on the sofa, maybe DStv was playing. A digital satellite TV 'bouquet' came as standard in the complex: a selection of sports channels, mostly American sitcoms and movies. This was pretty new to us in the new South Africa; so was the dial-up modem that gurgled as I tried to reach my university friends abroad. Over there I never watched TV, would never think of it. But here it was on all day, my mother waving at the Sky News anchors like they were old friends.

Every half an hour or so, an advert for the bouquet came on – why I could never understand, since you were already watching it. Perhaps it was just to pad things out, fill up dead air. It was like a highlights reel or montage of forthcoming attractions. Explosive blockbusters, Formula One cars spinning off the track, Hollywood catchphrases, canned laughter. A wacky compilation of bits and bobs, telling you how amazing this summer's viewing was going to be.

The security guards walked their loop, Tyler and I drove our laps, the highlights reel came around again. By the second or third time it was unbearable; beyond that it felt like I had been plunged into a hell designed just for me.

I had the same conversations with my mother, the looping conversations you have with someone who has forgotten what they said two minutes ago. I was unpleasantly surprised at my selfishness, my unreadiness to humour her, my impatience.

Spending time with someone who has dementia dissolves the carer's own sense of identity. This is well known but I didn't know it. I only experienced it, and as something horribly corrosive of what a human self, either hers or mine, might be. Why bother pointing something out, why bother telling a story, why bother saying or doing anything at all when it will soon be forgotten? There is no imprint, no recognition, no record of you or what you have done, no emotional return on investment. And why was I thinking like this – in such a hard-hearted, calculating way – about someone who had done so much for me, and given so endlessly of her time?

I strummed the same chords on my guitar. What about a bit of 'Redemption Song'? said Tyler, showing me how to pick out the opening riff. But I kept playing Ani DiFranco over and over. We were smoking zol behind a boulder, the enormous boulder at the far end of the complex that no bulldozer had been able to shift.

It's an old, old song, Ani sings, the story of a father and mother, who battle each other, over nothing. Fights around the dinner table, ominous silences, treading on eggshells as you try to figure out what's what. It's a story as common as a penny, son (the chorus goes, fading out on a repeat of the last line): It ain't really worth anything, to anyone.

Today there are some sixty million people living with neuro-degenerative disorders that affect the memory, and these are only the registered cases. A whole mid-size nation of amnesiacs, and by 2050 the number will triple. As human populations live longer, dementia has become commonplace. Almost everyone now has the experience of knowing or caring for someone with a condition like Alzheimer's. A situation like this is now entirely ordinary; but it is also utterly incomprehensible, wrenching, cataclysmic and quite literally beyond words. It was beyond my wildest imaginings, beyond anything that my father or I had been raised, educated or prepared for. As with the Gorgon's head, I still can't look at it directly, the sorrow and shame of what happened.

My mother's mind unravelled just as I was coming into young adulthood. The experiences were so misaligned, the one was such an ill fit with the other, that I simply placed whole tracts of experience under embargo. I was so intent on forgetting my mother's forgetting that now I worry about losing her altogether.

3.

A beetle with a candle on its back. A candle on the back of a beetle, stuck to its exoskeleton. It is a surreal, properly dreamlike image. Wax drips down onto the hard wing cases, the thorax.

Thorax, exoskeleton: schoolboy words. Our primary school teacher, Mr B, is explaining a memory technique. Ahead of the exams, he is inducting us into the ancient science of how to remember things – mnemonics is the technical word. As in Mnemosyne, Greek goddess of memory, mother of the Muses. The candle beetle is to help us remember that insects have *a waxy outer layer.* You need to form a memorable image, linking the two ideas. Which seems like a lot of effort for a not-so-important detail; but the other example he gives is better.

For numerals one to ten, you first learn the following rhyme: one: *drum,* two: *shoe,* three: *tree* and so on, all the way to ten: *hen.* Now say you are going to the shop and need to remember milk, butter, carrots, newspaper. One: a drum full of milk. Two: cover your foot in butter so it can fit in a tight shoe. Three: do carrots grow on trees? You make the links like that, the more outlandish the better. So, two is a good one, the foot covered in butter. Because you can feel that one: the slippery, buttery foot. Butterfingers, buttertoes.

Since Mr B's memory lesson, hundreds of things – titles, places, people, lyrics, germs of stories – have coupled and uncoupled from the drums and shoes in my brain, the heavens and gates, wine and hens. The technique is especially useful for when you don't have pen, paper, or phone to hand: all those crutches for memory which (as people have been suspecting ever since Plato's *Phaedrus*) are accorded 'a power the opposite of that which they really possess'. The invention of writing, Socrates warns, 'will produce forgetfulness in the minds of those who learn to use it, because they will not practice their memory'.

As mnemonics go, the one-drum method is very simple. But perhaps it allows a glimpse of that great mystery, how our minds preserve and salt away the world, the past. Memories work, and work best, in mutually reinforcing clusters. Remembering well is a multidimensional act, moving across different genres and grammars of knowing. Numbers make a sound, then rhyme builds a bridge to story-image. You must keep forgetting to keep remembering (the one-to-ten system must be flushed clean to take on new data). Maybe dreams are full of the odd chimeras, the links left on the cutting floor of memory. Such links are both arbitrary and deeply meaningful. Story is a technique for remembering itself. Nothing stands alone in the mind. Everything encodes something else.

4.

In a piece for *The New Yorker* titled 'The Comforting Fictions of Dementia Care', Larissa MacFarquhar explores memory-care units that seek to create calming but artificial environments for patients with dementia. In the United States, these are often modelled on an idealised town square. Picket fences, facades of clapboard houses and faux storefronts: a kind of nostalgic stage set or simulation of small-town America. Given that people with Alzheimer's often ask when they are going home, some facilities have fake bus stops. Patients can be taken to wait there (at least until they have forgotten what they are doing) for a bus that never comes.

At the heart of this approach – which goes by various euphemistic names: 'therapeutic fibbing', 'brief reassurances', 'stepping into their reality' – is a belief that it is better to lie to patients (if it will soothe them and allay anxiety) rather than try to 'correct' them or set them straight. Though once you have begun to go down this road – colluding in a kind of compassionate deception – where does it end?

Not just with fake bus stops: some facilities even have fake buses with a screen for movement. One home, MacFarquhar reports, has simulated a beach with heat lamps, sand on the floor and the sound of waves. Care homes around the world carry different political histories. Some in the Netherlands have warmer, more humid wings for those who grew up in the Dutch East Indies. Some in what was once East Germany have rooms that evoke Communism under the GDR. *Ostalgie*, as it is called there: nostalgia for the East, for the bad old days.

Reading this, I wondered what the equivalent would have been for my mother. What kind of *Truman Show* or *Good Bye, Lenin!* simulation may have set her more at ease? Surely not a mock-up of the various mining towns where we lived. This would have required serious machinery to mimic the daily tremors of rockfalls and underground blasting. Not to mention a huge supporting cast of mine workers, walking along the hard shoulder in overalls and gumboots, to recreate the rolling mass action of the 1980s. Perhaps even some zebras and ostriches to evoke the lush company golf course on which these animals roamed, its fairways watered with undrinkable effluent from the mine workings. It had a distinctive odour, that water, a smell that rose from the company lawns and parks and gardens. 'A subterranean pollen-scent of chemicals, as of the minerals flowering underground' – Nadine Gordimer's perfect, Proustian description brings back that whole, collapsing world for me. White South Africa was already its own kind of simulation, its own false utopia.

I realise that I know little about what would have constituted a home for my mother. She had grown up in Cape Town as one of six children (three boys, three girls) and would speak about making 'pine needle houses' in the forests as a girl. Her mother played Chopin and loved Edith Piaf (her namesake), wearing berets like the French singer. Her father prevented his children from going to the beach before 4 p.m. – he was ahead of his time, my mother said. Always apply sunscreen to the tips of your ears, she told me, a body memory that is triggered whenever I do. Or whenever I am stirring half a teaspoon of sugar into coffee. Try to taste the sweetness without all that sugar, she would say, the natural sweetness in things.

When her parents divorced, three of the children went with Edith up to Johannesburg and three stayed behind in Cape Town. My mother was going to stay with her two beloved sisters Audrey and Sally, but (as she remembered it) a last-minute switch was made in the rail station. Her father took back one of her brothers and she was placed on the train up north. Up to the cold, dry Highveld where her working mother had to send her off to boarding school. It was a moment she came back to again and again in her last years: the fear that she would suddenly – for reasons beyond her understanding or control – be sent away. Dementia disorders mine the fault lines and traumas of a life, the pain and emotions that linger even when the events that caused them may have been forgotten or become garbled. The siblings were not switched at the station, my aunt later told me, but it was true that my mother was later sent north instead of her brother.

She spoke often about happy times 'temping' in 1960s London and then Johannesburg, where she eventually became secretary to the chairman in a mining company's head office – as high as someone like her could go, I imagine. She first met my father because she couldn't read his handwriting. When she married him, company policy obliged her to leave her job: it did not tolerate wives being employed. I found this out years after she died, and looking back it seems to explain the arguments where she would threaten to go and work as a cashier in the supermarket, as a cleaner, whatever – she needed to get out and *do something*. She'd travelled the world, getting up to all sorts in Swinging London, lighting one cigarette with the end of the other. Now she was stuck here, feeling useless – something amplified terribly by dementia.

We weren't a home movies kind of family, but I still find it odd how little record I have of my mother during these years. No video, no audio, even though I was always carrying around a four-track recorder. I find I struggle to remember the sound of her voice.

'I became, as so many caregivers do, a record keeper of someone else's obsessions' – so writes Dasha Kiper in *Travellers to Unimaginable Lands*, a book about the cognitive challenges, even impossibilities, of relating to someone with memory loss. Memory is so integrated into every aspect of human life, she goes on, 'from thinking, to communication, to forming and sustaining relationships, to creating continuity, meaning and coherence', that its disappearance is incomprehensible: 'We simply have no cognitive framework that allows for its absence in others.'

I wish I had recorded even those, my mother's obsessions. Looking back on old journals, I barely mention what is happening to her. It did not fit the pattern of an early adulthood conceived of as a grand adventure, of travel and self-becoming. I simply did not have the language for it. For years I barely stopped moving, jolting around the world in buses and trains, writing it all down – but none of that means anything now. I was writing down the wrong things. Now I comb those old notebooks for the rare moments when I have recorded something she said, some direct speech. 'I just want to go lie and down over there,' she would say, pointing to the edge of the complex, the drop off where lawns and flower beds gave way to boulders, a firebreak, fynbos. 'I'll just lie down in the sun and not be a bother to anyone any more.'

It was a time of airmail rather than email. Sometimes I would cram into dirty UK callboxes (using international phone cards that ticked down so fast), but mainly my parents and I communicated via onion skin letters or aerogrammes. Aerogrammes were single sheets of paper, postage paid, where you were effectively writing on the back of the envelope. The sheet was then folded in three, gummed together and addressed in the allotted box.

My father would always start, then my mother would tack her message at the end, one that became shorter as time went on. 'Hi there, Hed. I spent today indoors watching TV', one of the earlier ones begins (she is writing in the wrong part of the aerogramme). Then, in the right place:

> I stayed in all day today – its definitely getting cooler, and I expect it must be getting warmer there. Are you still into food?
>
> Dad's very good at making money – one day he sells lavender, growing outside, then he collects pansy shells, and I noticed he is collecting bottles in the kitchen!
>
> He also collects a certain type of beach shell which he has no trouble selling.
>
> We can now have meals on the property but so far haven't availed ourselves much.
>
> We are excited you are coming home. I eventually played tennis this week, which I enjoyed. Hope you will take me on.

'Are you still into food?' – the only real clue that something is amiss, though the non sequitur makes me smile now. 'I expect it must be', 'availed ourselves' – fancy phrases that sound like my mother still has all her linguistic wits about her. But in fact they don't sound like her at all, she didn't speak or write like that. She was anything but pompous.

Maybe she is reaching for something to hide behind, the kind of language that comes preformed, where you don't have to think too much. Or maybe she is sending it all up – the highfalutin pretensions of letter writing, language and life itself. She always did have a keen sense of the absurd.

My mother loved tennis, and in terms of her physical effects (pompous phrase), her tennis racket is virtually all I have. It is a Prince Pro with a dark frame and a brown grip. Once, in the 1970s perhaps, it was cutting-edge, the era when my mother was wielding it from the baselines of the Rec Club (she was never much of a net player), dispatching her trademark cross-court slices. The grip seems to be the original: brown and worn smooth like old wood by the serves and volleys, the ceaseless changing between forehand and backhand, rough or smooth, *p* or *d*. The top of the frame has been scuffed by hard-surface courts, revealing the base material to be aluminium, silver below the dark paintwork in a band from ten to two. But the strings are in good condition, a healthy dental yellow that convinced me to try the racket out a while back.

Which I regret, because holding it up to the light now, I'm reminded that rackets retain small filaments of tennis ball fluff where the strings cross. And if I hadn't played with it, then those strands caught in the net of gut would unquestionably have been from my mother's wily cross-court slice – which was something she could do even very late into her condition. The shape and rhythm of that shot must have been laid down deep in the cerebellum, along with other motor skills, just up from the nape of her neck.

Couldn't we invent something for her to do? I wrote to my father from the airport as I was leaving again (always leaving: no sooner had I arrived at the complex than I was desperate to be gone again). Couldn't she wash shells or pebbles or something, the ones that were sold in the gallery?

By this stage my father had split into two people for my mother. There was her husband, who took her for walks and set up picnics on the beach for her birthday. And there was 'him', the man who worked in town in and left her out of everything, took her money and her car away. 'He' was in there, in the bedroom, and she was too nervous to go in – I would find her poised in the doorway in the middle of the night, then try to coax her back to bed.

She never thought she'd have children, my mother often told me. Getting pregnant with me at forty had been a surprise, a nice surprise. And that was how I felt with her: not carrying the burden of a parent's unlived life, but left to become myself. Though she had, she told me, suffered from post-natal depression, which made her difficult sometimes, moody.

'I talk to you like an adult,' she would say. 'I can't help it.'

5.

My father was working hard to start his own business, a small art gallery in town, so he was gone most days. Even Christmas Days, when he tried to snare some last-minute custom. I remember buying some pies at the Shell Ultra City – our closest shop. I didn't really know how the oven in the unit worked, so one Christmas lunch my mother and I sat down to some lightly charred chicken and mushroom pies.

She seemed vaguely relieved by this. 'It's too much bother and too expensive to do much cooking now,' she would say. This was part of a web of stories and sayings that she came back to, as explanation of why she could no longer work, drive, handle money, cook. 'The problem is that no one told me who everyone is.' 'Of course, I've always been a bit absent-minded.' She tried keeping track of it all in little red diary: 'I'm so organised I'm disorganised.' She'd always said that, in a light-hearted way. Now she clung to it as a kind of mantra.

Faced with a welter of confusing, unrelated experience, a person with Alzheimer's doubles down on what they think they know about themselves. The habitual, well-worn neural routes of the brain – its 'cognitive reserve' – are so powerful that this self-driving mode can disguise the progress of neurodegeneration, even to loved ones and carers. Or perhaps more accurately, it can blur the line between an existing personality and an increasingly fraught, compensatory simulation of it.

Though words like this – 'compensatory', 'simulation' – are loveless and sound wrong. So does 'dementia' (a heartless etymology: without mind) and 'neurodegeneration' (too clinical, too many syllables). Alzheimer's is like Marxism: it encompasses far too much, such an enormous body of human hope and pain, to be named after a single person. None of the words for it are right. They are too detached from the experience of watching a self facing its own decreation, and trying to reorganise, regroup, strategise, somehow endure. I'm so organised I'm disorganised.

When we did get out of the complex, when my father drove us to do one of the local forest or beach walks, then my mother would be very nervous in the passenger seat. Alzheimer's, especially in the early stages (which are in many ways the hardest to witness), unleashes all kinds of fear and anxiety. A nameless angst courses through the body like electric current, earthing itself via whatever is to hand. Each oncoming vehicle made my mother flinch, the trucks made her grab my father's arm. Cars merging, overtaking, people spilling across the road – perhaps they all looked like accidents waiting to happen, reasons to expect the worst.

When I was a small, riding the Highveld in her mustard Escort, I would stick my hands out the window and make shapes with my hand, scooping and flying it through the air.

Aerodynamic!

The steel-framed mirrors were cocked at jaunty angles. The windows had delicate little winders, and were propped up by these small triangular panes: Scalene! There seemed to be more angles and intricacies to things then, more crannies for memory to dwell.

My mother was a word person, a cryptic crossword expert. So what was the word, I asked, for that feeling of – well it was hard to explain. A kind of excitement, but in the body. Like a bubbly, fizzing feeling, that things would just keep getting better, that life was big, the future full. Or maybe just this steady current of well-being, of feeling invincible really, because I was raised by her and had her attention. What was the word for that?

I'm not sure, she said. Could it be: anticipation?

Biodegradable! I shouted, chucking a banana peel out the window.

These fancy new words allowed you to break the rules. Don't you think, I asked her, don't you think that from inside the car, it looks like the dashboard and bonnet is so much wider than the road? That was very true, she said, sounding impressed at this observation. It was all about perspective, she said.

Twenty years later, sitting in the passenger seat of an Audi 500, was she seeing a world in which her mind could no longer account for perspective? Such that everything looked out of kilter to her, overlapping or on a collision course with everything else. The car really was overshooting the road, was somehow occupying a space that it couldn't or shouldn't, the law of non-contradiction gone by the bye.

My mother had always been a nervous passenger. But then, this was not without reason. My father was overworking himself, trying to make the gallery a success. The stress of those years – losing his job, moving, dealing with my mother, running a business – it left him so tired that he would fall asleep at the wheel. He would begin to nod off as he was driving along the highway. First just little nods towards the steering wheel, little micro-naps that he would pull up and recover from. But then a deeper nod and maybe a little snort, which could send us edging towards a bridge or the Shoprite lorry barrelling towards us along the N2. At this point, I would do a well-timed little cough to get us back on track.

A polite cough, so that all of us could save face. Instead of saying: *Dad, for God's sake pull over!* That cough gives an indication of the level of emotional openness in our family, the small family unit on which the wave of dementia was now breaking.

6.

How to drive: an example of non-declarative memory, the kind of memory that (once you are used to driving) does not declare itself, becomes automatic, implicit, habitual. This is part of the brain's great ambition to relegate as much of human experience as possible to the unconscious – far less costly (in terms of energy) than conscious processing. Contrast the first experience of driving on a highway (and the utter exhaustion that follows) with how easy it becomes in time. Highway amnesia, highway hypnosis: terms for how the 'automaticity' of our mental processes takes over, so that you can drive hundreds of kilometres and barely remember a thing.

Then there is declarative memory – explicit or conscious memory – which takes two forms. Semantic memory: facts and propositions about the world in general (what that triangular sign means, with the road disappearing into mist: tar ends ahead). And then episodic memory, the kind of personal, recollective memory that attaches to a particular event or experience (*that drive*, with its whole cluster of sensory and emotional traces).

Not that memories for facts and those for events can always be easily distinguished. Autobiographical memory is slippery like that, since it straddles this basic divide. You may 'remember' something about your childhood because your parents told you about it later (early life memory tends to be collaborative). In which case something you did experience (episodic), or thought you did, might blur into the memory category of something that you did not (semantic). And if the kind of memory that seems so personal and unique may not be, then what does it mean to 'have' a memory in the first place?

That drive, from the mine into town when I am four, five, six years old, emerging from childhood amnesia into autobiography, self-mythology. But oh, how we were admired! She and I, me and her, in the orangey-yellow Escort. Didn't petrol attendants dote on the car? Didn't they constantly ask if she would sell it to them? Not today I'm afraid, and we were off again, nipping along between the sinkholes and the slimes dams. Somewhere there my father was at work, inspecting the cyanide tanks or the jaw crushers. But we still had hours to go, hours to be ourselves.

We are passing fields of maize and stopping at the Portuguese grocer in his roadside shack. Unforgettable, because he had pinups of topless women behind the scales. My first experience of pornography, furtively glimpsed behind the mealies and onions hanging from the roof.

Not that (remember) memory is a simple act of recollection. Even though I (seem to) remember those breasts very well, they are no doubt borrowing data from the many other furtively glimpsed breasts that followed (in *Scope* magazine, Pirelli annuals, then Mandela-era

Hustler and later the deluge of internet porn that renders these mags positively quaint). In the same way, the Escort is retrospectively tinted by my recent googling of vintage cars. All are part of a story that I have evolved about my mother and me, burning this cluster of images brighter into the synapses, strengthening but also altering it each time, while consigning so much else to oblivion.

7.

Many years too late, I began reading about dementia. The literature of Alzheimer's and related conditions is vast by now, a spectrum running from prose non-fiction to much more experimental, fragmentary modes.

Most straightforwardly there are there are memoirs by partners and carers, children or family members. Jonathan Franzen writes about the effects of Alzheimer's on his difficult father, a piece which begins with the author receiving an autopsy report on his father's brain (which had been donated to science). Reading the clinical language ('parasagittal atrophy with sulcal widening') and the weight ('1 255 gm'), Franzen cannot help but think of 'the familiar shrink-wrapped equivalents in a supermarket meat case'.

How to move from the brain as meat to our cherished notions of self, consciousness, personhood? And how long can the self (as we know it) be said to endure in the face of neurodegeneration? Almost all writing on dementia turns on such questions, eventually. The writer-carer is forced to wonder: *is* this self as real, as alive as my own? Or: where can selfhood be found and honoured in the absence of memory?

Some describe the condition as an agonisingly slowed-down form of dying that gradually evacuates being. Others persist in seeing evidence of individual personhood very late into the condition, even if only (in the words of Patricia Lockwood) as 'a line of light under a locked door'. The wrong metaphor, probably, but somehow it feels right. Responding to someone with Alzheimer's opens a small, saving gap between what you may know (conceptually) and what you might perceive (instinctually). Even a writer as hard-headed as Franzen is determined to see signs of his father's selfhood right to the end, asking us to widen our imaginations about where it might reside: 'Hour after hour, my father lay unmoving and worked his way toward death; but when he yawned, the yawn was *his*. And his body, wasted though it was, was likewise still radiantly *his*.'

A time of unexpected intimacy with a once distant parent – this is one of the common tropes of Alzheimer's literature, and a way of giving it some kind of moral or redemptive shape. As antidote to any such sentimentalism, there is *I Remain in Darkness* by the French Nobel laureate Annie Ernaux, an unflinching record of her loved and feared mother's decline. Never missing an opportunity to mention the smell of urine in the care home, her diary of the ordeal can sometimes feel like the flaunting of authority over a once dominant but now helpless figure: 'She has to watch television right away. She can't wait until I have cleared the table. She no longer understands anything, except her own longing.'

Why, Ernaux wonders, is she gathering the favourite sayings of a mother who can now barely speak? 'Literature is so powerless', she comments. And then: 'I am terrified to reread what I have written about her.' She records driving away from the care home after visits, listening to music at full blast on the highway. The need to pursue an affair, to feel sexual again, to put distance between herself and what is happening back there.

Then there are the rarer, first-person accounts written by those suffering from dementia, like Thomas DeBaggio's *Losing My Mind* (which I have never found the courage to read). Autobiography becomes autopathography, the self as refracted through the prism of disease; though in the case of dementia this can only reach so far. 'For how does the *I* observe the *I* that is going,' asks Nicci Gerrard, 'and how can language capture its own disintegration?'

In *What Dementia Teaches Us About Love*, she explores the 'emotional modernism' of the art that attempts not simply to observe and describe but to inhabit late-stage Alzheimer's: that 'desolate place of self loss' in which 'there is no central narrator, no coherent story, where things are fractured and the safe ground slides away beneath our feet.' In the wake of her husband's dementia, she finds the work of Samuel Beckett charged with a new meaning, as does Dasha Kiper: those 'nutty, obscure and flamboyant conversations' in a play like *Waiting for Godot*, the 'nonsensical misunderstandings, pointless quibbles, inconsequential mutterings.' The kind of talking that carries on even in the absence of anything to talk about ('This is becoming really insignificant,' says Estragon at one point). That is just to keep some channel open in the face of growing absurdity, sadness, silence.

A kind of broken experimentalism, Gerrard suggests, a jagged non-realism is better able to impart a sense of the condition as it advances. She gives the example of *The Father*, the recent film with Anthony Hopkins, adapted from Florian Zeller's play. The language of film – shifting sets, changes of actor, jump cuts – is used to evoke an experience of growing confusion and disorientation. Many found it wrenching, gruelling; but my reaction was envy: this is a best-case scenario. Hopkins has such a nice apartment! His daughter (Olivia Colman) is so devoted, his private nurse looks like a film star. He is obsessed about losing his watch, something worth obsessing about, not the little Taz plastic counters that came out of Simba chip packets and so worried my mother.

If anything, it is *Everywhere at the End of Time* by sound artist The Caretaker (Leyland Kirby) that I've found most equal to the gravity and remorselessness of neurodegeneration – no doubt because it moves beyond words altogether. Across six albums and almost seven hours, Kirby subjects old swing and ballroom records from the 1930s to increasing levels of distortion and sonic degradation. The nostalgic soundtrack (just on the edge of human memory) grows ever fainter, the enveloping noise ever louder. 'A brutal bliss beyond this empty defeat', 'Place in the world fades away' – these are track names in Stage 6, right at the end. By then there is only a buzzing, crackling drone, a wash of distortion that is beautiful, terrifying, terminally lucid.

Do you try to keep someone aware of the facts of their own life, no matter how bleak, and if so for how long? Or do you surrender to a parallel world of simulation and therapeutic lying? A world in which care homes hire improv comedians to help train their staff, with different parts of the facility referred to as 'on stage' or 'backstage'. One of the most haunting examples is something called simulated presence therapy, where loved ones are asked to compile an 'asset inventory' of a patient's happy memories, anecdotes and special interests. A 'chatting script' is then developed, a pre-recorded audiotape that impersonates one side of conversation, with timed pauses to allow for replies. 'There was a séance-like quality to these sessions,' MacFarquhar writes: 'They were designed to simulate the presence of someone who was merely not there, but they could, in principle, continue even after that person was dead.'

She seems unsure of the whole philosophy. What does it do to carers who must maintain these fantasies and falsehoods, who must preserve continuity as strictly as if they were on a film set? And what does it do to the moral standing of a person with Alzheimer's? Is it something you'd want for yourself, after all – being constantly lied to, having a waking dream elaborated around you – just to keep you calm? And (given that a future self with dementia would be so different to your present one) from what vantage point could such a decision ever be made?

The comforting fiction also opens up its inverse: the discomforting truth. That is, the intense frustration that results from trying to keep a dementia patient aware of reality. From trying in vain to reason with them, from not being able to help yourself, even while knowing that their behaviour is due to the disease.

It was not my mother doing all those bizarre things, I would write to my father, it was the Alzheimer's. I could never imagine that she was 'just being herself' when she made wild accusations or draped sopping clothes over everything, because her self was so fundamentally changed every time I came back home. This seemed so obvious to me then; but in time I have come to think a little differently.

To find oneself unable not to blame an Alzheimer's sufferer for what they do; to keep feeling (even while 'knowing' differently) that they are, in some way, just being themselves – this is also, in a way, to reaffirm their moral and human standing. It comes partly from trying to hold on to them – as an autonomous human being, a fully equipped moral self – for as long as possible.

Perhaps it was not just inflexibility or lack of imagination that made my father seem so ill-equipped to accommodate my mother's dementia, so unwilling to concede its alternative reality. Perhaps it was also him assuming that what she needed was what he, a fiercely independent, self-made man, would have wanted for himself.

To slide into the comforting fiction, on the other hand, is to tear up the contract of reciprocity, to default on the agreement that someone is just as real as you are. But eventually there is no choice in the matter.

8.

As my mother's anxiety subsided, as she entered the post-awareness stage, I felt better equipped. Quite well trained, in fact, for the serious business of submitting to a world where everything was (as she seemed to think one day when looking at photos from my travels) an avocado. Trees, sculptures, people in saris: to her, today, these were all avos. And we're going to go with that – avocado girls in avocado worlds – followed by a slow 'Hey Jude' waltz through the unit, *Na, na, na – NANANA-NAAAH!* – why not? Being serious does not mean being solemn: this was something I had learnt from her. Her utter lack of solemnity, her radiant ordinariness, had taught me a way to be with her now. How to roll with whatever comes your way, how to improvise. How to live (even in the face of all reasons to the contrary) an unembarrassed life.

Say it was some advertising jingle from her childhood that had floated up to the surface of her mind. We're going to dance through the unit doing 'the Pepsi jive'? Your arms (she shows me) go left, right, left right left. Sure, let's jive with that, all the way out the unit and through the gardens. Let's Pepsi jive all the way to the fuchsia, where Tyler is going to join us in this entry-level dancing, but give it a reggae skank.

Or was it time to belt out Edith Piaf again? *Non, rien de rien!* we would sing to each other, sashaying through the unit with dishcloths round our faces, really going for it. *Nooooooooohn, je ne regrette rien!* That much I understood, but from there on we were both 'yoghurting' out the lyrics – something I learnt from a French friend. *Il fait du yaourt* was when she and her teenage pals would mime English pop songs without knowing the words. You just go for a mushy, nonsensical approximation of English-ish syllables, all sound and no meaning. *C'est payéééé, balayéééééé, oubliééééééé … Je m'en fou de passééééééééé!* I don't care about the past – it's paid out, swept away, forgotten – although the

French is stronger. About the past, frankly I don't give a shit.

Lalalalalalalalala... My mother is stuck in these syllables, singing a mantra in the garden of the care home. It is much later in the disease, close to the end.

'Yes dear,' one of the other women says. 'We get the picture.'

'I think they're dosing her with too many drugs,' my father says. One of the women who bathe and change my mother is named Patience. There are other details that I don't want to record.

My mother lies in a wooden room where I feed her soup and peeled grapes. The care home is under the trees, in earshot of the highway. Cars and trucks driving through the night – but it is comforting somehow, a wash of sound. This is the place where her life, the life left in her body, will end.

9.

I was clearing out a cupboard when a small red book fell out of a box. The cover read 'Millennium 2000 Edition' – it was a diary. I opened it and saw my mother's name in caps. The front pages were covered in bits of her handwriting: phone numbers, addresses, reminders to call her friends – all clustered together in different inks and sizes. Also random names and words that she was (I think) trying to puzzle out the spelling of:

> Freddy / Mercury Murcurie
> perfectionist
> John Gull Guillgood 93 died.
> Dr John Grey psy men mars woman venus. Shoe laces stockings <u>New glasses</u> etc Owe N.B. Melody ^{rang} a ring next time She rang today. 9 3 TV3. ¼ to 3 collect Hed. 5c x 4 Passport No: Tim has. Medical Aid No: Not on anymore. 54 kg – my weight.

It is not a dear diary kind of diary. It is not confiding or reflective, and there is barely a mention of her condition. It mostly logs daily events, chores, money spent. 'Bought this book', the first entry reads on Monday 27 December 1999. 1 January has 'R50,54 (food bought)' but no new millennium's resolutions. If (as many suspect) human memory evolved less to record than to predict, then forgetting is just as corrosive to the future as the past. 'Walked to Ultra City for bread' is a typical entry. 'Walked to town got some sweets washed takies and windows.' 'Tried to do washing but useless.'

My mother's handwriting was rounded, easily legible. In its prime it looked both confident and approachable, smartly adult but without having entirely lost the loops of a more girlish hand. Unpretentious, I would say, which was something I loved about her, love about her, I should say, more so with each passing year. The wisdom of her humility is endless.

The handwriting does begin to change, though. The letters become detached, rather than linked up in cursive. Her v's and n's had always been very similar, and now they become almost impossible to tell apart. The earlier entries surely record a 'lovely drive', a 'lovely day', but then somewhere it shades into 'lonely day': 'Bought tuna mayo lonely day'.

15 February: 'New Iron!! Hell to use. Windy day I went nowhere Things go from bad to worse.' 4 March: 'Tim collected more stones! stones in the head. Would like to see the masterpiece eventually.' 31 August: 'Walked to beach & sat there. Bought some cakes & Carol gave me a lift. Kind person.' There are many names I don't recognise: a whole roster of people who looked in on her and out for her, a book of random kindness. But she keeps having her shoes and wallet stolen: 'Real crooks at the Beach Bar.' I imagine that she had misplaced them, but who can tell.

The entries thin out as the year goes on. The second-last entry (3 September) is: 'Hed rang – Croatia?' After this the weeks pass with only the diary's printed reminders. Armed Forces Day in Mozambique and Malawian Mother's Day pass in quick succession, so do the Independence Days of Swaziland, Lesotho, Zambia and Angola.

My mother's last entry (presumably filled in ahead of time) is on 20 November: 'my b/day'. But other than that, blank.

10.

What would one woman's death by memory loss weigh in the scale of extraordinary human disaster? What did my mother's feeling useless count against a world where young men still wait for work at the complex turnoff, and seldom find it? If only such questions didn't have to be asked. If only we had reached the place where different kinds of sorrow didn't have to be weighed against each other. One answer would be: very little.

In another sense, given that the world can only be experienced via one mind at a time, I still have reason to think that what happened to my mother was just about the worst thing that ever happened. I have only given glimpses of it here, leaving out the deeper forms of chaos and embarrassment that the condition wreaks in a family, even while feeling compelled to record something of her life and its end. Why transcribe the entries of a diary I can barely read for an audience of readers I barely know? Why write down anything at all, given that Alzheimer's delivers you, like nothing else, to the limits of human being?

My mother's dementia coincided with a time in my life that is linked to the so-called reminiscence effect, or reminiscence bump. That is, the period in one's late teens and early twenties that is most richly impressed in the mind, the life stage that people return to most often, and most vividly, as they get older. My sense was that, while memories of her from that time had been censored or embargoed, they were and are also there, strongly there, waiting to be cued. Writing means pulling on one thing to bring another, as yet unrealised, with it. The beetle of memory pulling the candle on its back; or the candle drawing out the beetle.

Writing is the slow, recursive process in which words are laid down, then reordered and revised, tested and retested against memory in the attempt to produce something halfway dignified, somewhere between a sentimental fiction and a truth that can seem too harsh, or too self-satisfied in its harshness. Sometimes I worry that I have forgotten all about my mother; other times I feel that I carry her within my every sound and gesture, the shape of every sentence.

Every few months there are stories about medicine being on the verge of a breakthrough for Alzheimer's disease. If it ever comes, the magic pill, and if this epidemic of forgetfulness then becomes historical, then how should it be remembered? How do you build a memorial to forgetting?

'Things go from bad to worse' – the relentless nature of the disease will give the lie to any comforting fiction that one may try to braid around it. Don't pretend that it will be all right, or that there will be a clear moral or a message. Don't try to make an optimistic plot out of it. I can write about the way my mother came to inhabit the present moment more fully, feeling the sun on her face as if for the first time. But then I must also record how she would, later on, sit out in the complex garden until she was badly sunburned. The staff tried, Tyler tried, my father said, but it wasn't like he could make her go inside. By the time my mother died, Tyler and I both had our driver's licences. For the funeral I picked him up in my father's Opel Corsa Lite (the Audis were long gone) and was touched by how smart he looked in his leather jacket. I realised that I had never seen him in anything but the complex uniform.

Equally, don't stay mired in sadness for too long. Since there is, finally, no way of knowing what happens in the mind of someone in the late stages of this disease. Also (I would say to my younger self), your anger and impatience is not only selfishness. That thing that feels like a moral tumour in your psyche, it also comes from wanting to hold on to a loved one as a complete person for as long as possible.

A memoir is not simply an account of how things were – that would be naïve. It is more an exercise in how you want the world remembered, a strengthening and laying down of certain neural pathways and now these strings of words, sentence by sentence unfolding on a page, until the end.

The utopia project

For some reason Maps took you the wrong way, so we gave directions by email or over the phone.

You could take the coast road, and where the mountains ran up close to the sea, there was a fold in the escarpment, like a deep green U. At the bottom was a cluster of thatched, whitewashed buildings surrounded by olive groves and paddocks. People would sometimes just turn up at reception, asking about whether they could hike or swim on the property – the kloof had beckoned them off the road. After heavy rains, a rill of white would appear high on the slopes. This was a waterfall that we warned people about: it looked closer than it was.

Or you could take the main road and turn off after Bela, the Moravian mission town. A dirt road wound through the foothills, through apricot orchards, citrus and almonds. Signs asked drivers to keep to 20 km/h, to avoid covering the fruit in dust, then you crested a rise and there it was. And when people saw it all laid out – the cloisters and the Meditation Hall, the gardens and the labyrinth, the fishponds and the farmhouse under those enormous trees that were always in motion, always shimmering as the wind blew in from the sea – then they tended to start thinking that *this was the place*. This was the place where your long-suppressed dreams of a different life might finally come into being. A better life, the counterlife that you should have been living all along.

And that was just the problem, said Maxine, the owner. No sooner had people arrived than they began to have designs on it: they wanted to make it into *their* version of the good life. Each week brought another round of guests or seekers, another genre of alternative living. Buddhist retreats and gut cleanse workshops, song circles and sweat lodges, tantric masterclasses (by invitation only) – they all passed through, each with their own dietary requirements.

Frankly, she was getting tired of it all. The hangers-on and freeloaders, the locals who made dreamcatchers and bad jewellery. People whose conversation was too vague, who had no real sense of the country they were living in, no politics. Then there was the yoga and wellness crowd who crunched up the driveway in their Subarus, all Lycra and smoothies. 'Thank yourself for taking this time just for yourself': this is what the teachers would intone while you lay there in Savasana. All this 'self-care', now what was that – some kind of neoliberal mantra? So, she wanted to transition to something more meaningful, more organic intellectual. Her father had been a historian of the Struggle, a political theorist, a thinker – we'd seen the library.

Max was an old friend of my father-in-law, who'd been a trade unionist and Trotskyite in the 1980s but was now more into spiritual transformation and what he termed 'plant work'. A generous man who liked to sweep you up in his latest enthusiasms, he would give his daughter and me birthday presents along these lines. And so we had visited a couple of times before, first for a mushroom ceremony (which was beautiful) and then for an ayahuasca song circle (less so). We stayed in the old farmhouse, our door opening onto the library. This was a small, square room with comfortable armchairs, a wood-burning stove and floor-to-ceiling bookshelves. Socialist books, spiritual books, ecological, counter-cultural, New Age, religious, historical, mystical, devotional, practical, impractical – that utopian library kept beckoning me back. On the lawn outside was a labyrinth: a snaking cement pathway overgrown with succulents and spekboom.

Mornings of writing and then afternoons on the land: digging vegetables, planting trees, cutting back aliens. This was the idea: a perfect balance between honest organic toil and the life of the mind. What happened is that we were drawn into the micro-politics of a retreat centre in a troubled country, and one that proved not so easy to retreat from. We saw, you could say, the back end of mindfulness.

Maxine had been running the place at a loss for years – as 'a moderately unsuccessful hotel' she said, showing us around after we arrived. She was a beautiful woman in her sixties. A bronze bust had made of her when she was young; it stood between the horse paddock and the biogas digester – that was what this heavy manhole lid in the ground was. And here was a new common room under construction – we were introduced to the team of builders, all from Zimbabwe.

Repairing the grass between the farmhouse and the kitchen was one of the first things we could do. There had been a wedding that turned into a three-day rave: the lawn was badly stomped on. The tool and garden shed was behind the chicken coop, with shapes of the different implements traced satisfyingly on a wooden board. There were caterpillars and chrysalids on the beams, the chicken wire, all over the shears and secateurs, even in the metal grooves of the spades – I'd never seen such a hatch before. You're always fed the line that the caterpillar wants to turn into a butterfly, Maxine said, but these ones seemed to be having a dreadful time. They were woozy and broken-winged on the fence posts, locked together at the abdomen, pecked at by the chickens.

It was the 'end of term', she explained, since the current cohort of volunteers was about to leave. This was a new system they'd been trialling. For three months it was free room and board, with off-grid living and mindfulness workshops provided by Julian. But you offered your mindful labour, or *dana*, to help maintain the property, water the gardens, run the kitchen, change the bedding of the paying guests and retreatants. In time they wanted to extend the volunteer system over an entire year, slowly transforming the place from a venue for hire into something more meaningful. But for now she needed a break, Maxine said, a retreat from her retreat. She was going to spend time abroad, visit Schumacher College, an ashram maybe. And we could slot in as volunteers, help Julian with his preparations for the Organic School.

Julian was Max's new boyfriend – slim and tanned, with silvery, shoulder-length hair, quite a bit younger than her. He was working as a kind of estate manager, taking care of the land, which he pronounced (with great reverence) *the lehnd* – he'd spent time in New Zealand, which had done something to his vowels. It had more intentional communities per capita than anywhere else in the world, apparently, except Israel.

Julian was into indigenous African cosmologies and reckoned this place was on sacred, energetic ground. The lines of rock strata all bent and converged on the U-shaped kloof, so if you looked at things from a hunter-gatherer perspective (which he often asked volunteers to do) you might think: now here is a place of shelter, sweet water, good things. And sure enough, there were stick figures, buck and water snakes etched on rock shelters all up through the slopes: a haunch here, a hand there. It was all part of a conservancy that was virtually its own floral kingdom. Sun glistened on the small-leaved fynbos; birds with long tails chased each other from flower to flower.

Maxine's house was upslope in the Afromontane forest. From a wooden deck in the foliage, she could look out over the Shangri-La she'd created and occasionally swoop down to expel everyone and start over. There had been many such purges over the years (my father-in-law told us) and several boyfriends – so I felt a little anxious for Julian. While guests and celebrants flounced around in robes, he wore those hiking pants with the zip halfway down, the ones you could turn into shorts if things got heated (and then have the problem of where to keep the unzipped cut-offs: I knew those pants).

Julian didn't say much but smiled about the plant work crowd. His thing was not psychotropic work but real labour, the kind that left the muscles in your back aching. He worked all day long: forking the compost heaps and tucking them up in blankets to speed decomposition; clearing wattle trees and feeding the woodchips into the hot water boiler. His dream was to create an Organic School here, a place devoted to permaculture, off-grid living, mindful labour and sustainability. And he really needed our help in drafting the Code of Conduct – you wouldn't believe the difficulties they'd had.

'The telephone book of most cities reminds us that utopia is always with us', writes one historian of the concept. The telephone book is gone now, but utopia remains. In an hour's radius of where I live you can find utopia as 1) bathroom tiles showroom, 2) supplier of domestic Astroturf, 3) vegan foods business specialising in dairy-free dairy, 4) heavily securitised old age home and 5) a rooftop restaurant, Utopia: Dining Elevated, at the top of a hotel called The Capital Mirage.

Utopia as meme, brand name, marketing widget. A word that can encompass everything from toilets to fake lawn, from nut-based cheese to Stellenbosch frail care unit (with PRIVATE PROPERTY: KEEP OUT! signs outside). Also note the switcheroo: it's not Utopia Elevated Dining but Utopia: Dining Elevated – which implies that the whole notion of eating at altitude has been rethought, the entire rooftop dining wheel reinvented, by the copy writers of The Capital Mirage.

It wasn't those utopias I was looking for. I was in search of real utopias, actual utopias. But it's a hard concept to get at, a contradiction in terms.

The first thing people will tell you about utopia is that the word means both 'good place' (*eutopia*) and 'no-place' (*outopia*). The original Latin was a pun, coined by Thomas More in his 1516 account of a perfectly governed island commonwealth off the coast of North America (which now reads a little totalitarian). In the nineteenth century, the great age of utopian writing, others play the same game: Samuel Butler's *Erewhon* is a scrambled version of 'nowhere'. Both books contain maps of a place that is hinting at its own impossibility.

Outopia suggests a place that is unrealisable, impracticable, impossible. This is a common, negative usage of the word, as in utopian dreams, something too idealistic to work in the real world (Marx and Engels famously dismissed 'utopian socialism' in favour of their own 'scientific' variant). *Eutopia* broaches the question: whose version of the good are we dealing with exactly, and at whose expense? It chimes uneasily with other eu- words in the English language – euphemism, euthanasia, eugenics.

In the five centuries since More dreamed up his island, utopianism has come to mean everything from literary genre to political theory to a whole range of experiments in living differently: communes, kibbutzim, co-operatives, eco-villages. But across it all the word holds in tension two very different attitudes to the world, and to human nature – so different, in fact, that it's hard to contain both in a single frame.

One is the earnest manifesto for social change and human betterment, a blueprint for total social overhaul, from Plato's *Republic* of philosopher kings to Marx's classless society. The other is a much more sceptical, ironic view of whether this would ever come about, how it might play out if it did, and who would be in control. 'There's always a little Hitler in there somewhere,' a friend used to say whenever I spoke longingly of going off to live on a commune. Utopianism mixes the deadly earnest and the unstoppably satirical. It throws together ideologues and ironists, authoritarians and anarchists. Literary utopias explicate brave new worlds but also implicate those who fall for them too easily.

In the wake of fascism and communism, in a world of religious and market fundamentalisms, eutopia warns of the violence that so often underlies impositions of a better world, and the atrocities justified by idealism or ideology. Page through *The Faber Book of Utopias* and there *is* a Hitler in there: John Carey's anthology includes an excerpt from the Führer's table talk, a conquered Ukraine reimagined as breadbasket of a racially purified Germania: 'We shall get between ten and twelve million tons of grain annually. I think we ought to build spaghetti factories on the spot.'

To count as a utopia, Carey suggests, 'an imaginary place must be an expression of desire. To count as a dystopia, it must be an expression of fear'. This makes them sound like opposites. 'But scratch the surface a little', writes Margaret Atwood, and 'you see something more like a yin and yang pattern; within each utopia, a concealed dystopia; within each dystopia, a hidden utopia' – 'each contains a latent version of the other'. The Czech writer Milan Kundera extends this line of thinking into a little parable of Soviet communism: 'Once the dream of paradise starts to turn into reality, however, here and there people begin to crop up who stand in its way, and so the rulers of paradise must build a little gulag on the side of Eden. In the course of time this gulag grows ever bigger and more perfect, while the adjoining paradise gets ever smaller and poorer.'

I take all this as read. But (just to put it simply for now) what I mean by actual utopias are those that are not (when you scratch the surface) actually dystopias. That is too easy. That move is all too common by now – artistically, politically – even a little complacent.

In cinemas, on bookshelves and streaming platforms, a whole flood of dystopian futures and apocalypses pour forth: slick HD disasters which not only imagine but even seem to obscurely desire the world's end. Dystopia had become routine, and post-apocalyptic wastelands reassuringly familiar – this is what academics and Marxists were saying.

Why are we so comfortable with dystopias? Have they become a kind of easy, feet up on the couch fatalism? Even if so many utopian dreams of the twentieth century went sour, we shouldn't give up on the utopian impulse. Because this, wrote Zygmunt Baumann, was a fundamental trait of the human project: 'To measure the life "as it is" by a life as it *should be* (that is, a life *imagined* to be different from the life *known*, and particularly a life that is better and would be *preferable* to the life known) is a defining, constitutive feature of humanity.'

But all those italics, those hectoring *Marxist* italics. Just on the basis of those italics, I felt that my utopia project would have to be something set apart from the language of the intellectual left, vast segments of which had (I felt) taken a wrong turn somewhere, had come to advance a joyless vision of life. Or one where joy was suspect, always at the expense of someone else, like some kind of ill-gotten surplus value.

In my day job, it sometimes seemed that imagining the worst was the surest way to get ahead. The end result of all this – this outflanking of competitors through ever more stringent, undeceived or dire imaginings – was turning the university (surely one of humanity's great utopian ideas) into a real downer. That was my feeling, anyway, as my sabbatical came up and I found myself wanting to be as far away from academic institutions as possible, spending time in places (whether real or imagined) based on a risky optimism rather than safe, professional pessimism.

So, the idea was to work from the other direction in the complex yin/yang of hope and fear, garden and gulag: to unearth traces of utopian thought and imagination and community from all the discontent. Not to indulge in cruel optimism or other forms of brittle positivity (investor confidence, Dining Elevated, etc.) – but rather to admit the worst, and then to work from there. To snatch utopia from the jaws of dystopia, so to speak. If only to say that there were alternatives, and that it could have gone differently with the human experiment (I would settle for the past tense). Another world was possible.

On the front page of a notebook, I copied out an epigraph. A bit of graffiti that appeared in Latin America at the turn of the millennium, and which says it all really: *Let's save pessimism for better times.*

Some people arrived and it was like they'd never used a rake before. You saw them pushing a rake like it was a broom. And he loved those people, Julian said, because they could learn with you. Others arrived and then asked for toothpaste and you say: Well, you signed on for three months, how much toothpaste did you bring? Three days of toothpaste. Then mummy and daddy must go and get toothpaste from town.

We were meeting with Julian to begin drafting the Code of Conduct. He was giving us a list of prohibitions, bugbears, snags – he had a lot of experience in this sector. He was going to give it to us straight. But then he wanted us to rewrite it into something gentler for the Organic School welcome pack, nuance it a little. We were also going to compile a What to Bring section, which was more like a What Not to Bring.

First off: no alcohol and no hard drugs. That sounded fair enough: we could all use some drying out. Though sitting on Maxine's wooden deck, discussing this over a glass of wine, I felt like a Communist Party member eating Western delicacies in his dacha.

Secondly: to get it across that there was no internet access. That also sounded okay – and clearly there was a big market for digital detoxing. But in fact there was an outcrop, called Signal Hill by those in the know, where you could pick up a bit of 3G under the milkwoods. A bit further upslope was a caravan where Brother Luke lived: an elderly man in robes who'd known some of the Beat poets, the Merry Pranksters and even been part of that Rajneesh experiment in Oregon – or so he said. He slept most of the day but always turned up for communal meals, where he tended to 'paw at' (Maxine's words) young women. We should just watch for that – though he was harmless really.

Thirdly: no marijuana. That was a tricky one. They'd tried all sorts of approaches. First, if you do it after hours, then fine. But invite someone with you. Don't be secretive, be ceremonial. Or go for a walk. Still didn't work. People were stoned all day, not present, not mindful. And there were power tools involved: chainsaws, wood-chippers, not to mention the danger of igniting the biogas digester. So, they clamped down, asking for total sobriety, clear minds.

But I knew that Joe and Verity, who worked in the kitchen, were smoking spliffs behind the tool shed – I knew that sweet, insinuating smell anywhere. If Julian's Toyota Hilux started descending from the slopes, its tyres xylophoning over the wooden bridges, then they went to the bird hide on one of the swimming dams. It was the perfect place, said Joe, a shy guy who scrubbed the pots and did the namaste greeting a lot. You were nicely concealed but could see anyone approaching.

'Let's go birding' came to have a secret meaning, which was satisfying to the birders among us. In the world beyond, cannabis had become a corporate empire, with CBD oil retailers and vape shops now looking like iStores. But here one could still feel a bit of an outlaw, hiding away from Julian and Gabriel, indulging in what Verity (who wore feathers in her dreads) liked to call 'ritualised transgressions'.

Gabriel was Belgian and very loyal to Julian and the whole Organic School vision (he also wore the zippable pants). He got up at sunrise to gong for early meditation, devotedly watered the agapanthus beds at sunset, and was skilled on the driveable mower. He loved this country, he told me, people were friendly. But his family back home teased him, asked if he'd joined some kind of cult.

This was another thing to get across in the Welcome Pack, said Julian, that they weren't a cult. Or a party venue. No more parties, definitely no more trance parties. The neighbouring guest farm had complained, and none of this was helping the Organic School's application to be zoned as a place of religious observance. Also, what must that 'music' be like, Julian asked, for the birds, the frogs, the snakes, the voles, the beyond-human presences, the multi-species entanglements that we shared the valley with?

He was a passionate guy, ecological – I liked him. But as he kept reeling off the rules – correction: not rules, but guiding principles that volunteers would voluntarily choose to be guided by – I wondered how we were going to massage all this into a welcome pack that didn't seem draconian or at best (at worst?) passive aggressive.

We were confronting some age-old utopian tensions between freedom to and freedom from. Where does your right to swing your fist – to crank up the bass bins of a PA rig – begin to impinge on my nose, on my right to enjoy the sound of frogs, or string quartets, or silence? Or anything at all, Julian said, since tech now offered such powerful and portable ways to amplify one person's ego and destroy someone else's life.

The only thing they would tolerate going forward was non-electrified, non-amplified music generated by either a) the breath or b) the playing of *non-annoying* acoustic instruments: e.g. singing, using the piano in the Med Hall or the other instruments hung on its walls: guitars, violins, mandolins, zithers, koras. But no djembes. And definitely no drum circles. Those were like catnip for the people they were trying to shake off.

Next was no gossip. No gossiping or 'chit chat' between volunteers and guests or retreatants. This seemed to be straying into dangerous territory. Who was going to draw the line between chit and chat? Imagine a world where every conversation had to be earnest and meaningful – I couldn't think of anything worse. And how could you outlaw gossiping, which was such a deeply human activity?

Indulging in it with Tessa (a dancer, who ran reception) and her partner Gary (a photographer, who looked after housekeeping) had given me some good backstory. Like when Gabriel had found ambiguous stains on the meditation cushions after the last sacral chakra opening workshop. The energetic space of the Hall had been so compromised that Maxine flew a group of monks out from Sri Lanka, who did a week of solid chanting to purge and then repressurise the venue. They'd also left behind a lot of tinned jackfruits, which Namaste Joe was now trying to work into every dish, despite our objections. Following a walk-out of the previous chef, he'd somehow taken charge of the kitchen.

Gary laughed at the whole mindful labour thing. It was a bit of a pantomime, really, some entry level chores for people who'd never learnt to clean up after themselves. Since in fact a garden and domestic service was bussed in once a week from Kwanokuthula to do most of the work around here. Each afternoon he would drop the builders back there, driving them in Julian's Hilux. One day he asked me to do it and must have seen the look on my face: I was going to be driving labourers in the back of a bakkie now, like a fully fledged white farmer? Don't worry, it was twin cab, Gary said, so we could all ride together inside. My conscience would be safe.

'Just drop us at the 80s,' said Denzel the foreman as we approached the location on the edge of town. Why go back there, I thought? A second later I realised he meant the 80 km/h signs at the side of the road. I was more than happy to drive right up to their doors, but Denzel said better not: the locals were hard on foreigners here, didn't like them having jobs, they would walk from there. Just drop us at the 80s.

Ja, it was a bit of a bubble, Gary said as we changed sheets and pillowcases. This part of the world wasn't the easiest place to set up an intentional community, a gated community was a surer bet. He and Tessa were leaving soon, going back to the city – but it was mainly because of the kids.

Utopianism: A Very Short Introduction remarks that intentional communities 'are often seen as wonderful places to be a child and terrible places to be a teenager'. This spoke directly to the experience of Tessa's two children. Four-year old Maia was living in paradise, dancing across the lawns in a tutu, counting the frogs in the dams, riding on her cool dad's tattooed shoulders as he showed guests around in Thai threads. But for Lisa, who was seventeen, and the child of a different father, every minute among these nerds with lame pants seemed agonising. She could barely raise her gaze enough to greet you, and would spend all day on Signal Hill, waiting for bits of her real world to buffer, or waiting for her dad to come and pick her up in his Audi Quattro. It had a picture of himself on it – firm jaw, hard, competent face – with one of those real estate taglines: 'I am Whale Coast'. He made a point of never taking a step beyond the gravel parking lot, and often wouldn't even get out of his vehicle, especially if he saw any celebrants floating around in robes.

Scanning the shelves of the library, I wondered what to read. It was an eclectic selection for sure: Plato's dialogues next to Credo Mutwa's *Indaba My Children*; Jan Smuts's *Holism and Evolution* rubbing shoulders with Chomsky and Chairman Mao's poetry. John Ruskin's *Unto this Last* sat alongside Krishnamurti, Fanon was up against Gandhi. I paged through Ramachandra Guha's biography of the Mahatma's South African years at the Phoenix ashram near Durban. 'Beetles everywhere, spiders, ants in the milk', wrote one long-suffering devotee: 'No baths, water bad, people half naked, filth too. Lift a plate and you will find an insect underneath, snakes hanging from the tree, you have not only to tolerate this but love the insect life, you may not destroy any life.'

One shelf was pure political economy and class struggle: left-wing texts and people's histories from the liberation struggle. I guessed this was the core collection from Maxine's father. But since then, there had been an open-minded exchange policy: take a book, leave a book. So, all the hard-nosed historical materialism had been infiltrated by more esoteric and (to use a word Julian liked) 'woo-woo' texts: guides to this or that spiritual path, self-actualisation manuals, ways to transform the world from within your own consciousness.

The dimensions of this square, cosy library made you feel that, given enough time, maybe you could get through everything. But as so often happens when you look at all the books you thought you wanted to read, you don't feel like reading any of them. They seemed too worthy, too nebulous, or too self-righteous – the kind of books you knew would be filled with musts and oughts.

My eyes scanned the shelves until I found a tattered old biography of George Orwell. Paging through I came across a 1937 letter by his wife, Eileen Blair, explaining to a friend that they now had a little dog and called him Marx. This was 'to remind us that we had never read Marx, and now we have read a little and take so strong a personal dislike to the man that we can't look the dog in the face when we speak to him'.

Orwell was famously hard on middle-class cranks, writing that the mere words 'Socialism' and 'Communism' seemed to draw towards them with magnetic force 'every fruit-juice drinker, nudist, sandal-wearer, sex-maniac, Quaker, "Nature Cure" quack, pacifist, and feminist in England'. But that problematic crabbiness made the optimism that was there all the more real, I felt, and all the more nourishing. It was a strange thing, and not talked about much: that the writer who had dreamed up the most famous, most pitiless dystopia of them all could write so well about happiness.

As we pulled up rotting lilies from the swimming ponds or chased baboons out of the orchard, I began to think of the experience here as an Orwellian pastoral – but in two opposed senses of the word. The first was the negative, Big Brother sense. This came from the feeling that even within this paradise, someone was always watching you, always monitoring your virtue. But actually it was still more subtly totalitarian: not that you were being watched and monitored but that you *wanted to be*. If you were doing something virtuous, you wanted to be seen doing it. A rather shabby realisation about yourself: that you were 'doing the work' (one of this place's catchphrases) not for its own sake, but for some kind of social currency. We called this high-vis *dana* – as opposed to the tasks where you were far away in the fynbos or upslope (low-vis *dana*) and so could not harvest the self-satisfaction of knowing that people were clocking your labour.

High-vis *dana* was digging trenches around the vegetable beds that were located next to the main driveway. There were five raised beds clustered in a circle, each bordered by wooden planks, five variations on a trapezium. The job was to dig a 20 cm-wide trench round each, then fill it with woodchips from Julian's temperamental boiler. The woodchips were to keep out pests but mostly to create a moat that halted the kikuyu, which always seemed poised to take over everything around here ('This whole place is a war against grass,' Gabriel told me as he climbed on the mower). The tangible progress of digging these trenches and filling them in was very satisfying – you could see what you were doing and so could everyone else. Until eventually you forgot about all that pettiness and were drawn into another world.

Of sunflowers and artichokes, gooseberries and golden rod. Of mother spiders rushing away their egg sacs, and the white grubs that swifts and hadedas would land and peck for. The little flashes of red or blue were wing cases shed by escaping beetles. Once, sadly, my spade severed the tail of a small grass snake, its underside coloured like a white anchovy. Forking the strips of dug-up turf onto the first compost heap, I apologised for this to the mole snake, the grass snake's kin that generally took the sun on one of the four heaps (there was a progression from the new, raw stuff all the way to the dark, mature compost, nicely tucked up under its blanket). Later I realised that the kikuyu strips could be used, like a skin graft, to repair the lawn that the wedding ravers had stomped on. How satisfying to be part of a circular economy, an ecology where nothing was wasted. And then back to drawing earthy borders round the five geometrical beds, like putting five perfect paragraphs down on the page.

Here was the other, positive, sense of the Orwellian pastoral. He was a man who loved digging in the earth, keeping chickens and generally enjoying the sensory pleasures of a physical world. 'Outside my work the thing I care most about is gardening', he wrote in response to an author questionnaire in 1940, 'especially vegetable gardening'. In an essay of 1946, he noted the toads that he sometimes found hibernating underground, and how this animal 'has about the most beautiful eye of any living creature'.

Is it wrong to take pleasure in things like this, Orwell wonders? 'To put it more precisely, is it politically reprehensible, while we are all groaning, or at any rate ought to be groaning, under the shackles of the capitalist system?' *Ought* to be groaning – exactly. This was the expected code of conduct in the seminar and committee rooms where I worked. Orwell goes on: 'If a man cannot enjoy the return of Spring, why should he be happy in a labour-saving Utopia?' And then ends on the beautifully wilful note – the note I always loved and listened for in his writing – that 'they can't stop you enjoying it. This is a satisfying reflection'.

The Meditation Hall was the heart of the place, a whitewashed building with high eaves and a thatched roof. It looked a bit like a rustic chapel, but instead of stained glass there was a clear window set under the roof beams: one square, transparent pane through which you could see the slopes of the kloof, grasses rippling in the wind.

During the mushroom ceremony held there, I understood (as we listened to gorgeous strings and choirs via Bluetooth speakers – what a miracle: our daily reality really did involve living out the wildest dreams of previous eras) that the green slopes were somehow continuous with the flanks of the eland who grazed on them, those glossy creatures who were in turn shaded delicately on rocks by the First Peoples of these valleys; and that the same energy undulated through the slopes and trees and through time, making us all one with the fruiting body of the eternal earth mother. The celebrants were mostly elderly people who lay down on the floor in sleeping bags, listened to the music and (one of them told me) came to a different relationship with death.

During the ayahuasca song circle, I experienced a kind of panic boredom because I didn't know when the session leader, a pony-tailed guy called Brendan, was going to stop talking. 'I don't really want to say much,' he began, 'since what we're about to experience – the teachings, the learnings – well, it's really beyond words.' Sure enough, two, three hours later he was still lecturing us about his experiences in the Amazon and the revelations granted him by its magical vines, whose only effect on me was a low-level nausea. The only thing he asked was that no one left the venue before the ceremony was over (because it could break the energetic seal). But that was, in effect, asking everything. We were locked in all night, made to sing the 'hymns' he had written and then printed out in a little laminated hymn book – he was trying to start 'a congregation' in the area. If ever you fell asleep, one of his helpers would shake you awake and point out the stanza you were supposed to be singing: that you should soar, soar, soar with the wings of an eagle, or that God is love and love is everything and everything is love.

Going through this life entailed drinking in so much beauty and bearing up under so much pain – and that was okay. You could make peace with it. This seemed to be the gist of the mushroom ceremony for many of us, as we entered that state where emotions 'arrive in all their newborn nakedness, unprotected from the harsh light of scrutiny and, especially, the pitiless glare of irony'. This is how Michael Pollan puts it in *How to Change Your Mind*, his book on psychedelic experience and the brain: 'Platitudes that wouldn't seem out of place on a Hallmark card glow with the force of revealed truth.' He goes on to say that there was nothing supernatural about his psilocybin-heightened perceptions, nothing that he needed an idea of magic or divinity to explain:

> No, all it took was another perceptual slant on the same old reality, a lens or mode of consciousness that invented nothing but merely (merely!) italicized the prose of ordinary experience, disclosing the wonder that is always there in a garden or wood, hidden in plain sight ... Nature does

in fact teem with subjectivities — call them spirits if you like — other than our own; it is only the human ego, with its imagined monopoly on subjectivity, that keeps us from recognizing them all, our kith and kin.

That was beautifully put: the prose of ordinary experience being italicised, made emphatic, its innate sacredness revealed by wonder and expanded perception (so different from the 'italics mine' of pushy academia). The teeming strangeness and otherness of the other-than-world, pressing in, pressing in. The chickens eating the caterpillars, and us eating the chicken eggs with their bright orange yolks — disgusting and miraculous. The quadrophonic bird and frog song that issued from the forest and the swimming ponds at dusk. The sociable weaver birds, *clearly* communicating with each other, chatting, gossiping, lifting off in a swarm together and then, in a split second, magnetised back onto the stems of the rushes, silent. 'Nature does in fact teem with subjectivities — call them spirits if you like — other than our own.'

But most of the time it wasn't so beautifully put. Most of the time it was the Hallmark platitude. 'Everything is ready to acknowledge you, if you're just open to it, even a stone' — this was Brendan verbalising the same sentiments as Pollan, but now it sounded ridiculous (how could a *stone* acknowledge anything?) Especially when one of the acolytes (who had been waking me up all night) leapt in to agree and began telling us how a tree snake in the forest 'had done a little dance' for her (no it *hadn't!*). Brendan listened and nodded as if he already knew this, had expected it since the dawn of time.

All of which is to say that I shared Julian's (and Orwell's) impatience with the plant work crowd, even while beginning to realise that his Organic School Welcome Pack (which we were now having daily meetings about, as if he needed to decompress after two decades in the intentional community sector) was wildly over-reaching itself.

No romantic relationships between volunteers. A controversial one, he knew, but Julian wouldn't budge. There were rumours down in the valley about this being a kind of sex cult. There always were, around any commune — people out there were so uptight and salacious, they projected it all onto you. So, they needed to 'change the brand' (he had these lapses into corporate speak), to keep the tantric and pelvic floor crowd away.

Then food. When it came to dietary requirements, Julian closed his eyes and tilted his head down, silent. He placed thumb at one temple and middle finger at the other, covering his eyes. The issue of food, I gathered, was that intense, that fraught. Let's just say that people projected a lot onto food, Julian said, a lot. They wanted to feel catered for, fine. But then individually, as if they were clients or customers. Everyone wanted to customise an experience that should actually be communal; some of the plant work crowd even stipulated no salt. Now what was that about? Some people needed no onions. Some needed bone broth with every meal. There were always issues in the kitchen, always. It was kind of a major power base.

The kitchen power was definitely going to Joe's head. He was rolling out ever more bizarre dishes, and not hearing a word against them. A Thai green curry pasta salad. A Spanish omelette sprinkled with cranberries. Rocket topped with turmeric and a slick of coconut oil fried kale. This is the kind of thing we were having to carry out to guests, and also to Denzel's crew of builders who (the looks on their faces seemed to say) were having all their worst culinary stereotypes confirmed. Joe was obsessed with not wasting food – if something had been opened it needed to be finished – but this led to an epidemic of wastefulness. If a R500 tin of olives had been opened, it would be olives on everything until the tin was finished. Salads became so strange – collages of boiled eggs, grapefruit segments, olives – that they seemed like something forked off the compost and dumped on a plate. Joe would not hear a single criticism: he had swelled up from Namaste Joe to a kitchen tyrant in a week, like one of those Grow Monsters you chuck in a kid's bath. I tried to joke with Verity about it, but she was too kind, too understanding. Joe was a bit on the spectrum you know, a bit neurodivergent. You just had to get used to him – he meant well.

To deal with human oddity with no recourse to gossip – this was the hardest edict of all. All interpersonal niggles, Julian told us, should be resolved via a process of talking circles that involved a talking stick – when you were holding the talking stick, only you could talk, and everyone had to listen. A central tenet of the future School: criticism was all well and good, but if you wanted to indulge in it, you had to do it to someone's face.

Finally, the question of expulsion, rustication, excommunication, he would leave us to find the right word. It would all work via consultation and the mutual criticism talking stick sessions. The party in question would have input, the group would have input. Then Julian would have input. It did happen, it would happen. He'd seen it with the volunteers, it was a difficult process. They would have a breakdown at some point, they were supposed to, it would come. You close the escape hatches one by one: alcohol, internet, chocolate, chit, chat. And they realise there aren't escape hatches really, that there's no escaping yourself. That there's no need to escape. That everything you need is already present.

It didn't come as such a surprise to hear that the Organic School had imploded a month or two after its inauguration. I don't know what the full story was – I only got it in bits and pieces, in text messages from Tessa and Gary, Joe and Verity. But it seemed that Maxine had come back from her sabbatical and found a mutiny in progress against Julian. The Organic School volunteers, she said, would probably have stayed the course and made less of a fuss about the food if they'd had to pay for the experience rather than having been given this incredible opportunity for free – that was capitalism for you.

Julian said that the intake was just not emotionally ready for what he had to offer. The pandemic lockdown had also led to unforeseen pressures and intensifications. Protests closed the coastal road more often, so did fires and floods. There had been a mutiny against Julian and his talking sticks – too controlling – and huge problems with the woodchip boiler. It needed electricity to ignite, but the country was being plunged into ever more power cuts (some feared a collapse of the national grid). Julian's vision wasn't as self-sufficient as he liked to think, and eventually Max asked him to leave too – he'd moved down the coast to try it on with another community. From now on, her vision was rewilding, reforesting, environmental repair. She'd bought the adjoining farm and was going to create one of the biggest pockets of indigenous moist coastal forest in the country.

The only person left over was Gabriel, who still gonged the start of every day, watered the beds at sunset and walked the labyrinth, that snaking concrete path on the lawn between the library and the Meditation Hall. A labyrinth is different from a maze, of course: there are no choices, and so there are no wrong choices or dead ends. You simply walk the path in your own time, arrive at the centre after a series of detours and diversions.

This place could have been the ideal place, I thought, and could still be. But only if you could be the ideal you – that was the catch.

I thought about Orwell and Gandhi, whose biographies I had sunk into in the library, whose lives I found so moving. Shortly before his death, when he was working on *Nineteen Eighty-Four* in a remote cottage on the island of Jura, Orwell reviewed the Mahatma's autobiography. 'Reflections on Gandhi' was the last essay he ever wrote, about a figure at once so similar and so different from himself. Thinking about the life of this living saint, who demanded such asceticism and abstinence from his followers; who warned that friendship could lead you into wrongdoing (and once pressured his sick wife and child to refuse the chicken broth recommended by doctors); who, ultimately, located his idealism and politics in a world other than, better than, this one, Orwell reflects:

> This attitude is perhaps a noble one, but, in the sense which – I think – most people would give to the word, it is inhuman. The essence of being human is that one does not seek perfection, that one is sometimes willing to commit sins for the sake of loyalty, that one does not push asceticism to the point where it makes friendly intercourse impossible, and that one is prepared in the end to be defeated and broken up by life, which is the inevitable price of fastening one's love upon other human individuals.

Walking into the labyrinth, I was often impatient, with scattered thoughts and the urge to take shortcuts, to leap over the spekboom dividers and get it over with. But by the time I walked out, the mind had quietened and surrendered to the hairpins and doublings back; to the realisation that progress would be slow and convoluted, leaving a trail like you see made by insects under tree bark, or worms in the silt of the dam. I remember walking there afterwards, up the valley to the second of the two swimming ponds, and counting frogs at the bottom of the pier. Then down the wooden steps into the water, apologising to the spider who couldn't help but spin a web across them during the night.

The lonely planet

The Dictionary of Imaginary Places, compiled by Alberto Manguel and Gianni Guadalupi, comes in at 2 000 entries and over 700 pages – a tribute to the deep human urge to make up other worlds (and draw maps of them). Paging through, you might recognise names from childhood: MIDDLE-EARTH, EARTHSEA and NARNIA are there. So are KÔR, LILLIPUT and the ISLAND OF THE ROC. JURASSIC PARK and HOGWARTS were added in the second edition.

Then there are worlds encountered later in life: Gabriel García Márquez's jungle village MACONDO, with its plagues of amnesia and butterflies; the Pacific island of GONDAL, dreamed up by the Brontë sisters. Many islands of course: an island is the most available model, the starter pack, for dreaming up a distant, self-contained elsewhere. UTOPIA and EREWHON are there; so are ATLANTIS and AZANIA, LOTUS-EATERS ISLAND and CALIBAN'S ISLAND (see PROSPERO'S ISLAND).

'We agreed that our approach would have to be carefully balanced between the practical and the fantastic', Manguel writes in the foreword:

> We would take for granted that fiction was fact, and treat the chosen texts as seriously as one treats the reports of an explorer or chronicler, using only the information provided in the original source, with no 'inventions' on our part.

The straight-faced approach suits the genre of utopia. The defining characteristic of a literary utopia is 'its nonexistence combined with a *topos* – a location in time and space – to give it verisimilitude' (that is, the semblance of being real). This sets it apart from more free-floating visions of paradise, nirvana and the Golden Age. The better places of myth and religion tend to occupy another plane of existence; utopias have a more worldly address. Which is what makes Oscar Wilde's lines so apt: 'A map of the world that does not include Utopia is not worth even glancing at, for it leaves out the one country at which Humanity is always landing. And when Humanity lands there, it looks out, and seeing a better country, sets sail. Progress is the realisation of utopias.'

So where on earth to locate a utopia? Where to place the non-place? You can opt for the close at hand – a secret valley, as in the Chinese fable of the Peach Blossom Spring – or the other side of the world. With the circumnavigation of the globe, the antipodes become a favoured location. Thomas More's *Utopia* and Samuel Butler's *Erewhon* impersonate travelogues to places as far away as possible from their first readers – the New World for More, New Zealand for Butler – and here the utopian imagination becomes entangled with colonialism and empire. Brave new worlds for some mean dispossession and enslavement for others.

As more and more of the earth's surface is mapped by cartographers, speculative worlds migrate to Arctic wastes (Mary Shelley), the planet's hollow core (Jules Verne), the deep ocean (Verne again) or an exoticised African interior (H. Rider Haggard). Some are relocated into the past or future with time machines, or shifted into alternative streams of history: all strategies used in nineteenth-century bestsellers by Edward Bellamy, William Morris and HG Wells. Or (another refuge for the speculative imagination) what about a counter-history where Africa, Asia and the Americas were never colonised?

With space travel in the twentieth century, the astronomical solution comes to dominate: moving off-world and inventing new planets altogether. And so the literary tradition of utopia merges with science fiction, a genre in which absolutely everything (you would think) can be reimagined. Though in a piece called 'Do-It-Yourself Cosmology', Ursula K. Le Guin issues a warning about what SF fans call world building:

> As soon as you, the writer, have said 'The green sun had already set, but the red one was hanging like a bloated salami above the mountains,' you had better have a pretty fair idea in your head concerning the type and size of green suns and red suns – especially green ones, which are not the commonest sort – and the arguments concerning the existence of planets in a binary system, and the probable effects of a double primary on orbits, tides, seasons, and biological rhythms; and then of course the

mass of your planet and the nature of its atmosphere will tell you a good deal about the height and shape of those mountains; and so on, and on.

If you're bored by the labour of figuring all this out, she continues, then you shouldn't be writing science fiction. A great part of the pleasure of SF, for both writer and reader, 'lies in the solidity and precision, the logical elegance, of fantasy stimulated by and extrapolated from scientific fact'. This gets at something important in what makes an imaginary place seem real: that it is somehow self-consistent and true to its inner laws.

Other planets, however, are not included in the *Dictionary of Imaginary Places*. Given the vast scope of the imaginary universe, the editors had to establish certain limits. So, while Le Guin's island archipelago of Earthsea is well represented, her other (science fictional) universe does not appear. There is no mention of the most unlikely, most convincing better place of them all – the only one I've ever been tempted to leave Earth for anyway.

Anarres *is a fictional planet in* The Dispossessed, *a 1974 novel by Ursula K. Le Guin. The work received both Hugo and Nebula awards and is regarded, along with* The Left Hand of Darkness *(1969), as one of Le Guin's masterpieces, and a landmark in twentieth-century science fiction.*

Anarres is located, together with its neighbouring planet Urras, in the solar system of Tau Ceti, a real star at a distance of just under twelve light years from Earth (or Terra, as it is referred to in the novel). Urras is the Old World: state-controlled, hierarchical, patriarchal, unequal but lush, materially rich and beautiful. Anarres is the New World: anarchist, communal, feminist, egalitarian, but arid and ecologically poor.

A century and a half before the novel opens, idealistic revolutionaries from Urras have gone into exile and settled Anarres. The dry satellite planet becomes the setting for a social experiment based on the principles of mutual aid, communalism and social equality. On Anarres, the three great barriers to human freedom as identified by nineteenth-century anarchist thinkers – the state, organised religion and private property – are absent. The Dispossessed *was, Le Guin commented, her attempt to write an 'anarchist utopia'.*

Writing a readable utopia – putting down on paper a convincingly better world than our own – is famously difficult. Human improvement, contentment and perfection are not promising literary subjects. They tend towards the static, bland or blank ('happiness writes white', as the saying goes); whereas narrative needs problems and complications, antagonism and change. Contentment is best evoked in contrast to some other, more miserable, state; but what if everyone is homogeneously content? And then: anyone or anything too perfect and well-adjusted is likely to tip over into satire. Any greatly improved world may just sound too wholesome and boring. 'The newspapers of Utopia', wrote Arthur C. Clarke in *2001: A Space Odyssey*, 'would be terribly dull'.

Written utopias tend to be structured as a kind of guided tour of the world in question, with someone showing someone else around, explaining everything. These works may be dressed up in a kind of narrative, but what they really need to do is get across lots of information. This can make them feel clunky or pedagogical, as if you're sitting through a lecture (or reading Wikipedia). They are, in my experience, almost impossible to get to the end of.

Le Guin plays with this whole tradition in a short story called 'The Ones Who Walk Away from Omelas', one of her most famous. It imagines a summer festival in a coastal city that she tries to evoke as the most fortunate and beautiful of places, even as she wrangles with how difficult this is. 'The trouble is', she writes, 'that we have a bad habit, encouraged by pedants and sophisticates, of considering happiness as something rather stupid. Only pain is intellectual, only evil interesting'.

The first half of the piece is an invitation to help co-imagine this paradisal place. Do you want ancient parks, moss-covered walls, horses, parades, music, trains and trams? Or more modern technology, floating light sources, fuelless power, a cure of the common cold? Feel free to add or subtract as you like. Still, the narrator worries that Omelas so far strikes some of you as goody-goody: 'If so, please add an orgy. If an orgy would help, don't hesitate.' Drugs? Why not, why be puritanical? Let there be drooz, which brings lightness and brilliance, then dreaminess and languor, but is not habit-forming. What else? Let there be victory parades, but not for miliary victories (there are no soldiers): 'The joy built upon successful slaughter is not the right kind of joy; it will not do; it is fearful and it is trivial.'

If this still fails to convince, then the speaker asks us to imagine one final detail: that locked in a windowless basement somewhere in the city is a single suffering child, sitting alone in the dark:

> They all know it is there, all the people of Omelas. Some of them have come to see it, others are content merely to know it is there. They all know that it has to be there. Some of them understand why, and some do not, but they all understand that their happiness, the beauty of their city, the tenderness of their friendships, the health of their children, the wisdom of their scholars, the skill of their makers, even the abundance of their harvest and the kindly weathers of their skies, depend wholly on this child's abominable misery.

The terms are very strict: not even so much as a kind word may be spoken to the child, who sits in its own excrement, whose back and buttocks are mess of festering sores. Most people who visit the child eventually go on with their lives, or come to accept that the happiness of thousands depends on the misery of one. But there are some, just a few, who never accept this, who start walking down the streets and out the city gates:

> They go on. They leave Omelas, they walk ahead into the darkness, and they do not come back. The place they go towards is a place even less imaginable to most of us than the city of happiness. I cannot describe it at all. It is possible that it does not exist. But they seem to know where they are going, the ones who walk away from Omelas.

The story has been taught in thousands of school classrooms, mostly as a prompt for a debate about utilitarianism, or a glorified version of the trolley problem. Should you divert the train so that it kills only one person instead of more? Should ethical action be based on the principle of the greatest good for the greatest number?

But reading the story again, it strikes me how Le Guin introduces the pivot, in the first instance, to make her made-up world more plausible: 'Do you believe? Do you accept the festival, the city, the joy? No? Then let me describe one more thing.' As if (by the end of the twentieth century) a vision of a better place is almost unimaginable unless it is at the expense of someone. As if this is has become a crucial, structural aspect of what we take as reality: some hidden suffering that we know must be there, but do our best to suppress, ignore or rationalise away.

'The Ones Who Walk Away from Omelas', published just before *The Dispossessed*, reads like a philosophical preparation for the novel. Anarres is built on the life and thought of a woman, Laia Asieo Odo, who led the rebellion on Urras, and whose teachings form the basis of the social system on the new world (its inhabitants also call themselves Odonians). In her notes, Le Guin described Odo as one of those who walked away from Omelas. In other words, someone unable to accept that social well-being should ever come at the expense of anyone, not even a single person (perhaps not even a single living creature).

And so Le Guin is also walking away from a whole tradition of written utopias. Mostly these begin with that guided tour or blueprint of a better society; but gradually (in reading the fine print) you realise that its beneficence rests on certain silences, on some kinds of people being shut out. Or some other 'externality' (as economists would put it): some harm being passed on elsewhere, out of sight.

In *The Dispossessed* Le Guin tries something different: she begins with the principle that nobody is excluded, that nothing is hidden – and then works out the parameters of her dry, difficult world from there.

Plot and narrative structure

The Dispossessed *tells the story of Shevek, a brilliant Anarresti physicist, who travels to Urras to advance his scientific research. Going against the Terms of Settlement (and against the wishes of many on his home planet), Shevek wishes to re-establish contact between the 'sister-worlds' of Urras and Anarres.*

The novel begins with Shevek's departure from the Port of Anarres on board the space freighter Mindful. *One plotline concerns his experiences in Urras, where he is feted as a visiting scientist at an eminent university in A-Io (one of three warring powers on this planet: the others are Thu* and Benbili). The other narrative strand goes back in time to relate his upbringing and coming of age on Anarres: his education, relationships and his struggle to balance personal initiative with social responsibility.

Social, economic and political organisation
On Anarres, society is organised according to principles of mutual aid, voluntary association and absolute non-coercion. Economic activity is divided into syndicates and federatives, with work postings advertised via an automated system called Divlab: the administration of the division of labour. The network of administration and management is called PDC: Production and Distribution Coordination. This (as Shevek explains to his hosts in Urras) is 'a coordinating system for all syndicates, federatives and individuals who do productive work. They do not govern persons; they administrate production.'

Pravic, the rationally devised language of Anarres, makes no distinction between the concepts 'work' and 'play', but the term 'kleggich' refers to drudgery: the kinds of menial or manual labour that most Anarresti volunteer for one day out of every decad (the ten-day cycle which forms the weekly unit on the planet).

The portrayal of Anarres is drawn from the author's wide research in social and political theory. Reflecting on what led her to write The Dispossessed, Le Guin remembered how the novel took shape in the aftermath of protests against the Vietnam War:

> But, knowing only that I didn't want to study war no more, I studied peace. I started by reading a whole mess of utopias and learning something about pacifism and Gandhi and nonviolent resistance. This led me to the nonviolent anarchist writers such as Peter Kropotkin and Paul Goodman. With them I felt a great, immediate affinity. They made sense to me in the way Lao Tzu did. They enabled me to think about war, peace, politics, how we govern one another and ourselves, the value of failure, and the strength of what is weak.
>
> So, when I realised that nobody had yet written an anarchist utopia, I finally began to see what my book might be.

'A whole mess of utopias' – bringing together utopia and mess feels counter-intuitive, liberating. Le Guin's phrase made me want to do the same thing: to spend a year reading through a whole mess of utopias. Not to search for a rationalist blueprint of perfection, but rather to sink into a confused and fertile jumble, a compost heap of books, ideas, people, places, failures, better failures. One of the pleasures of *The Dispossessed* is slowly piecing out how the novel refracts our own world's utopian past. It is a book that shimmers with forgotten possibilities.

Le Guin's thinking, she often said, was deeply shaped by the Native American societies written about by her father (an anthropologist) and mother (a biographer and historian). Her science fiction uses the anthropological imagination to access the *longue durée* of human history (most of it lived out in small, self-regulating communities). 'I'm interested in anthropology because I'm interested in human possibilities', the anarchist thinker David Graeber remarked, 'and in a way, there's always been an affinity between anthropology and anarchism, simply because anthropologists know that a society without a state is possible. There's been plenty of them.' Things (in other words) have not always been as they are (and so could, one day, be otherwise again?).

If utopias often shade into dystopia because of a creeping authoritarianism – some Orwellian Party, Huxleyan world government or Atwoodian theocracy – then Le Guin walks away from this tradition too. The challenge she sets herself in *The Dispossessed* is to imagine a better social system but one without any kind of centralised power structure (though the plot does turn on whether some kind of social conformity is subtly reinstating itself on Anarres: this is what Shevek seeks to leave behind).

The social contract of Anarres draws on everything from the Taoism of ancient China to the thought of Peter Kropotkin, the 'anarchist prince' who turned against his aristocratic upbringing in late-nineteenth-century Russia. There are many similarities between Le Guin's Odo and Kropotkin, who argued that selfishness, aggressive competition and the survival of the fittest were precisely the wrong conclusions to draw from Darwin's theory of evolution. As a young man, Kropotkin travelled to Siberia to study geography, glaciers and animal behaviour, as well as the local peasant communities. What he saw there – the way animal communities cooperated and shared resources to survive in harsh conditions; the resilience and collective decision-making of village communes – led him to write *Mutual Aid*. It is a book that takes aim at the crude social Darwinism that has been used to justify everything from imperialism to eugenics to the free market. Shevek echoes Kropotkin's core argument at a cocktail party in Urras, when someone claims that the law of evolution is that the strongest survive. 'Yes,' Shevek replies, 'and the strongest, in the existence of any social species, are those who are the most social. In human terms, most ethical.'

Sometimes he can sound a little too earnest, this innocent abroad. At other times he hits back with cunning intelligence. When one of his colleagues on Urras talks about the 'politics of reality' – how Anarres only survives because it has no rival neighbour states, and how freedom only exists if you have the guns and economic power to back it up – Shevek the scientist lands a stinging riposte: 'You put your petty miserable "laws" to protect wealth, your "forces" of guns and bombs, in the same sentence with the law of entropy and the force of gravity? I had thought better of your mind!'

Like his anarchist contemporary Mikhail Bakunin, Kropotkin argued (against Lenin and the Bolsheviks) that an authoritarian Party would never achieve a just society: a unity of ends and means is a key principle in anarchist thought. Kropotkin's anarcho-communism differed from Bakunin's collectivism, however: it did not demand that an individual must work to access necessities like shelter, clothing, food. On Anarres, these are freely provided – in communal domiciles, depositories, refectories – and any work or activity is to be undertaken voluntarily, without any form of coercion. For those unwilling, there is the option to drop out of society and live as a nuchnibi, beyond the realm of the social conscience.

What to do with the lazy person – a recurring question in anarchist thought, which does not want to force anyone to do anything. Anarresti society suggests that when work is done not for profit but in service of mutual aid, there is no shortage of willing labour. It is a utopia not of ease, but of adversity. And here Le Guin's vision accesses something borne out by our own world: the immense human energies that are unleashed, in times of crisis, by voluntary organisations – from the Red Cross to Doctors Without Borders, from Gift of the Givers to the Royal National Lifeboat Association. The English lifeboats were Kropotkin's favourite model of anarchism in action. They showed how camaraderie and local knowledge were far more effective in saving lives than hierarchy and centralisation: 'There are no embroidered uniforms', he wrote, 'but much goodwill'.

Le Guin also names Mohandas Gandhi, from whose life and thought comes the principle of Sarvodaya: well-being for all. There is something distinctly Gandhian in the non-affluence, even asceticism, of life on Anarres (also in the importance of doing one's own kleggich, or dirty work). It is a technologically advanced society but one that has chosen a path of contraction and resilience, of equilibrium rather than growth.

How hard can one cut back on material goods and still envision human flourishing? What is the bare minimum required for a fulfilling life? What would days be like if our world's resources really were divided equally? 'God forbid that India should ever take to industrialism after the manner of the West', Gandhi wrote in 1928: 'If an entire nation of 300 millions took to similar economic exploitation, it would strip the world bare like locusts.' It is a truth that modern environmentalism often finds difficult to say outright: that universal 'progress' in the image of a global elite is impossible, insupportable, suicidal.

Here is another departure from more conventional dreams of a better world: Le Guin is testing a utopia not of abundance but of scarcity. On Anarres, contentment comes not from the proliferation of goods but the reduction of wants (here, the Odonians follow Epicurus, the philosopher for whom bread and cheese was as good as a feast). At Shevek's college farewell party, we are given a description of eats that are all the more delicious for their rare simplicity (people have been saving up their daily allowances for weeks). Spiced wafers, little peppered squares to go with the smoked fish, tiny salt shrimp, piles of crisp sweet-potato chips, preserved fruit from the Keran Sea.

Couples wander off afterwards to 'copulate' in the double rooms allotted for this (everyone else is in dorms). There is no word for fuck in Pravic, nor for rape, since the principle of consent – both political and erotic – is so ingrained in social norms. Though in imagining this utopian Esperanto, Le Guin struggles a little with the wholesomeness problem: 'It is hard to swear when sex is not dirty and blasphemy does not exist.'

Published in 1974, *The Dispossessed* comes in the wake of the 1960s, tinged with the communes and 'drop cities' of American counterculture: back-to-the-land social experiments based on personal freedom, pleasure, sexual liberation, self-reliance and a rejection of hierarchy. But often Anarres seems to owe more to an earlier, more sober moment in American utopianism. In *Utopia Drive*, a road trip through this nineteenth-century history, Erik Reece writes that the Shakers have a good claim to be the most successful utopian experiment of them all. Their communities lasted for over a hundred years, based on equality, celibacy, peaceableness and the communal ownership of all goods. There is simply no criterion, Reece writes, by which we can say that they failed: 'We might say, in retrospect, that the larger American culture failed them.'

Shaker villages, he points out, were exceptional for what they *didn't* have: a jail, a courthouse, a police station, a lawyer's office, a bank (very much like Abbenay, the main city of Anarres). Shaker settlements amazed visitors with their simplicity and spotlessness, their inventions (clothes pin, condensed milk, Lazy Susan, flat broom, mop ringer, circular saw), their starched white linens and beautiful woodwork, the endless sweeping of floors, perches, kerbs so that 'the very dust in the road seemed pure'. Perhaps Shaker design is so beautiful, Reece goes on, precisely because the Shakers did not believe in beauty. As one elder put it: 'The divine man has no right to waste money upon what you would call beauty, in his house or his daily life, while there are people living in misery.'

When Shevek arrives in Abbenay for the first time, it has this minimalism to it: a city where form evolves from function and the dignity of labour is central, always visible. He walks to his shared domicile past unwalled workyards and small-scale factories with open doors. Buildings are built low due to seismic tremors; beyond them are the wind turbines and parabolic mirrors that provide power. There are no slums, no advertisements, no locked doors. Nothing is hidden.

For those who have left Omelas, perhaps this is the place, the city where one can live a decent life at nobody's expense. 'Abbenay was poisonless', writes Le Guin in some of the book's simplest, most beautiful lines: 'A bare city, bright, the colours light and hard, the air pure. It was quiet. You could see it all, laid out as plain as spilt salt.'

Geography, environment and ecology

Anarres has one continuous landmass and three main oceans (the Sorruba Sea, the Temaenian Sea, the Keran Sea). The seas have not been connected for several million years, and so their life forms have followed insular courses of evolution, with a diverse range of fish and other marine organisms.

On land, however, there are few endemic species. The planet's climate since the settlement of Anarres has been shaped by a millennial era of dust and dryness. The long beaches of the Southeast region are fertile, supporting fishing and farming communities, but beyond the arable coastal strip are the dry plains of the Southwest: an expanse that is largely uninhabited (except for a few isolated mining towns) and known colloquially as the Dust.

Flora on Anarres are mainly spiny scrub or semi-desert species like moonthorn. The dominant plant genus is the holum tree, used to make food, textiles and paper. Old World grains and fruit trees have been imported from Urras but grow only in the higher-rainfall regions of Abbenay and the Keran Sea. In terms of terrestrial fauna there are only bacteria (many of them lithophagous) and a few hundred species of worm and crustacean on Anarres.

> *Man fitted himself with care and risk into this narrow ecology. If he fished, but not too greedily, and if he cultivated, using mainly organic wastes for fertilizer, he could fit in. But he could not fit anybody else in. There was no grass for herbivores. There were no herbivores for carnivores. There were no insects to fecundate flowering plants; the imported fruit trees were all hand-fertilized. No animals were introduced from Urras to imperil the delicate balance of life, only the settlers came, and so well scrubbed internally and externally that they brought a minimum of their personal fauna and flora with them. Not even the flea had made it to Anarres.*

The star Tau Ceti can be seen with the naked eye from both hemispheres. It forms part of the constellation Cetus, the Whale, which sits near the other water signs of Pisces and Aquarius. It is similar to our own sun in terms of mass, brightness and metallicity: our closest solar analogue.

When astronomers draw up lists of where to search for extraterrestrial life and Earth-like exoplanets, the Tau Ceti system is often near the top. This is also because of its age, eight to ten billion years, which may have allowed sufficient time for complex life to evolve. There seem to be at least four rocky worlds in Tau Ceti's orbit, and one or two of them are thought to be 'Goldilocks' planets. They are at a distance from their sun where water could exist in liquid form – not too hot, not too cold, just right – and this puts them in the so-called habitable zone. 'These are places I'd want to live', writes astronomer Margaret Turnbull, 'if God were to put our planet around another star'.

By putting Anarres around Tau Ceti, Le Guin is following her own advice about DIY cosmology. *The Dispossessed* is operating (in some sense) within the parameters of scientific possibility. And it has coordinates – a topos – within our known universe. But if Anarres is theoretically possible and possibly habitable, it is only just so. 'Nowhere in the geography of utopia', wrote one reviewer, 'is there an island apparently so fundamentally hostile to human flourishing'.

When Shevek leaves Anarres for Urras, he is reversing the usual trajectory of utopian literature. He is travelling not *to* the New World, but *from* it. Not towards utopia, but away, back to the Old World, the dystopia that his people once walked away from.

Or, at least, this is what he has been brought up to think. Anarresti schoolchildren are taught that Urras is a nightmarish place of injustice and inequality, that its inhabitants are heartless 'propertarians'. They learn about a mythic figure, the 'Beggarman'. They can barely imagine that 'body profiteers' sell sex, or flaunt their sexuality, for a thing called money. Vice versa, many on Urras see the Anarresti as hairy, unkempt puritans: 'starveling idealists' whose social experiment is really an economic colony that can only exist because of mining exports that travel on space freighters from Anarres to Urras. The double planet system is used to show how each society needs an Other to define and construct itself against – 'Our earth is their Moon', says one character, looking from Anarres to Urras, 'Our Moon is their earth' – and it is not always easy to see where the truth lies.

Shevek has grown up in a world where wood is never burned for warmth, where people eat two meals a day and books are printed with tiny characters and narrow margins. Organic evolution has produced no insects here, no quadrupeds, nothing more complex than fish and non-flowering plants. It is a lonely planet.

This generates some of the most beautiful, most counterintuitive effects of the novel. When Shevek arrives in Urras for the first time, he is driven from the spaceport to the city at night. He wonders about the thicker darkness flowing endlessly along the road. Could they have been moving, ever since they left the city, among trees, among (the foreign word comes to him) 'forest'? For an instant, he glimpses a face in the darkness of the roadside foliage:

> It was not like any human face. It was as long as his arm, and ghastly white. Breath jetted in vapour from what must be nostrils, and terrible, unmistakeable, there was an eye. A large, dark eye, mournful, perhaps cynical? Gone in the flash of the car's lights.

An animal? Shevek asks. 'Yes, an animal. By God, that's right! You have no large animals on Anarres do you?' A horse, his minders tell him – but we as readers get the haunting description before the word.

At the university he is settled into 'his' room (another foreign concept, since his native language does not have possessive forms: in Pravic one even refers to 'the mother' rather than 'my mother'). He marvels at the 'elaborate shit-stool' in his private bathroom and is puzzled by the material that covers the armchairs: 'a non-woven brown stuff that felt like skin'. He is mortified by having someone clean up after him.

On the first morning he opens his window and sees the most beautiful view of his life. The mix of colours, cultivated shapes and natural contours give an impression of complex wholeness such as he has never seen. The farmlands of Anarres are like a crude sketch in yellow chalk compared to this. This is what a world is supposed to look like, Shevek thinks:

> And somewhere, out in that blue and green splendour, something was singing: a small voice, high up, starting and ceasing, incredibly sweet. What was it? A little, sweet, wild voice, a music in mid-air.

This is the other, quieter, first contact story that Le Guin is telling. The Urras press is full of headlines about the arrival of the 'Man from the Moon'. But this visitor's first experience of forests, birds and other mammals makes the book a kind of ecological fable – uncanny but weirdly familiar. The lush natural history of Urras (so unnatural to Shevek) retroactively builds the world he has left behind, where these life forms have never come into being.

When he sees the 'deep, dry, dark gaze out of the darkness' – the face of the never-before-seen horse – it makes him think of his partner Takver, who he has left behind on Anarres. She is a fish geneticist, immersing herself in the oceans for the interspecies kinship that is so rare on the planet, longing for experiences beyond the human boundary. When Shevek visits the laboratory and its fish tanks, he is awed by the evolutionary diversity: 'Their variety was bewildering.' It had never occurred to him that life could proliferate so wildly: 'So exuberantly, that indeed exuberance was perhaps the essential quality of life.'

But the seas of Anarres are as full as the land is empty. It is 'a queer situation, biologically speaking', says Takver: 'We Anarresti are unnaturally isolated.'

The Hainish cycle and the Ekumen

The Dispossessed is the fifth book-length work in what is now referred to as Le Guin's 'Hainish cycle': a loosely linked series in which the known universe was peopled by an ancient interstellar civilisation from the planet Hain.

This larger backstory is revealed late in the novel when Shevek completes his scientific research. Worried that this will fall into the hands of a militaristic state on Urras, Shevek flees to the Terran embassy. Here he places in the public domain the equations that will enable the building of the ansible, a technological device that allows instantaneous communication between any two points in the universe.

The ansible provides (in Le Guin's other novels) the basis for a federation — sometimes called the League of All Worlds, at other points the Ekumen — that is trying to link all known humanoid societies. It seeks to understand the various paths taken by these civilisations, given different environmental parameters, different social arrangements, and even different trajectories of genetic modification and organic evolution. And so, while The Dispossessed *is the fifth Hainish novel that Le Guin published, it provides the backstory to the cycle (in terms of internal chronology, it can be placed right near the beginning).*

The Terran ambassador Keng offers Shevek safe passage back to Anarres, but the novel ends before he reaches his home world, and we are left uncertain about how he will be received there, whether as hero or traitor. The Dispossessed *ends as it began, with a journey that links two worlds, its structure echoing the lines from Odo that appear on her grave in Urras: 'To be whole is to be part; true voyage is return.'*

Imaginary worlds change as they move through time and space. When *The Dispossessed* appeared in 1974, most readers responded to the questions of political economy that the novel activates – all too human histories. But today, it's the ecological loneliness of Anarres that seems most haunting to me. A world without birdsong. A place where spring is silent and fruit trees must be pollinated by hand (now happening in parts of Terra, as insect populations collapse.)

'There is no Planet B' – a slogan from protests about climate breakdown, air and water pollution. About deforestation and damaged soils, hunger and food insecurity: all the linked crises that follow from human action crossing various planetary boundaries. Atmospheric CO_2, biodiversity levels, the nitrogen cycle, biogeochemical runoff into the oceans – in all these planetary processes, industrial and economic activity has (according to some earth scientists) crossed from the safe operating space of the Holocene into the uncertainty of the Anthropocene, an era when human action has taken on the parameters of a geological force.

Planetary boundaries can be defined (in the ominously downplayed language of peer-reviewed science) as 'levels of human perturbation of the Earth System beyond which Earth System functioning may be substantially altered'. One of the nine boundaries identified by the Stockholm Resilience Institute is 'Novel entities': a term for all the synthesised chemicals, excavated ores and industrial by-products whose presence in the biosphere is new, and whose effects on organic life are barely known. Earth's inhabitants are, in other words, living through an experiment at planetary scale, and there is no precedent, no analogue and no control – no standard of comparison for checking the results.

In the last few years, Planet B has become a more literal talking point, given that news feeds are full of billionaires building rockets, promising to colonise Mars and make humankind (as CEO of SpaceX Elon Musk likes to say) a 'multi-planetary species'. Musk is a science fiction fan who wants to name his Mars rocket The Heart of Gold in homage to the spaceship in Douglas Adams's *The Hitchhiker's Guide to the Galaxy*. He likes to brag about being a utopian anarchist, but Musk's brand of utopianism seems more like the conventional one: a belief that human technology and market forces will solve all problems, a blind faith in geoengineering and the ability to terraform other worlds into habitability, a disregard for any planetary or biological limit. Adams sends up the whole idea of 'custom-made, luxury planet building' by the super-rich in *The Hitchhiker's Guide* (and The Heart of Gold is, after all, powered by an Infinite Improbability Drive). But the champions of the new, privatised space race don't seem to get the joke – or they do, but the satire bounces right off, maybe it's even a little flattering – and they take their DIY cosmology very literally. Detonating thermonuclear weapons above the poles of Mars, Musk has suggested, should warm the planet up nicely.

There is something very old-fashioned about this future. As historian Jill Lepore writes in her account of X-capitalism – the extreme, extraterrestrial capitalism that feeds on images of apocalypse and wants to take humanity beyond the Earth – such visions seem anachronistic, even antique. If the tech and engineering titans of Silicon Valley are in thrall to science fiction, then it is often the SF that stops before the 1970s, before the genre was reinvented by writers like Le Guin, Samuel Delaney and Octavia Butler. Musk's SpaceX and Jeff Bezos's Blue Origin often seem more like something from the Cold War or the 1950s, a kind of intergalactic empire building that harks back to nineteenth-century imperialism. 'I would annex the planets if I could,' Cecil Rhodes liked to say: 'I often think of that. It makes me sad to see them so clear and so far.'

If there really is no Planet B (no magical escape hatch to exit our own world and all its problems), then reading science fiction at its best involves a kind of double vision. One lens of SF's aesthetic machinery, writes Kim Stanley Robinson, 'portrays some fiction that might actually come to pass; it's a kind of proleptic realism. The other presents a metaphorical vision of our current moment, like a symbol in a poem'. Speculative fictions create worlds that we inevitably read against our own: as corrections or counter-histories, as alternate futures or different social hypotheses. But at the same time they could also *be* our own, metaphorically speaking: tweaked, coded or disguised versions of our actual world that can make us see it anew, going beyond what realism can do.

Through one lens, the biological isolation of Anarres reads like an estranged, poetic symbol of the Anthropocene. Or the Eremocene, as biologist EO Wilson termed it: the Age of Loneliness. What does it mean – philosophically, psychically – that so many of our companion species are going, going, gone? How does it feel to be living through the sixth mass extinction event in earth history, but the first in which a single species, *Homo sapiens*, is the main protagonist – its cause and its witness, instigator and archivist?

Moving between Anarres and Urras, *The Dispossessed* is full of echoes and transmutations of our own world: its aridity and lushness, its inequality and solidarity, its loneliness and its wonder. But then towards the end of the story comes a jolt: Shevek flees to the Terran embassy on Urras, and suddenly we are given the real Earth back.

The Terran ambassador Keng tells Shevek that they are both aliens on Urras, but that perhaps he is more alien than her. Because for her and for all Terrans who have seen it, Urras is the kindliest, most various, most beautiful of all the inhabited worlds: 'It is the world that comes as close as any could to Paradise.' So, if Shevek sees her Paradise as Hell, can he imagine what *her* world (that is, our world) must be like?

> We controlled neither appetite nor violence; we did not adapt. We destroyed ourselves. But we destroyed the world first. There are no forests left on my Earth. The air is grey, the sky is grey, it is always hot. It is habitable, it is still habitable – but not as this world is … You Odonians chose a desert; we Terrans made a desert.

The reappearance of Earth as a 'real' variable within the novel's complex utopian maths – as the third term in what was until now a binary equation – makes for an ambivalent ending. Does it mean (as Keng suggests) that the inhabitants of Terra forfeited their chance to become Anarres long ago? Is Shevek's world, after all, utopian in the negative sense of an impossible dream? Or is this to take the novel too literally, and (as he argues) to misunderstand the nature of hope, time and change?

The double lens of this science fiction – both semi-plausible universe and impossible, poetic fable – evokes the odd challenge of thinking ecologically in the twenty-first century. Ours is a moment when individual human beings must reckon with vast collective action problems, must open their minds to geophysical changes far beyond the human scale. But how? If this is the end of the world as we know it, then psychologically the experience can feel like a combination of 'it will never happen' and 'it *is* happening' – but not quite as imagined, and not quite as real.

Perhaps it is only by accepting that the worst will happen, or has already, that some kind of hope and change might be unlocked. This is the poetic theorem – irrational, paradoxical, hard to express in non-fictional prose – that I glimpse in Le Guin's novel. Only in realising that climate breakdown will not be 'solved' via existing political and economic realities can a different future begin to take shape. It is a future that will require cultivating love for a damaged planet, 'a non-human-centred and perhaps impossible love for a world that is no longer suited to human thriving'. This is the unearthly emotion that Anarres prepares us for, I think, as Le Guin's lonely planet moves deeper into the Anthropocene. 'We cannot come to you,' Shevek tells Keng:

> You will not let us. You do not believe in change, in evolution. You would rather destroy us than admit our reality – rather than admit that there is hope! We cannot come to you. We can only wait for you to come to us.

The Dispossessed is half a century old in 2024, but it speaks powerfully of a world that needs to imagine as a world, as an earthly community beyond the nation state. It is a book I have read and reread, in everything from lurid SF covers to a classy Library of Congress box set. *The Hainish Novels and Stories* collection comes in two volumes, with a picture of Le Guin on each. On volume one she is youngish and elfin, wearing an androgynous SF blouse/trousers combo and holding (always likely to surprise you) a pipe. On volume two she is the elderly, legendary Le Guin, swathed in a medicine blanket: the Arch-Mage of Portland, who (a few years before she died) became a meme for remarks she made in a 2014 National Book awards speech:

> We live in capitalism, its power seems inescapable – but then, so did the divine right of kings. Any human power can be resisted and changed by human beings. Resistance and change often begin in art. Very often in our art, the art of words.

The haircut is the same in both pictures, though: a sleek bob that landed fully formed on her head like a UFO, and which in its own way always seemed to be making a career-long statement about SF and gender.

In her introduction, Le Guin says she's not so sure about the Hainish label. It implies a coherent fictional universe with a well-planned history and timelines early in the process: 'I failed to do this. Any timeline for the books of the Hainish descent would resemble the web of a spider on LSD':

> Irresponsible as a tourist, I wandered around in my universe forgetting what I'd said about it last time, and then trying to conceal discrepancies

with implausibilities, or with silence. If, as some think, God is no longer speaking, maybe it's because he looked at what he'd made and found himself unable to believe it.

Here, she contradicts her earlier strictures about DIY world-building, and the demand that any imagined universe must stay true to its inner laws. But why not? The right mixture of constraint and freedom, of discipline and rebellion, seems close in spirit to her ambiguous utopia, and close to the heart of creation itself.

Otro mundo

On the flight I tried to read up about the crisis – oil money, corruption scandals, threats of impeachment hanging over the president – but it was hard to follow.

I connected in São Paulo, taking a bus from one airport to another. The city was vast, the terminals alone seemed to go on for kilometres. An electric storm boiled up in the dusk and there was a plane moving through it, high up there with its headlights on.

The association held an annual conference, one year Montreal, the next Gothenburg. Now Porto Alegre, a city that had hosted the famous World Social Forum at the turn of the millennium. So said the conference helper who got us on the airport shuttle and pointed out the sights. Another World is Possible – if we remembered that slogan? The graffiti on the overpass was from those days. The city was known also as a place where many Germans had fled after World War II.

Interesting, said the person next to me. She was Clancy, a PhD student from Atlanta, here to present on James Baldwin. As we drove through the city, I kept seeing the word ALUGA on buildings and hoardings.

The conference helpers, all young student volunteers, were dressed in black jeans and long-sleeve tops. And so the conference organisers at the local Catholic university began referring to them as the Teenagers in Black. As in: If you need any help, just ask our friendly Teenagers in Black! Or: Thanks so much to the Teenagers in Black for making this such a wonderful event!

I figured it was just a statement of fact, or a Hollywood reference gone slightly weird in translation. But Clancy said she found it worrying how quickly that phrase had become part of the conference lexicon, how it had persisted. Was it just her?

I got the sense she was looking to form some kind of cabal, one that would define itself in opposition to the main organising committee (mostly older American profs in blazers). But at the welcome drinks we met Gaspar, a Chilean guy in leather jacket and skinny tie: much better cabal material, which Clancy soon realised.

The next day I was on a panel with Li Mae, a media communications lecturer from the North China University of Technology. Just before the session, a Teenager in Black came with a request from the organising committee. In the interests of not delaying the bus to lunch, would we please cut our presentations from fifteen minutes to twelve?

You Africa, me China, Li Mae said afterwards. All this way for twelve minutes? *And* the chair of the panel had been checking her phone under the table as we presented. No manners.

Would I mind being in a photo with her, Li Mae asked, just to prove to her director back home that she really was on academic business? I pretended to ask a question as she stood in front of her PowerPoint. She was pleased with the picture. I was a good actor.

Dr Zoe Khan was the chair who'd been checking her phone during the panel. She was sorry, so rude, but a scandal was breaking loose at work. Or at least someone was doing their absolute best to make it a scandal – she would explain later. She was from England and taught at a college in a small seaside town. Ten or so years older than me, I guessed, elegant in long boots and a chunky belt.

We delegates were booked into a Sheraton that formed part of a high-end shopping complex. Walking out the foyer took you straight into a concourse of gleaming boutiques and lingerie adverts. Women in high-waisted underwear dangled on banners, two storeys high, from the upper galleries.

My room was on the eleventh floor, with big windows. Not used to having a TV around, I sat on the edge of the bed and looked at the flatscreen, mouth slightly open. A twenty-four-hour news channel played, with its stock graphs and scrolling tickers. Evidently the crisis was intensifying. The right-wing interim leader of parliament had just dissolved the Ministry of Culture and appointed a cabinet made up entirely of white men.

There was an insert on some abandoned mega-project outside the capital, the small-town mayor pacing across a helipad on top of a building. We were told that international CEOs would be landing here all the time, the subtitles read, but now everything is empty. Then another insert: musician-activists were taking over derelict buildings and creating free schools, with help from Cuba. On the building opposite the hotel was that sign again: ALUGA.

A place gripped by some commotion that you didn't really understand – Zoe said she felt it too. Our panel was having dinner at a small bistro near the hotel, on a street lined with jacarandas.

On the day she'd arrived, she'd gone for a walk in the neighbourhood, which was clearly affluent. But just down there, outside one of the cafés, she saw two men get into an argument that almost ended in physical violence – a police officer, a woman, arrived to break it up. Zoe didn't speak the language, but she felt sure that the argument was about politics, that it was related to the crisis here. Something about the way they spoke, these well-dressed men, raising their voices in long, bitten-off sentences.

As far as she could tell, the right-wing faction had contrived a corruption scandal to undermine the left-wing government, a government that had come to power by campaigning against corruption. The opposing faction had been working to destabilise the state, fomenting violence in the north of the country and vilifying the president, who was now facing a grotesque situation. Her political adversary – the man leading the campaign for impeachment and trying to prosecute – had been a security operative under the old military dictatorship. He'd interrogated her when she was a student activist and (she claimed) tortured her. The charges against her now were a diversionary tactic, intended to draw attention away from the much more widespread forms of patronage and extortion that her opponent had presided over in the state where he'd been governor.

This was the picture Zoe had of it anyway, via the news outlets and commentators that she read. But those in the opposing camp no doubt had an entirely different and halfway plausible narrative. That the president was a hypocrite, leading an anti-corruption campaign while using national oil companies to enrich herself and her allies.

That she was trading on her long-ago credentials as a freedom fighter, playing up this interrogation sob story for political kudos.

This country was vast, a major political bloc of the continent, of the globe. Not unlike China, she said, looking at Li Mae, who seemed a little unengaged by the story so far (though perhaps I just couldn't read her cultural cues). The stakes of what was going on here right now were enormous, were geopolitical, geophysical. If the right-wing faction prevailed, it was almost certain that remaining environmental protections would be scrapped, that miners and ranchers would slash and burn more of the forest more quickly. All of which could send the whole region, maybe even the planet, over a tipping point. That was the situation, and yet – here was the point she was trying to get to – in her world, in the small academic department where she worked, barely anyone was talking about it. Instead, they were consumed by micro-dramas of outrage and punishment that played out week by week on the seafront arts campus, one that had a reputation for being fiery and progressive even though it was set around a placid estuary where you could hear the spars of small boats at anchor, clanking gently in the wind.

If you worked there, she said, then you were expected to participate in these dramas. That's why she'd been checking her phone during the panel, because of all the emails that were pinging through from work, messages that one was expected to react to in real time. A lack of response could be interpreted as siding with whatever was being deplored at the time, so if you wanted to stay onside, you were effectively chained to this feed. Generally, she managed to keep a little aloof from these blow-ups. She was diplomatic like that and could normally placate all parties, but this time it was more difficult. A senior colleague had written an email that another, more junior, colleague had construed as racially offensive; and now that younger colleague was making a huge fuss about it – it was even front page of the local papers. Because of her background, she was being summoned as an expert witness in this affair. That was the feeling she got, anyway. An uncomfortable position to be in, since she went back a long way with the older colleague.

She was sorry to go on like this, but she felt that talking might help her work through it all – the impeachment crisis and the email crisis, if we didn't mind – and work out what to do. We knew how it was when you travel and can tell people things that you might not normally speak about, because you won't see each other ever again.

I felt a little disappointed when Zoe said that. She seemed forceful and interesting, dressed in stylish clothes that I guessed might be newly bought from the hotel-adjacent mall. She was careful about addressing her remarks to both me and Li Mae – her face turned slowly between us like a desk fan – but I wondered how much of it my co-panellist was following. Li Mae could certainly make herself understood; she had that drive to communicate that bends language to its will, and had made it very clear to the waiter, across several language barriers, that the food was over-salted – but for all that, her English was not great.

After lunch, Li Mae said she was tired and going back to the hotel to lie down. Zoe and I walked to a small neighbourhood park and sat on a bench. It was a dog park, the animals and their owners walking the perimeter or gathered around a fountain at the centre. As two non-dog owners, we reflected on how complex and opaque these interactions often seemed to be: between dog and dog, owner and dog, owner and owner. On how the loudest, most aggressive interactions between animals were often shrugged off as nothing by their human masters. Whereas something much more silent or hard to spot, at least to the outside observer, would produce a sudden rupture or reprimand, with someone lifting their pet up and walking pointedly away.

To run amok – this was the phrase that caused all the trouble. At a time when student protesters were shutting down classes, when feelings on campus were running high, the older professor had sent an ill-judged email to his class of four hundred undergraduates. It read: 'i will be deliver [sic] lecture tomorrow at 9am as usual. please note protesters may disrupt and likely to run amok!'

Zoe had never given much thought to the phrase before; it wasn't one she used. She knew that it meant to run wild, or out of control, to go crazy. But lodged within it was a particular etymology, a particular history – like a little bomb with a time fuse.

The older colleague's email manner had always been patchy – lower case, often misspelled – as if he'd just tapped out a reply on his phone at the traffic lights, or while waiting to collect his kids from school. He was just a few years away from retirement but had two young children, which he was clearly finding exhausting. He had a slightly patronising, maybe supercilious, air, especially if you didn't know him well enough to realise that a lot of this was shyness. In the past, he'd had a reputation for hitting on students and colleagues. This had happened to her when she'd first arrived, but he'd backed off quickly enough. He still winked at her occasionally – gave her a slow, over-familiar wink – but she'd noticed that he did this with everyone. She read it as a clammy form of camaraderie: unprofessional and (like his email manner) something only a male academic would get away with, but not (in her view) the end of the world.

His nemesis was a new hire from the States, a much younger man who arrived speaking that civilisation's particular left-wing lexicon, most of it concerning the ever-present legacies of racism, injustice and trauma. His research was on the Dutch East India Company and slavery in the Indian Ocean world – with a particular focus on where I came from, in fact. That city had once been a brutal slave port, but this (he said) was brushed under the carpet. The British press kept voting it the world's top tourist destination, which sickened him.

Soon after arriving, this colleague was caught on camera defending some student protesters. The police arrived on campus and attempted to move the students from an occupied building, kettling them in an access road and causing at least one panic attack. Her new colleague was there to face them down in a dashing and courageous fashion. The footage went viral, and many on the Progressive Academics message group swooned a little, watching this fearless and elegant man, in his chunky glasses, wispy scarf and beautifully tailored jacket, taking on the police. What a rush.

From being a softly spoken, even deferential person, the junior colleague swelled up overnight. Soon he was shouting down and denouncing other faculty and colleagues wherever possible – he seemed hugely energised by it all – chasing that moral rush in all kinds of places. But it must have been harder and harder to come by in a small university town. And so when the older professor's email arrived – screengrabbed by a friend of the student and posted online, where it started to draw attention – it presented an opportunity.

Furious emails began arriving from the younger colleague. Running amok (or amuck), he explained, was a phrase from ancient Javanese and Malaysian cultures, referring to a blind, murderous and suicidal rage. He attached his articles on how this culture-bound syndrome had proved so useful for dehumanising colonial and Orientalist stereotyping. When the people of southeast Asia were enslaved and transported across the world in the seventeenth century (to the Cape of Good Hope, for instance), 'running amok' had become widely used by white settlers, colonists and Company officials – a way of framing political resistance by enslaved peoples as crazed, futile or irrational. As animalistic and bestial, in fact, which was why the professor's use of it with regard to BAME students was reprehensible and violent. The Progressive Academics (he insisted) needed to issue a statement distancing themselves and condemning such racially coded language – there was not a second to lose.

An official apology was duly issued within 48 hours via the college's press office (far too slow for the younger colleague, who saw a conspiracy of silence at work). In the press release, the senior colleague was quoted as saying that his email had been 'appallingly ill-considered and hurtful', and that he was 'deeply ashamed at his lapse of judgment'. There was something off about that language, Zoe felt, a tang of show trials or Maoist self-criticism. In any case, she'd imagined that such an overblown, even craven apology would be the end of it.

Now that my session was done, I stopped attending other panels. As did everyone else, it seemed. We went shopping or on guided tours of the city's famous freshwater aquarium. The whole thing began to feel like a ghost conference, a charade. The world was falling apart because of this kind of attitude.

I made myself go back for the plenary session. The American profs kept making the case that the field of study they were all here to talk about should be taken seriously as a field of study. That it had been unfairly neglected by mainstream scholarship, and that steps needed to be taken to redress this. Everyone in this world seemed to like feeling sidelined, overlooked, underappreciated, everyone all at the same time – but how was that possible?

The chair of the organising committee was a big man in a suit who tended to sit in the back row, paring his nails with a nail clipper – a gesture that was hard to interpret. Perhaps it implied that that the chair, as founder of the annual conference, had already made his contributions to the field and was now resting on the seventh day, that others should now take his seminal insights forward, go forth and multiply. The chair had withdrawn from his creation, leaving space for Young Turks in leather jackets like Gaspar – though perhaps that expression was no longer appropriate and would not go down well with Clancy, let alone the new hire in Dr Zoe Kahn's seafront arts college, a man she seemed (as I listened between the lines) fascinated by and even obscurely attracted to, or who was at least taking up a lot of her mental bandwidth and even (she had let slip) appearing in her hotel room dreams.

Whatever the case with the chair and his nail-clipping, there was clearly a whole intellectual ecosystem that had grown up around this conference as it moved from Montreal to Lisbon, from Kraków to here. And you couldn't just waltz in as an equal; you had to do a few tours of duty first, pay your dues. This was what the enduringly frosty reception from Gaspar seemed to suggest. Though I also got the feeling that Gaspar regarded me as irretrievably tainted by where I came from, like an apartheid-era orange. I was surprised not to encounter this kind of attitude more often out in the wide world; frankly, I found it encouraging that the sentiment was still out there. Whereas someone like Zoe, more open and empathetic, seemed to assume that of course my politics were okay, that I was a suitable audience and that she could continue with her story over lunch the next day.

The thing that might seem hard to understand, she said, was how quickly the new hire developed his towering hatred of the older colleague, how quickly the senior prof became a symbol of everything that was standing in the way of a better world – when to a casual observer the man was just a tired, mild-mannered father, soon to retire. But there was another dimension to this story, one that she might as well outline now since the queue for the dessert buffet was quite long.

As a teacher of young people, she felt, you could choose to be either a mythologiser or a demythologiser. You could mystify a subject and make it seem like the preserve of an elect few; or you could demystify it and make it seem open to all, make it open source. The first kind of teacher wanted to be a guru, to have acolytes. The second kind would consider this a failure, since their aim was to allow, as fully as possible, the slow unfolding of whatever potential was latent within different human individuals – or, at least, to begin this process, to guide it a little and then get out of the way.

The younger colleague was in the first category, all for espousing doctrine and cultivating disciples, a coterie of student admirers who became his eyes and ears in the college's seminar rooms and lecture halls. There would be secret caucuses in his office at which this group would report back on all the things that other faculty had done wrong. Though she suspected that the intel came almost entirely from a young woman who had a tremendous crush on the newly arrived lecturer, something the student had posted several thinly disguised blog entries about in Zoe's creative writing workshop. To get closer to her scarf-wearing, socially just instructor, this student was looking for transgressions and infractions everywhere. This was her currency, and it was subject to inflation. Physical intimacy between these two (who would have made a gorgeous couple) was out of the question: any lapse would transform the younger lecturer into a version of the older. Instead, their bond was to be forged in the furnace of moral rectitude; they came together in holy sanctimony towards all errors in the fallen world around them. The older colleague was, in Zoe's reading, at the receiving end of a massive exercise in erotic sublimation and displacement.

The upshot was that the blandest remarks, things that could have been said in any halfway robust classroom discussion, were now interpreted as deeply problematic. Had the senior colleague really wondered whether it might sometimes be necessary to use the master's tools to dismantle the master's house? *Aloud?* Had he really made a joke about traumatic content at the beginning of a lecture, and suggested that students easily offended by difficult subjects might not be best suited to the study of literature? *At a time like this?* Bits of banter, in other words, Socratic questions, dad jokes – these were regarded by the younger colleague as virtually on a par, it sometimes felt, with the kinds of hateful politics that were pitting the right-wing interim leader of this country's impeachment crisis against all the gains that had been made under the left-wing president.

A mild provocation in a seminar room and an ecocidal demagogue on the other side of the world – these seemed to be equivalent in the brain of the younger colleague. Or more than this: the tipping of an enormous tract of the earth's surface into socio-environmental chaos was actually an unforgivable distraction from the much more pressing issue of an ageing professor's email manner. The younger colleague now took up whole meetings with harangues about how enmeshed they all were in unexamined structures of historical violence. Which was probably true: who knew what ships had set out from the placid, deep-water harbour that the campus was built around? But ultimately, she wondered if this history was best addressed in the way that he was addressing it: by mauling whoever was closest to hand and easiest to maul. Mails about timetabling or venue allocation would ping back with a blizzard of tracked changes pointing out the crypto-conservative assumptions in every phrase. Wasn't that the feeling now? That whatever you did, the most ungenerous, censorious reader was standing right over your shoulder, or had even taken up residence in your brain?

Sometimes she thought about it via the following metaphor. Some kind of bacterium or microbe has been genetically engineered to eat up all the plastic in the ocean. A good idea, in theory, but when introduced into the ecosystem, the experiment runs out of control. The microbe, the bacterium, whatever it is, also begins to eat away at living tissues, or uses up all the oxygen. It moves through the food chain, poisoning krill and corals, fish and birds. Now imagine a microbe engineered to destroy all forms of racism, patriarchy, inequality, homophobia, misogyny and all the rest. But we live in a world of unintended consequences. This experiment in political bioengineering goes awry somehow, perhaps because it feeds on any kind of affront, any sense of slight or humiliation – it rewards that and secretes more of it the same time, creating a feedback loop. In its wake is a kind of dead zone, eutrophic, no real signs of intellectual life. She didn't know if that was the right way of putting it. The metaphor was a bit out there, but it came to her during the aquarium tour.

For the final conference dinner, we were bused to a steakhouse franchise at the bottom of an empty sports stadium. This costly structure, one of the helpers informed them, was left over from the World Cup. Dish after dish came out, all meat. Steaks, ribs, chops, loin – overcooked and tough. Espetadas: cubes of beef rammed onto skewers that dangled vertically on their little stands, dripping juice and gravy. Skewers of chicken hearts, stinking terribly.

Zoe was seated at a table with Gaspar, Clancy and the chair. She was talking to them all easily, animatedly, and they were all listening. It was a gift to move between audiences like that, I thought. I wondered what they would make of the story of the younger colleague. Clancy, I imagined, may also have been outraged by the email. But Gaspar, I liked to think, would have regarded it as a storm in a bourgeois teacup, a distraction from his South American socialist commitments. Perhaps it was an issue that would have divided them or, more optimistically, led to some honest conversations and a deepening of their conference romance. The chair, I felt sure, would consider himself above having an opinion on the matter, and remain silent. But perhaps this was indulging in exactly what Zoe's story warned against: the assumption that you could predict anything someone would do according to what category of person they were, and that nothing would ever escape this gravitational field. Nothing would ever surprise you, would ever be new or unexpected. Everything would be translated back into a version of what was already known. It was, as her aquarium metaphor suggested, a bleak way of approaching the world, a desolation.

It was bad meat – stale, grey, tasting old – and the delegates were not making much headway. But the dishes kept coming. Here comes my salty, said Li Mae. She had kindly presented me with a Chinese Tea Gift to say goodbye, since she was leaving for the airport right after dinner. So was Zoe: I would have to face the last day all on my own. Meat kept piling up on meat. It was a level of conspicuous meat consumption that outdid anything I'd seen back home. How much forest must have been cleared for all this? How much slashing and burning? I felt queasy and went to stand in the corridor.

Back at the hotel mall I went shopping for lingerie, for some of this high-waisted underwear. Is she my size, the shop assistant asked? Bigger in the breasts, hips? Smaller? I thought I glimpsed Zoe browsing in the rails, wheelie suitcase at heel, but felt it would be too awkward to say hello or goodbye here. I also shopped for lip balm since the travelling dried you out so much. Again a shop assistant was more than helpful, recommending a particular strawberry one. I crossed back to the hotel bar and joined an after-dinner reception for someone's book launch. I sat in the middle of the bar, smiling approachably. But people detoured around me, shot a glance and then hurried on.

Back in the hotel room, I saw that the strawberry lip balm was more a lip stick – perhaps there had been a problem in translation. There was a smeary red circle round my mouth. This is how I'd been sitting in the foyer, smiling at everyone like some clown, blowing my chances at ever becoming a conference insider. Though in fact the chair was the one person who'd come to talk to me in the foyer. And for the first time since the conference began, the big man had seemed mildly intrigued by something.

I lay awake with embarrassment, meat regret and too much wine. In the middle of the night, some screengrabs and a long voice note pinged through from Zoe, who was waiting to connect in the capital. She wanted to finish her story, if I didn't mind, if only to hear how it sounded when spoken to a stranger on the other side of the world, totally out of context. Also because, she felt, it had a cautiously hopeful ending. I sat on the bed and listened, watching the muted flatscreen TV.

In the last few days, the Black, Asian and Minority Ethnic Society at the college had issued a thoughtful statement on the email and moved on. The younger colleague, however, was not letting go. He was doubling down, getting more incensed, more rhetorical. When the chair suggested a departmental tea to decompress, discuss things and maybe move on (with some delicious cinnamon buns made by her young daughter), he fired off a two-thousand-word email at 4:53 p.m. on a Friday, cc'ing all staff and students, condemning the kinds of wilful amnesia he saw at play here. Was he supposed to forget all the hurt and pain the email had caused him and just carry on as if nothing had happened? It made him sick to his stomach to even *think* about gathering for tea, a social ritual so steeped in imperialism, at a time like this. And frankly he regarded the offer of cinnabuns as typical of the quiet violence that lurked within the supposed benevolence of a liberal consensus, that insidious form of civility that wanted to whitewash its murderous past. If legitimate protest at this institution was to be deemed 'running amok', then he had no choice but to inhabit that stereotype himself.

It was at this point, Zoe said, that the women of the Progressive Academics WhatsApp group had taken him aside. They were tired of it all, they told him: the machismo, the grandstanding, the male-on-male feuding, the endless emails. They wanted to exit the circuits of antagonism. They had to work here. The tea had been a turning point, a beverage that (as Li Mae's kind gift had underlined) was surely part of the global heritage of hot drinks, not just a signifier of colonial nostalgia. The younger colleague had been hurt and surprised at being outflanked like this, via feminism and commodity analysis. It seemed to shrink and quieten him down overnight. Apparently, he was now looking to move back to the States.

But that wasn't really the note she wanted to end on, Zoe said. She'd told this story as if the younger colleague was an idiot. In fact, he was a funny, charming and intelligent man, a person with strong moral feelings, but one who'd been overtaken by a surreal and self-corrosive mania. It was a mania that required the artificial prolonging of a real emotion. Cant, in other words, which was something so typical of this moment, when anger had become digital currency, and so useful to people like the dead-eyed right-wing interim leader of the country she was now exiting. Such a gift to bad actors who were always looking to show up the pomposity and hypocrisy of their left-wing opponents. She knew it was a long voice note she was sending, killing time here in the transit lounge, but there it was. Behind the story of the impeached president was the story of the email; and behind the story of the younger colleague's outrage was the student whose crush couldn't speak its name.

Beneath all of this was another story again, Zoe said, one she hadn't mentioned yet. But it concerned someone she had met in the past year, the man she'd been buying lingerie for in the mall – for his benefit, she meant. This man was a ceramicist she'd met at a residency in India, at some kind of intentional community there. He showed her how ceramic glazes worked. Different chemicals and oxides were applied to produce different colours during the firing process. But it was still so unexpected how the plates and bowls turned out, what textures and tints would result, what reactions took place within a furnace burning at thousands of degrees.

Since meeting him, it had been like one long conversation – a single, freewheeling, uncensored conversation – and one so far removed from the pre-agreed talking points that everyone was supposed to live their lives by now. He would never allow her to drag all that into the kitchen or bedroom – not in an any earnest way – and had nothing but amused contempt for people who did. He was fierce about it. She had some friends, she knew, whose partners would happily wheel out words like patriarchy and privilege over a midweek meal, who allowed it all to keep gushing into their lives, warm internet juices running down their chins. But through some extraordinarily good fortune, it seemed she had met someone with a secret life and a funny mind. Someone she was going back to now, and then they would travel together to another country, neither his nor hers, just say the word, the rest was understood. And that's why in the taxi to the airport she'd begun to cry a little, out of sheer happiness and gratitude.

The whole last day I spent walking through the city, trying to get beyond the slick cafés of the hotel district. I could hear a protest somewhere, chants echoing off buildings, but could never seem to find it. I walked until lost and went into a shop for directions – but it was no use. Much as the staff wanted to help me, I couldn't explain. Internet? I asked, but they had none. Sheraton? I said, but they looked blank. The exchange left me elated. I was utterly lost.

I kept on walking – along busy roads and below underpasses, through industrial estates down to the river – and for so many hours that it felt like I'd walked back into a younger version of myself. Anonymous and adrift, back to a time before you needed to have opinions on everything, to pronounce on anything.

A chemical smell came off the river. On its bank stood an overgrown structure where people were living rough. WORLD CUP FAN ZONE read a faded sign – which felt like stumbling across the Statue of Liberty in *Planet of the Apes*. For days it felt like I'd been moving through a semi-distorting mirror, a world where some elements were familiar (the jacarandas, the meat, the crisis, the mall) but others cryptic, indecipherable. OTRO MUNDO ES POSSIBLE – that was easy enough to understand, but ALUGA? There it was again: ALUGA and ALUGA.

What did it mean? Impeach? Vote? Believe? Resist? Fight – as in ALUGA CONTINUA? I could have looked it up, but I didn't, still haven't.

Monsoon raag

I

Marx, Lenin and Ho Chi Minh go to a wedding. It sounds like the start of a joke, but the story was in the papers when I touched down in Kerala. In this south Indian state, the Communist Party was elected in 1957 and has governed for most of the decades since. Names like this are common among its members. The troika of wedding guests had gathered to watch their friend Engels marry Bismitha at a boutique hotel, with Marx flying back for the celebrations from Dubai.

There are four international airports in Kerala, all with direct flights to the Gulf. So, it's easy to reach this small pocket of historical anomaly, where hammers and sickles appear on the damp, beautifully mouldering walls of Fort Kochi, and red flags fly over rice paddies in the backwaters. There are five supposedly Communist countries left in the world (Cuba, China, Vietnam, Laos and North Korea). But Kerala is the only non-autocratic, free and fairly elected variant: a place with 95 per cent literacy and some of the best healthcare in India. Private property was never abolished here, religion never banned. Hindu and Buddhist temples sit cheek by jowl with Catholic basilicas; there are mosques near the ancient synagogue of Mattancherry.

In the old town of Fort Kochi, the mix of Portuguese, Dutch and British colonial architecture was vaguely familiar – as if parts of Cape Town had been reshuffled, tropicalised and daubed with beautiful Malayalam script. Local politicians addressed each other as comrade, which also reminded me of home. As did the facetious deadpan with which Party members debated whether the name of a proposed worker-owned amusement park, 'Malabar Pleasures', was appropriate (given that pleasure was a bourgeois concept, the name was later changed to 'Incredible Park').

But (by contrast) in Kerala there was no wind, little alcohol and a prevailing sense of public safety and peace. The locals I met seemed to have an easy confidence in their own past, their place in the world. The Malabar coast had been a centre of world history for centuries: protected from inland incursions by the long range of the Western Ghats, open to global sea routes.

Malabar was where Chinese treasure fleets and European trading empires had come for pepper and spices; the place that Vasco da Gama found a sea route to, rounding the Cape and reaching Kerala in 1498. This allowed the Portuguese (later the Dutch and English) to cut out the middlemen in places like Egypt, the Gulf and Venice, the route through which Indian textiles, spices and artworks had been flowing for centuries. Ivory figurines of *yakshi* fertility spirits had been found in the ash of Pompei; Roman legionaries at Hadrian's Wall were using Indian pepper. The world had always been more surprising, complex and cross-stitched than one gave it credit for – something I came to Kerala to remind myself about. Though this time my real destination was elsewhere, or a different kind of elsewhere: a utopian community called Auroville in the neighbouring state of Tamil Nadu.

In 1516, the first editions of Thomas More's *Utopia* appeared in Antwerp. Styled as a hoax travelogue, it pretends to be part of Amerigo Vespucci's reports on *Mundus Novus*, the 'New World'. But in the frontispiece of some editions, there is a woodcut of an imaginary 'Utopian Alphabet' that points in a different direction:

ὁ ⊖ ⊕ ⊖ ⊖ ⊙ ⊃ C ⊙ ⊙ ⊗ △ ⌐ ⌐ ⌐ ⌐ ⌐ □ 吕 ⊞ ⊟ ⊟ ⊡ ⊠
a b c d e f g h i k l m n o p q r s t u x y z

Looking at this again, I felt there was something familiar about these letters, especially the curving, oval forms of *g* through *l*. This déjà vu, I learnt, may well have a world-historical basis. Inventing his alphabet, More was most likely inspired by the letter forms of Malayalam. These had reached Europe in the preceding decade, via the accounts of Da Gama and other travellers to Kerala and Goa. Five centuries later, I also felt drawn to hand-copy bits of this graceful script from the damp, decaying walls, even though the text (which I could not read) probably said STICK NO BILLS.

Utopias come in waves, historians agree, generally in the wake of major social and economic rupture. More's tract emerges from the epochal collision between Europe, the Americas and the Indian Ocean world. After the American, French and Industrial Revolutions, thousands of religious and communal experiments are founded in the nineteenth-century United States ('We are a little wild here with numberless projects of social reform', Ralph Waldo Emerson wrote in 1840: 'Not a reading man but has a draft of a new community in his waistcoat pocket'). With the First World War comes the Russian Revolution and the triumph of the Bolshevik version (or perversion) of Communism. Auroville was the product of a later wave of social dreaming: a spiritually attuned, counter-cultural quest for new social formations in the wake of the Second World War.

In the mid-twentieth century, a wave of decolonisation and liberation begins to break across the world: visions of national unity and self-determination like that which leads to Indian independence in 1947. But alongside the grand nationalist struggles, there are also smaller, community-based visions of a better world. The global flowering of post-war communes and intentional projects includes California's drop cities, Japan's anti-consumerist Yamagishi movement, the kibbutzim of Israel. By the 1960s, more than ten thousand experiments in alternative living have emerged across the planet. It is a 'golden age of utopia', writes Akash Kapur, a moment when youth and hippie movements in Europe and America are turning to the East as 'a salve against the broken materialism of the West'. Auroville, he goes on, emerges at the tail end of this era, 'though it will, ultimately, outgrow and outlive many earlier projects'.

Founded in 1968 on a barren piece of land near the town of Pondicherry, this 'City of Dawn' has lasted fifty years and counting. The 'pioneers' of the 1970s – seekers drawn from all over the world – planted millions of trees, transforming the ecosystem back into tropical forest and fertile farmland. Auroville (I had read) was a world leader in sustainability, in small-scale agriculture and renewables, also education, low-cost building and earthen architecture. It billed itself as the world's longest-lasting international conscious city. Residents didn't seem to like the word 'utopia': it came with too much baggage. Auroville was more like a social experiment, a living laboratory of alternatives. 'For those who are satisfied with the world as it is', wrote the Mother (the project's spiritual figurehead), 'Auroville obviously has no reason to exist'.

There was no hard boundary, no fence. The place didn't announce itself in any grand way. There were just gradually more bakeries and more white people on scooters and motorbikes, emerging from the forest on red dirt roads. I sat and watched them for a while, eating a croissant (which was excellent: Tamil Nadu was once part of French India, not the British Raj).

The peri-urban clutter thinned out; so did the plastic bottles and other trash that cakes the Indian subcontinent. Then, in the greenery, you began to see different architecture: a low-key, earth-coloured modernism glimpsed through the foliage. Terracotta walls, concrete arches and domes. Geometric villas, ramps and roofs in ferrocement and compressed earth bricks. The names of Auroville communities began appearing on signs in English and Tamil: Certitude, Aspiration, Sincerity. It was like living in a subtropical allegory: take a left at Transformation, then Existence will be on your right.

Centre Guesthouse was spartan but earthy, with coloured glass and latticed brickwork. Brushed concrete flagstones under the banyan trees, deep-set and moss-covered. Something about the red soil staining the bottom of walls reminded me of home: a 'rest camp' in a Lowveld game reserve, perhaps, with the same mugginess and lushness. A touch of brutalism in the bungalows, but sensitively done, and no braai areas, no scorching of flesh. The meals served in a small common room were pure plant: spiced potato fritters and curled courgette salads. Delicious thin dahls and dosa pancakes, the bitterest of pickles and a slice of papaya on the side. A poster advertised a Sound Bath at one of the cultural pavilions dotted through the settlement.

I biked to the Auroville Library – small, minimalist, beautiful – and browsed its shelves. The fiction section was a bit thin, but it had a copy of Ursula Le Guin's *The Dispossessed* (with a stamp, AUROVILLE LIBRARY, on the title page). A science fictional utopia embedded within an earnest attempt to build a real one, both dating from the 1970s – this was pleasing. As was the Auroville Library of Things just down the road (ALOT: Abundance through Sharing), housed in a shipping container. Here you could check out items or appliances that you might want to borrow but didn't need to own. Drill or tent, suitcase or sound system.

Why wasn't the whole world set up this way? Was this place just a collection of good ideas in a forest, with delicious vegetarian food? Part of me wanted not to learn any more, and so keep my vision of a workable and slightly exotic utopia intact. Another part of me was curious about how it had come to be, and what its history might reveal.

'Auroville is a live-in research campus', read a sign at the Visitors Centre: 'Not a tourist destination!' But the community attracts thousands of visitors each year, most of them making the trip to see the Matrimandir (Temple of the Mother) at the heart of the settlement. Everything radiates out from this dimpled, golden orb – like a giant metallic golf ball teed up on concrete stilts. Normally, there was an elaborate ticketing system for day visitors to access it (also special socks). But the Temple – not devoted to any specific religion, more a space for personal meditation and reflection – remained closed to visitors after COVID. Only Aurovilians were allowed inside, and I got the feeling they quite enjoyed keeping the day-trippers out of their marble-lined sanctum. Within the inner chamber, a beam of sunlight strikes a globe of optically perfect glass, channelled down from the roof by a computer-controlled heliostat.

Alongside the Matrimandir are landscaped gardens and the open-air amphitheatre where Auroville's inauguration was held on 28 February 1968. Its focal point is an urn containing soil from each of the 124 nations and 23 Indian states whose delegates attended the opening ceremony. Also sealed in the urn are the words of the Auroville Charter ,which on the day was broadcast in sixteen languages via All India Radio:

1. Auroville belongs to nobody in particular. Auroville belongs to humanity as a whole. But, to live in Auroville, one must be a willing servitor of the Divine Consciousness.
2. Auroville will be the place of an unending education, of constant progress, and a youth that never ages.
3. Auroville wants to be the bridge between the past and the future. Taking advantage of all discoveries from without and from within, Auroville will boldly spring towards future realisations.
4. Auroville will be a site of material and spiritual researches for a living embodiment of an actual human unity.

The Charter – which, like many utopian documents, seems to say both everything and not all that much – was drafted by Mirra Alfassa, a French woman of Jewish, Egyptian and Turkish heritage who came to be known as Sri Ma, or the Mother. Too old to attend the opening ceremony in person, in February 1968 she read the words into a microphone from her room in the Sri Aurobindo Ashram in nearby Pondicherry.

On any visit to Pondi or Auroville today, you will see pictures of the Mother together with Aurobindo Ghose, or Sri Aurobindo: the anti-colonial Bengali leader turned religious sage who fled from British authorities to the French-controlled enclave in 1910. I had filled up my scooter at the Sri Aurobindo Service Station, where pictures of this famous duo appeared above every pump. Aurobindo is in white beard and raiment, so serious and spiritually composed that he might almost be tipping into a vast cosmic boredom. The Mother has kind, kohl-lined eyes and a knowing, mask-like face; but her expression is less guru smirk than shy smile, with rounded cheeks and some front teeth showing. (Another, much bigger banner behind the petrol pumps thanked Prime Minister Narendra Modi for a successful vaccine rollout.)

In Pondicherry, Sri Aurobindo and the Mother had a fabled meeting, formed a spiritual partnership and established an ashram that still attracts visitors from all over the world. Its grey-painted walls are visible all along Pondicherry's seafront promenade and in the old colonial quarter still referred to as *la ville blanche* or 'White

Town'. When I visited, ashramites of all hues could be glimpsed in their outdoor uniform of belted PT shorts, on their way to various sports grounds for some calisthenics or physical jerks. The Mother was a noted tennis lover and would play most days on courts near the promenade: 'as if she was playing with the whole universe', an acolyte would later recall: 'Every ball was as it were the universe and she was beating the universe as it were with her racket.'

Following Aurobindo's death in December 1950, the Mother secured land for Auroville as a place where the 'Integral Yoga' of his voluminous writings could be made manifest. This is not yoga in the downward dog sense; it refers to a much more ambitious programme of spiritual and physical striving, one that extols active participation in the world, not aesthetic withdrawal from it. Manual labour, the Mother wrote, was something indispensable for inner discovery: 'To let the consciousness organise a bit of matter by means of one's body is very good.' A Committee for the Yoga was established to extend the Ashram's vision and oversee the building of Auroville. Although in time the Ashram's younger, counter-cultural creation would rebel against its founders.

A sound bath is not easy to evoke in words. The overlapping, omnidirectional richness of tones and overtones. The swells, sustains and slow decays of a soundscape made from skin, gut and gourd, brass and breath.

We were asked to enter the pavilion and lie down on the mats provided, laid out in a large circle around which the instruments were arranged. There were gongs, bells, flutes, chimes, cymbals, sitars, tablas, harmoniums and other things I did not recognise.

We lay on our backs, looking at the ceiling, facing away from the performers. They weren't performers, they were more like more like facilitators: students from the Sound Research Institute who walked briskly around and among us. What a relief: to have no conductor or virtuoso, no centre demanding your attention. Just these impersonal technicians coaxing unheard-of things from their equipment, swinging gongs and chains and cymbals over our heads, moving fast enough to create stereo and Doppler effects. The sonic bath ebbed and flowed.

Flutes gave way to fizzing drones, chords became blank and buzzing ambiences. Blocks of sound slowly resolved into melody or abstained from it once more.

At one point I hear an engine starting up outside. Typical – even in this paradise of sound one can't escape the petrochemical din, the signature tune of our civilisation. Then I realise that the noise – deep, whirring, menacing – is from knotted cords, like sound lassos, being swung round in the air above us: *vooooerrrr-vooooooeerrr!* Resonators with dangling springs make thunder. Filled tambourines give the soft collapse of waves, shells and seedpods become dripping water. 'We give thanks for this full, rich, heavy monsoon,' the Institute's director intoned in a slow, emphatic voice: 'The earth is full to the brim.'

The whole body was an ear, he always like to say, since the water and cerebrospinal fluids of our bodies conducted soundwaves faster than our conscious hearing. He took me on a tour of the Institute, where every strut of the balcony could be played like a xylophone, where the steel wires used in construction were tuned for plucking. We were seldom aware of how many layers there were to the soundscape that swathed us every day, and what it all might be doing to us. Which is why he asked all students at the Institute to make time to listen to the world, and to keep a sound diary. It was a very different, much deeper way to remember a journey than just snapping pictures from the same places that everyone else took them. Sounds might often be meaningless – or rather, less easy to cram with easy, obvious meanings. I should try it, he said. And then asked if I had met Zuckman – who was also from my country. The director smiled and shook his head. I must meet Zuckman.

'There should be somewhere on earth a place which no nation could claim as its own', the Mother wrote in a 1954 piece called 'A Dream'; 'Auroville belongs to nobody', says the Charter. The language is dreamy, universalist, apolitical. But of course, the community was to be built in an actual, historically complicated place.

This was the difference between Le Guin's vision in *The Dispossessed* and the story of Auroville, I figured. In the novel, one of the most complicated variables of the utopian equation has been subtracted. Le Guin's anarchist utopia takes shape on a lonely, previously uninhabited planet, whereas the 'divine anarchy' of Auroville (as the Mother liked to put it) would manifest in a country dense with history and conflicting claims on the land – and this in a part of India that had, technically, remained a French possession until 1962, long after the rest of the country had thrown off British rule (it was only in the wake of the Algerian War that France finally ceded its territories to the Indian state, just six years before Auroville's inauguration).

This history was somehow bound up with the whole project, but in an ambiguous, double-edged way. Auroville's spiritual-socialist communalism was a clearly a reaction against imperialism and capitalism; but at the same time, it was positing a faraway (non-Western) place as the favoured location for a new world – a colonial reflex at least as old as More's *Utopia*. The Mother liked to refer to local Tamil communities from which the land had been bought as 'the first citizens of Auroville', but one wondered how they'd felt about that. And weren't some of the place names – Forecomers, Sustenance, Adventure – a bit like those the Voortrekkers had scattered across the Karoo?

Zuckman pointed to other examples – Gaia, Sacred Groves, Joy of Impermanence – where the Voortrekker analogy broke down. The challenge, he said, was to stop seeing everything as a version of something that already existed. I should leave all that behind, make space for the new.

We were on our way to Pondicherry in a Hindustan Ambassador, one of those classic 1950s-looking cars you see all through India. But this one had been modified, he said, so that it ran on recycled ayurvedic massage oil. He was taking me to a micro-brewery in town, as if to show that this place had everything from back home and more.

Sometimes I wondered if Zuckman was stretching the truth a little. He was such an evangelist for this part of the world. He was older than me but looked more youthful; he glowed with a zealous optimism that I associated more with the corporate sector. But so far everything he'd said – about being a Sanskrit scholar, about leaving Muizenberg to come and run his software company from Auroville – had checked out.

Over some craft beers, I told him about getting lost on the muddy jungle paths that morning and asking directions from a guy who *also* happened to be from Muizenberg – what were the chances? This guy had a dog, a hippie paunch and a patchwork moon bag. But nothing good to say about the place. They'd tried to kick him out, these Aurovilians. They were like an exclusive club that you had to apply to. He'd been turned down three times. Not enough money, he couldn't buy his way in. They'd even had a problem with his dog. But he didn't care, it was mainly just rich Europeans with second homes here. He was leaving tomorrow anyway, going to Rishikesh.

Zuckman said that getting lost was part of the Auroville experience. Everyone got lost on the jungle paths, the maps were deliberately vague. It was so you could discover the place on your own terms. As for the guy and the dog – it had three legs, correct? He knew the guy. They'd had to kick him out – he was selling drugs, bhang and so forth. Also, his dog had attacked someone in a nearby village. Bad scene. There was a reason for the screening process here. You could start as Volunteer, then move up to Newcomer on a trial basis, finally becoming a fully fledged Aurovilian in time (as long as no-one vetoed your application). At the time, Auroville's population of permanent residents was 50 per cent locals and Indian nationals, 50 per cent people from abroad. Yes, maybe some of the foreigners were wealthier, but then money flowed into local co-ops and community projects, like the workshop that made this Auroville paper (he gave me a notebook) without felling a single tree.

Zuckman invited me to his flat for dinner, up a stairwell in a kind of ochre-coloured, foliage-circled council estate. It was simple but lovely. This was the kind of housing that could be provided once you had qualified as an Aurovilian – though you weren't the owner of the property, only its 'steward'.

Zuckman served up buckwheat dosas with jaggery and bitter home-made chocolate. At the same time, he tracked the progress of an Uber delivery man halfway across the world (he had ordered pizza for his wife and kids back in Cape Town). He tuned up a harmonium from Mysore while showing me a series of YouTube lectures that he'd done on Auroville. All my governance and finance questions would be answered there – the place was impeccably run. He was now consulting via Zoom on a planned intentional community back home, a mini-Auroville near Mossel Bay. This was the role he increasingly saw for himself: seeding and incubation.

The next day I spent walking ever-larger loops from the Matrimandir, watching for its metallic glint through the trees. It did look very cult-like, that golden orb (like 'an expensive but rather vulgar gift from another galaxy', one journalist had written). But otherwise, Auroville had a low-key, eco-minded feel, like a place that had outgrown or moved beyond the esoteric vision of its founders.

I passed sports fields that echoed with the screams of delighted kids. I hung around in the doorway of the co-op, the Pour Tous Distribution Centre (PTDC), where residents signed for local produce without handing over any money. Participants pay a monthly subscription instead of being billed, though individual consumption patterns are tracked. 'People are made aware if they regularly "over-consume"', the Auroville website explains, 'and a common understanding is then reached on how to solve the problem'. Notices made it clear that visitors were not allowed in. 'But it's okay to pet the cat!' said a woman who sounded German, pointing to an animal on the stairs outside.

I went past the Solar Kitchen and looked at the big parabolic mirror on its roof, gathering heat to steam all the rice and vegetables. They didn't take money. I would need to load funds on an Aurocard, but the Finance Office at which I could do this was only open at certain, very limited hours. This mixture of idealism and extra-step bureaucracy – somewhat pointless but somehow symbolic – seemed quite central to the Auroville experience: a gesture at preserving some distance from India's supercharged market economy. Businesses and land speculators were trying to cash in on the community from every direction, I was told, trading on its name: Aurogreen, Aurohotel, Aurobeach Resort. What was the relation between an intentional community and the wider world that it had set itself apart from? And what happened when that world wanted back in?

I found the Auroville Archives and browsed some histories of the project, illustrated with pictures of the original landscape. Villagers herd cattle through eroded canyons; the only trees visible are spindly palmyras on the horizon. I found the black-and-white pictures of Auroville's early days hypnotic. Foreigners in loincloths dig wells alongside local villagers, or carry away excavated earth on their heads in baskets. People with long hair are making dams, building soil bunds, scrutinising architects' models that seem both futuristic and traditional, geometric and thatched. Everyone looks underfed but radiant with purpose. A young Indian woman's face filled the picture: she is walking through a field, no doubt on the way to do something meaningful – build a clinic, paint a school, fire a kiln. Her expression, serene and beautiful, seemed almost historical. I wasn't sure anyone looked or could look that way any more: suffused with such optimism and openness to the future.

Not that these early days were easy. Memoirs describe the heat, the harshness of the land and its self-willed character: 'take your eyes off something for five minutes and it either begins to crumble, collapses, disintegrates, gets stained, gnawed by rats, stolen, or chewed by termites'. Feelings of dereliction and decay haunt these accounts, a sense of gathering entropy and the best laid plans going to ruin. 'Before the seeds could sprout / Ants dragged them away', writes R. Meenakshi in a poem translated from Tamil:

> Before the spike of corn could ripen
> And bend with grains
> The parrots devoured them.
>
> I am in hunger,
> Leaning against the green branch of a tree.
> I am a woman farmer.
> My hands are sobbing

There are diaries of slowly coming to understand the land, the local ecosystem, intuiting some natural order that goes beyond mere neatness or decorum: 'I began to feel, for example, that this particular area wants to remain wilderness, untidied, while over there that tree is calling for space; that this swarming chaos of trees, vines and bushes are at ease with each other while that innocent-looking creeper wants to strangle everything in its path.' In his memoir *Better to Have Gone*, Kapur evokes the early years through letters written by an idealistic young American, John Walker, to his father (bemused but intrigued) back home. The early Aurovilians became 'accidental ecologists', writes Kapur, planting trees and bunding soil to survive, to create shade, grow food and prevent runoff:

> They are amateurs, informed by common sense and persistence rather than scientific knowledge. Because there are no seeds on the plateau, they must travel to nearby forests, places where the land is more fertile, to jump-start their efforts. They go by bus and spend days walking around with just a flask of water, maybe some peanut brittle for sustenance. They wear leaves on their heads to shield them from the sun, and they study the forests, trying to understand what grows, and when and how it grows. In the droppings of monkeys, pangolin, loris, and other wild animals, they forage for seeds, which they store in paper bags. Back in Auroville, they spread the seeds out and attempt to identify them, then set out to re-create the ecological matrices they've just seen.

This story of environmental repair reads almost like a parable: a group of Adams and Eves grubbing around in animal dung for clues about how to reverse-engineer Eden. A load of naïve and unserious hippies (their critics had charged), who didn't stick to the plans; but it was the naïveté of these 'idiot savants of endurance' (supporters argued) that had produced this paradise of ecological restoration.

In the archives there were also many pictures of the Matrimandir under construction – that Tower of Babel in reverse, in the words of the Mother – its globular structure slowly emerging from concrete stilts and scaffolding. And then reproductions of the Galaxy Plan, the original vision for Auroville drawn up by French architect Robert Anger. It presents a city of 50 000 people spiralling out from the Mother's Temple in a kind of LSD-tinged modernism, as if Le Corbusier had been crossed with a psychedelic mandala. This City of the Future was to be a place of monorails, moving sidewalks and intricately designed, interlocking zones – residential, industrial, cultural, international.

Meticulously planned city or accidental Eden: these two different myths of origin informed the project's sense of itself, with long-standing tensions between so-called constructionalists and organicists. Today, Auroville's population is about 3 300 and its built environment has mostly taken the different, more ad hoc path of the accidental ecologists. But there have always been those wishing to expand and densify Auroville, returning it the grander ideal of the Galaxy Plan.

Given that both the Mother and Sri Aurobindo passed away before Auroville was properly established, in the 1970s the community also had to confront, Kapur writes, a quandary that has faced many intentional communities: What happens when the founder dies? 'What structure, what kind of governance, can replace the charismatic authority that has initiated and held these places together?' Auroville's first full decade of existence, he goes on, was 'a tumultuous, fraught time'. The project was riven by a conflict between the centralised planners and the ad hoc improvisers. And Kapur's depiction of the standoff between the Ashram Committee ('older, tradition-bound and predominantly Indian') and the Auroville hippies ('many of whom have been forged by Western street protests of the 1960s') reads like some scrambled, parodic version of the imperial frontier, where natives have become colonial bureaucrats, and the colonising hippies have gone native. The Aurovilians are half-naked with matted hair, 'they have oozing sores on their legs, and their digestive systems are riddled with worms, amoebas, giardia, and other parasites that enter through the cracks of their bare feet'. The planners from the Ashram are in starched white shirts and tight khaki shorts: 'They are meticulously talcumed, comb their hair with coconut oil, and bathe with sandalwood soap after their forays onto the sweaty plateau.'

The evolving battle, Kapur writes, 'represents a curious amalgamation of the trivial and the epic, its stakes both trifling and monumental' – something I recognised from other historical accounts of utopian communities. If, after all, you sincerely believe yourselves to be involved in forging a new path for human consciousness, then even the most mundane questions – who's doing the washing up? why hasn't the grass been cut? – come to be charged with the most profound, world-historical importance. At the same time, there is something properly menacing that lurks behind the events in Auroville. The national backdrop is Prime Minister Indira Gandhi's Emergency from 1975 to 1977, which lends the events in Tamil Nadu an atmosphere of fear and violence Behind the Mother's vision of Auroville being governed via 'divine anarchy' lies the spectre of the state suspending human and democratic rights.

A decade later, the conflict between Auroville and Ashram reached a kind of resolution. In 1986, the status of this international, cosmopolitan enclave was safeguarded by an appeal to the Indian High Court. It ruled (contrary to the wishes of the Ashram) that Auroville was a spiritual but not a religious project. The verdict meant that the state was able to intervene in the community's governance, and to grant a special Auroville visa for foreigners. This removed the power of decision-making from the Ashram authorities and seemed to grant the project its independence. But the appeal to the state – a paradox for a supposedly post-national utopia – has come back to haunt the project.

Over 2 000 kilometres to the north, in the state of Gujarat, there were growing concerns about a proposed revamp of Mohandas Gandhi's ashram in Ahmedabad. This was the place where the Mahatma had lived from 1917 to 1930 on the banks of the Sabarmati River, and to which he vowed never to return until India was independent (Gandhi's assassination in January 1948, by Hindu nationalist Nathuram Godse, meant that this never happened).

An ambitious upgrade of this heritage site was now being run directly from the prime minister's office. The government was set on a flashy theme park, local Gandhians complained, with car parks and food court. This was all part (critics suggested) of Prime Minister Modi's penchant for grandiose construction projects to co-opt the heroes of India's liberation struggle into the fold of his Bharatiya Janata party. The Ashram memorial trustees had already batted away 'some incredibly stupid ideas': a Gandhi hologram that would rise out of the river at night;

a massive steel spinning wheel that could be seen by passing planes. It was a cynical ploy, Gandhi's biographer Ramachandra Guha suggested, given that the BJP was opposed to everything that the Mahatma stood for (and that some of its members openly celebrated his killer). And now it seemed that the government was coming for Sri Aurobindo's legacy, and for Auroville.

In February 2018, Modi delivered a speech at the Matrimandir, marking the community's fiftieth anniversary celebrations (Aurobindo's one hundred and fiftieth followed in 2021). Soon after my visit, a Modi loyalist named Jayanti Ravi was appointed to head Auroville's governing board and began driving expansion and road-building programmes within the area, and to develop it as a global destination for 'spiritual tourism'. The result has been an ongoing crisis, and new tensions between constructionalists and organicists, those two conflicting utopian visions of the twentieth century.

The government-backed planners want the city of 50 000 people that Auroville's original founders had envisioned. A new 'masterplan' was to be implemented, one that entailed building a new ring road and bulldozing anything that stood in its way: the Auroville Youth Centre, water catchments and hundreds of trees. The pictures I saw did not look good: huge muddy gashes through the forest; the brick-paved roads that allowed water to percolate through now replaced by thick concrete slabs. There were reports of smashed-up houses and residents being manhandled by private contractors.

'This place is something very beautiful that India has so magnanimously offered and we cannot have decadence and stagnation any longer,' Ravi stated. Another government appointee accused Auroville residents of being 'grossly deficient' in achieving the Mother's vision. It was 'decadence' for 3 300 residents to live on 3 000 acres of land in a country as densely populated as India, said government spokesman Sindhuja Jagadeesh: 'Many people have become attached to their comfort in the greenery, but we are supposed to experiment and evolve.' This place was supposed to be a bustling city and global spiritual tourism destination by now, the planners argued. They dismissed the Auroville of today, *The New York Times* reported, as 'an eco-village where a visitor can get a good cappuccino but not the change in consciousness its founder hoped for'.

The organicists – led by the working committee of the Residents Assembly – responded that this development was hasty, unsustainable and non-participatory. In the midst of unprecedented heatwaves on the plateau, they were sending out newsletters and press releases declaring an SOS: the world's oldest international conscious city was under grave threat. Trees were being bulldozed at night and the Youth Centre targeted. Guesthouses were being pressured to become part of an Auroville 'hotel chain' and entry fees would be now charged for various sites. 'Opposers' had been locked out of their email accounts and servers; visa support had been revoked, meaning that some people had to leave the country. Computers had been seized, Auroville committee members had been detained under draconian legislation that was being used to stifle the press elsewhere in the country. There were sit-ins and unity walks, standoffs and crisis meetings. 'To refuse to adapt the masterplan because it would be "blocking the Mother's dream" smacks of spiritual authoritarianism,' one Aurovilian told the *New York Times*: 'I don't think it was the Mother's dream to destroy the living environment around us.'

'Every utopian venture', writes one historian, 'is eventually interpreted as a referendum on human nature'. Is our corruption innate, or rather the result of a badly organised society? But this question is impossible to answer. No twenty-first-century community could wrest itself free enough of the wider world – social, economic, ecological – to provide a neutral testing ground, or ideal laboratory conditions, for this kind of enquiry. Any attempt to do so could be framed as its own kind of failing, like the charge of elitism or escapism that was now being levelled at those Aurovilian NIMBYs blocking 'development'. I could see the logic of this accusation – against a small, cosmopolitan community 'attached to their comfort in the greenery' – but also the depressing, deathly politics behind it. That every place on earth should be surrendered to the modern market economy, should submit to national GDP and growth and become like the MG Road that ran through every Indian town (and would horrify the man it was named after).

A few years before, I'd never heard of Auroville. Now, I found myself compelled by this small experiment halfway across the world, rooting for it, compulsively following the headlines in the international press: Build a New City or New Humans? A Utopia in India Fights Over Future. Or again: Bulldozers, Violence and Politics Crack an Indian Dream of Utopia. Even the optimistic Zuckman, with whom I kept in touch, had to concede that a pact with government might not be a good strategy for intentional communities.

On one hand, it seemed easy to reject the top-down vision of the constructionalists in favour of the organicists and their ecological ingenuity. Today, the 1950s drawings of a City of the Future plonked down on a plateau above the Bay of Bengal seem (as with other planned cities from that era, like Brasília and Chandigarh) ingenious but rather facile. Why assume, after all, that mere geometrical order (orderliness, rather) will produce social harmony and cohesion? Critics of mid-twentieth-century modernism had argued just the opposite: that tangled streets and pathways – irregular desire lines through cities or forests – might signal a far deeper kind of social organisation and resilience.

On the other hand, the creation of a lightly inhabited eco-village within a densely populated, rapidly urbanising country was bound to create tensions. Auroville's spiritually guided, post-industrial version of a liveable future was unfolding within the secular and headlong rush to modernise the Indian economy. People who came to this place for a peaceful retreat, an escape from the world – they didn't last long, Zuckman said. Auroville was more like the opposite: a petri dish, a magnifying glass for dilemmas that the world at large was facing.

I flew home from Kochi, which meant a journey back to Kerala. First a bus journey where I watched a cow chew its way through a knee-deep drift of plastic waste at a roadside stall (I filmed the cow doing this: a reminder not to romanticise India from afar). Then a train journey of noise, diesel fumes, creepy men harassing women. Then a taxi to the airport playing some of the worst, stupidest pop music I had ever heard.

The early morning chanting, the forests and red earth of Auroville, the sound bath and the dripping leaves – all of this was receding fast. Already it felt very far away. The brute facts of the world were reasserting themselves, stronger and more inevitable with every passing minute. The taxi swooped past enormous malls and new apartment blocks under construction: FLATS FOR RENT, FULL AIR CON. Auroville, the heritage precinct of Fort Kochi – the whole lot, it seemed to me, could easily be tucked into just a single block of this vast city. Which was one of so many vast cities, which was where most people would grow up and live their lives now. The whole idea of a utopian journey seemed illusory again, misguided, wrong-headed, always destined to fail.

On the flight home I turned back to a passage in Akash Kapur's book, one that provided its title. John Walker's elderly father is writing to his son, one of the Auroville 'pioneers' of the 1970s who has left a promising life in America to go build the City of the Future in a faraway place:

> I cannot thank you enough for your letter … I have read it twice and intend to read it again. It told me so much about your thinking. I admire you on your pilgrimage. May it have a good ending. But no matter, better to have gone on it than to have stayed here quietly. At the end of my life I realize that there is nothing worthwhile except love and compassion and the search, which I have not made, for reality.

II

The days would begin with singing, but we never quite knew where it was coming from. Male voices in unison drifting into our room while it was still dark, at the edge of waking. Early morning singing or chanting in Fort Kochi, voices coming from ... we could never tell, exactly: maybe the Basilica, the rooftop meditation hall beyond the football pitch, the Young Men's Buddhist Association over towards Mattancherry. Days were edged by this unison singing, in and out of sleep, the sound of people beginning the day together.

'Join us for a morning raag,' said the man at the Kathakali Theatre, bringing his palms together, bowing slightly, dropping his voice to whisper: 'Most welcome.' He had one of those voices that tickles the eardrum, that creates ASMR-like shivers even at a distance, that you want never to stop.

The idea is distinctive to Indian classical music – that certain sounds and performance styles are associated with certain times of day, or seasons of the year: morning, evening, the heat, the rains. But it seems (once you have heard it) utterly logical, beautiful, impossible to do without. A raag, or raga, is not a scale (because many ragas can be based on the same scale), and neither is it a melody (because the same raga can yield an infinite number of melodies). It has no direct translation in Western music theory, but with it comes the idea that certain patterns of sound have specific effects on the mind and body, that they colour things, hence the Sanskrit origin of the word raag: concerned with pigments, tinting, dyeing.

A morning raag is not *about* the morning; a monsoon raag is not *about* the rain (at least not in the way Beethoven's *Pastoral Symphony* attempts to represent a storm in music). A raga is not about the world, writes Amit Chaudhuri, but *of* it. Because of this, he goes on, the primary space of the raga is not the concert space: 'it's situated really in a time of day or season, and – in contrast to how we experience music in a concert hall – a significant leakage in both directions is allowed: the raga's into the world, and the world's into the raga. For this reason, every sound – birdcall; a car horn; a cough – is continuous with its textuality and texture'.

What happens (I wondered) if a raga is sung or performed at a time of day that it's not meant for? The result, writes Raghava Menon, is music subjected to a kind of 'jet lag'.

At night, the younger guy who takes over the reception desk at Raintree Lodge watches series or movies on his phone. The tinny noise keeps us a little awake, slows down our Wi-fi connection to almost nothing. But he is such a friendly guy, all alone all night, so we never tell him to stop. Never get his name, but he has a topknot, so we call him Man Bun Man, which somehow gets put to the tune of The Beatles' 'Nowhere Man': *Man Bun Man ... don't worry ... Take your time, don't hurry ...*
    Raintree Lodge must be the most photographed hotel in Kerala. All day there are shoots happening on its front doorstep, against the vines and creeper-covered balconies of the front façade. We suspect there is something we don't know about: that is has been the location of a famous film or music video. Perhaps some undeleted images still exist of us walking through a door to join the happy couple or the fashion model, unintentional photo bombers. We even learn to recognise the sound of a shoot from our upstairs room: the particular call and response of instruction, question, suggestion, preparation, action …

'In Hindustani classical music', writes Chaudhuri, 'improvisation is deferral. If a raga is a cluster of progressions and relationships, I, as a performer, will delay – without disfiguring the raga's form – a straight-forward portrayal of these interrelationships for as long as possible … I'll delay the expected; the audience will await the expected but partake intensely of the delay. I won't come to the point. My not coming to the point will be synonymous with the pleasure of improvisation'.

'Nowhere Man' is a song I just woke up singing one day. Anna, my wife, keeps a record of these, what she calls my 'morning jukebox', trying to discern what it might be revealing about my subconscious life. It's random, though: one day Ronan Keating ('Life is a Rollercoaster'), another day the song a fellow protester tried to teach us as we advanced politely on parliament: *uZumahhh! uGuptahhh!* Then a question along the lines of: where is all the money you ate?

Seeing Rabindranath Tagore on the shelves of Idiom Books sets off an overnight chain of association that draws up an obscure EP by Bonnie Prince Billy, 'Get on Jolly', his slow, wonky setting of the love poems from *Gitanjali*, full of drones and warbles and guitars fed quietly through a reverse pedal:

> I am here to sing thee songs. In this hall of thine I have a corner seat.
> In thy world I have no work to do; my useless life can only break out in tunes without a purpose.

Travel means relinquishing control of what music is playing around you. In the tourist strips you hear an unpredictable cross-section through globalised pop culture. Who would've thought that Phil Collins would be so popular in south India? 'Another Day in Paradise' comes around often, even in a chunky house remix. Ed Sheeran's 'Shape of You' is everywhere. Waiting in an understaffed café, I am amazed by the length of Jack Johnson's back catalogue. He goes on and on with his gentle post-surf strumming and crooning, asking why newsreaders didn't cry when they talked about people who die.

Brass band music from the school next to the café where I am working. Boisterous music-making, with lots of cymbal-clashing and squawking and showing off. The trumpets and trombones and tubas carry that tongue-in-cheek, over-the-top, magnificently childish and comic sound that brass instruments can have – a truly joyful noise. Bits of school assembly drift out through the grilles and brickwork, becoming part of the soundscape of a town. Children practise their English in emphatic call and response, or recite the national pledge with gusto:

> India is my country and all Indians are my brothers and sisters.
> I love my country and I am proud of its rich and varied heritage.
> I shall always strive to be worthy of it.
> I shall give my parents, teachers and all elders respect and treat everyone with courtesy. To my country and my people, I pledge my devotion. In their well-being and prosperity alone, lies my happiness.

Even before the early morning chanting: the sound of streets being swept (and swept and swept and swept).

A yoga lesson under a tin roof at the top of a building, a late addition to the monsoon falling. Being amid, watching, hearing heavy rain is one of the great highlights of this journey, after the long drought back home. Hitting the world in their millions, the droplets activate other dimensions, change your perception of space, colour and smell. In child's pose, in corpse pose, I lay there listening to it fall on the bus stop and the Reading Rooms, the roof and the pavements, each contributing their distinctive note in the soundscape, the rainscape.

I thought back to a documentary, *Notes on Blindness*, that I had seen a few years before. The audio track of the film was a taped diary recorded in the 1980s by a man named John Hull, an Australian theologian and academic who chronicled the experience of losing his sight. This audio diary was then worked into a film and sometimes 'performed' (perfectly lip-synced) by the actors playing him, his wife, his family. The most beautiful passage describes him preparing to leave the house one evening, then opening the front door to find rain falling:

> I stood for a few minutes, lost in the beauty of it. Rain has a way of bringing out the contours of everything; it throws a coloured blanket over previously invisible things; instead of an intermittent and thus fragmented world, the steadily falling rain creates continuity of acoustic experience.

He goes on to give the loveliest, most intricate description of this soundscape, remarking that while he knows the local phenomena of shrubs, footpath, front gate, culvert to be there in theory, normally they give no immediate evidence of their presence: 'I know them in the form of prediction. They will be what I will be experiencing in the next few seconds.' By contrast, the steady rain, transmitting its acoustic data, 'presents the fullness of an entire situation all at once, not merely remembered, not in anticipation, but actually and now'.

At this point, the film shows droplets cascading down over study desk, sofa, dining room table, a domestic monsoon:

If only rain could fall inside a room, it would help me to understand where things are in that room, to give a sense of being in the room, instead of just sitting on a chair.

This is an experience of great beauty. I feel as if the world, which is veiled until I touch it, has suddenly disclosed itself to me. I feel that the rain is gracious, that it has granted a gift to me, the gift of the world.

Have I grasped why it is so beautiful? When what there is to know is in itself varied, intricate and harmonious, then the knowledge of that reality shares the same characteristics. I am filled internally with a sense of variety, intricacy and harmony. The knowledge itself is beautiful, because the knowledge creates in me a mirror of what there is to know. As I listen to the rain, I am the image of the rain, and I am one with it.

But what I really wanted to record from the yoga lesson was the shocked, under-his-breath expression of our teacher – 'Oh-my-God!' – as he let go of my legs and my attempt at a headstand crumpled towards the floor in a second. The same thing happened to Anna just afterwards, to be met by an identical 'Oh-my-God!' It was so different from the relaxed commands that he had been issuing in a hypnotic, nasal voice, 'Ree-lax, ree-tain,' a voice that steadily and strangely bent up through different pitches, like a filling bottle of water, as he counted out the holding of breath '… One asana two asana three …'

In south Goa: hammering. Wooden beach huts were being constructed ahead of the peak season. In Palolem there was also a small sawmill near our guesthouse. The hammering and sawing was so ubiquitous along the coast that eventually we acclimatised, and reading on a beach seemed incomplete without a friendly thudding in the background. 'Man is a creature that can get accustomed to anything', wrote Fyodor Dostoevsky, 'and I think that is the best definition of him'.

Tea! Coffee!

Anyone who travels in these parts will hear the calls of chai sellers on street corners, on railway platforms, in carriages. It is the audio equivalent of a sunset picture at the Chinese fishing nets, or being snapped on that bench in front of the Taj Mahal. A spot where the fabric of the visible world has been worn so thin, like a map where people have pointed out, in the sense of rubbed out, the You Are Here.

But now we are kayaking around a small islet in the late afternoon, and we bump into two young guys who are flailing their paddles around and laughing about how bad they are. They say they are from Kerala but working in Dubai, and when we remark that we have met many Keralans who work in Dubai they say oh yes, have you heard the one about when the moon guy got to the moon and said, 'One small step for man ...' and then a voice piped up, 'Tea! Coffee!' And then they laughed hugely and kept failing to pilot their boat round the islet. 'Us Keralans get everywhere you see ...'

There are many Russian tourists in Goa (there is a direct flight from Moscow). We joked about taking our place as a minor partner in the BRICS alliance: Brits, Russians, Israelis, Czechs (or Croatians or Chechnyans), South Africans. Travel, for some members of the alliance, did not mean relinquishing control of the music around them. Often, a group of Russians would set up a smartphone on the table of a beach bar and begin playing their own music – tinny EDM or house beats, like a radio transmitter picking up frequencies from the motherland.

Silent cows. Silent disco. After the millennium, legislation was passed to curb the infamous trance parties that had taken hold on Goa's beaches since the 1970s. There have been several 'rave crackdowns' since. Now, you see the revellers behind the boulders at the end of the beach, headphones on, strutting, marching, two-stepping, alone together.

To get away from the sawmill, we moved into a treehouse in a jungle. Each night we heard the plastic bag in the bin rustling, but okay: it was an open treehouse and other organisms were coming and going. On the fifth night, I realised that there was no plastic packet in the bin. It was my packet of dirty laundry rustling, or being rustled. I switched on the light to see a large mouse headed across the floor.

'There are two of them, no it's pregnant, no it's a rat, no – it's got your sock!'

It was carrying off the second of my (favourite) green socks. At this point, Anna laughed for a long time, reflecting on what a long-term project this had been, almost a civil engineering project, night after night. In the morning, I found boxers scattered through the foliage below the tree house. The green socks were never recovered.

Crows and dogs. Crow fights and dog fights. On the beaches, in the alleys, from neighbouring villages at night. When we live in the treehouse, there are other bird sounds. Anywhere else it is the soundtrack of the Anthropocene, the Ed Sheeran of the bird-singer-songwriter world, our shadow species: crows.

Hooting and your changed relation to it – learning not to take it personally. How many shades of meaning can be compressed into a single sonic gesture, a single automotive squawk. Watch yourself, excuse me, here I am, coming through, seen you, thank you, on your way, no worries.

Moving from south India to south Sri Lanka, song-like Malayalam (just a beautiful word to say) turns to the more staccato, percussive Sinhalese: to the outsider, some conversations can sound like a drum solo, free jazz.

On the train journey down the coast from Colombo, the gangway between the two carriages is clanking as we go over bumps. It is an extraordinarily loud and unpleasant sound. All the casually violent noise we absorb: what does it do to us?

A commuter from Hikkaduwa tells me about when the tsunami hit the Matara Express just around here at 9:30 a.m. on Boxing Day 2004. Eight other trains on the line were held back, but one could not be reached by the signal operators, and kept advancing towards the wave. It was the worst rail disaster in history: over 1 700 lives lost. Two carriages survived in working order and are still used on the line, marked with a painted wave.

On my Kindle, I had been reading an extract from a book about the Japanese tsunami of 2011, about how coastal communities rebuilt and reckoned with what had happened. A survivor remembered:

> It was a huge black mountain of water, which came on all at once and destroyed the houses. It was like a solid thing. And there was this strange sound, difficult to describe. It wasn't like the sound of the sea. It was more like the roaring of the earth, mixed with a kind of crumpling, groaning noise, which was the houses breaking up.

The line from Colombo to Galle was repaired and runs close along the ocean. Between the hotels, fishing boat harbours, beach shacks, petrol pumps and Buddhas, you see small cemeteries in the grass, under the coconut palms, small memorials, upturned stones, faded murals.

The two overlapping gangways keep clanging – an unbearable, unbelievably violent sound. I wonder if it's just me, but then a fellow tourist gets up and begins filming the phenomenon. It stops as soon as he points the iPhone at it.

'Stay there,' his friend says. 'Stay there and keep it quiet'.

Sitting outside our room on the shared balcony at the guesthouse, I think I hear the couple next door having sex. They came past, said hi, went into the room and then it began. It makes me into the sonic equivalent of a voyeur, an écouteur (though that also means earphone in French). They are young but it sounds like good, mature, relaxed sex. Lots of talking and laughing, unhurried, and then the occasional sharp intake of breath. It could have been something else – one dabbing a cut on the other's body with Dettol, or clipping toenails, anything intimate and attentive.

Walking along the walls of the Dutch Fort in Galle when the call to prayer sounds from the mosque that is draped in fairy lights. The man has skills. On the third *Allah hu akbar*, he slides up to a keening, perilous, high note right at the limit of his head voice, skirls around in this ecstatic zone, loops and glissandos down again.

The sun is calling it a day out there, beyond the petrochemical fug that slides over the Indian Ocean from the subcontinent. The event is being solemnly saluted from the ramparts by hundreds of outstretched arms and tripods, raised phones and selfie sticks. This sunset of 17 November 2017, a pretty average one, is probably generating more data than the whole of human history had until the 1970s. Two billion digital images are uploaded every day. Each sunset adds terabytes more data; each one, refracted via the vast compound eye of the human race, must be stored in some air-conditioned server somewhere, digitally warehoused in Oregon or South Korea or Bengaluru.

Thousands of pics slide across our eyeballs each day, most given no more than a microsecond, no real purchase. Doctored and cosseted by those putting them up; consumed, swiped over in an instant.

I thought that collecting sounds instead of sights might offer something less … premeditated. Roads and train lines and the walls of coastal forts convene the world quite strictly, usher us towards particular places to stand and look, point and shoot. Sounds cut across space and cut in at inopportune moments. They cannot, by definition, be picturesque? They may often be meaningless, or less easy to cram with easy meanings: songs that have no purpose. It's easy to look the other way; it's less easy to block out a sound, which can be maddening, inescapable, unbearable. They go on happening in the dark.

The next day I realise that this call to prayer must be a recording, downloaded from elsewhere, Karachi or Qatar. The notes loop and curl in exactly the same way each sunset.

One afternoon there are thunderstorms in three directions – inland behind Galle, over to the east above the Peace Pagoda, bearing down on us from Hikkaduwa – each with different lag times. As people who grew up in a place of lavish electrical storms, Johannesburg, and now live in a place where you get maybe one a year, Cape Town, the sound of thunder rolling languorously around the horizon, taking so long to subside, for us it is like a tapping on a membrane of the subconscious, sounding out something half-heard, half-remembered, a noise field of intense, amorphous significance.

We watch and listen from the ramparts, hearing the *shush* of the fresh water meeting the salty sea just before it hits us. The sea is warm, so is the rain. The thunder has moved on, a few seconds elapsing after the flash. We float in the water off the walls of the Fort. The rustling of the seabed, the droplets striking your face and forehead – both are louder than usual, the water tapping on bone.

Listening to rain approach, set in, ease off, recede – day after day.

One of the young women who cleans rooms and prepares breakfast at the guesthouse has an unfortunate voice, one of those voices that sounds cracked or half-broken: half young girl, half old woman, not quite having coalesced into young adult.

These tiny young women are ordered around by a larger, older woman, Mrs Wickramasinghe, who sits on a sofa downstairs, directing operations from an iPad. She is sharp with her staff, matriarchal, but laissez-faire with us.

She is surrounded by several Dell computer screens that are divided into multiple CCTV feeds. One is of the kitchen upstairs, so she may have seen me talking to the fish. A big pale fish with bulbous forehead, full lips and a pained, humanoid face, suspended in a tank that seems too small for it.

'I think the tank is too small for it,' says Mr Wickramasinghe, a lawyer, as he cleans the filter for the fourth time, 'but it's my son's fish, and he wants me to keep it.'

His son is studying medicine in Belarus; his daughter is doing business management in Australia, and is coming back home tomorrow for a holiday.

We look at the fish again when its caretaker has gone, and it looks back at us with wide eyes. Suddenly its whole body is convulsed with emotion, or agitation, or some kind of communicative passion – it is unmistakeably trying to tell us something.

As we are crouching there at eye level, it opens its mouth, wide and soundless.

Something, we never quite work out what, plays out a wheedling version of Beethoven's 'Für Elise' early in the mornings and late at night. It has that sound of the ice cream van: bending, wonky, Doppler-affected notes. Alarm clock, elaborate rickshaw hooter, doorbell? It remains a mystery.

There are very elaborate hooters in south Sri Lanka: multipart klaxons on buses where the driver can obviously choose to go for the simple, the super, the super-duper, and then finally a button that activates something like a baroque chorale. The timbre evokes a quaint and archaic moment in the evolution of smartphones, the 'polyphonic ringtone', back in the day when mobiles still rang.

One of the most intriguing and ambiguous sounds of the trip is that made by local surfers as they paddle out among the beginners. It's a bit like an owl hoot, a bit like a whistle, but hard to attach a definite meaning to. It's not the internationally recognisable hoot of 'Get off my wave' since they do it when they are just waiting; it doesn't seem to mean 'Set coming' either since the noise and swell don't correlate. Finally, it just seems to say: 'Here I am,' a gentle assertion of localism without wanting to put off the tourists, a warm-water warning.

The clunking sound of a gear change on an auto-rickshaw: *ker-chunk*. When travelling in south Asia you will soon discover if you are a Royal Enfield man or a scooter man. Or a tuk-tuk man. Mrs Wickramasinghe has organised one for me to hire, a caramel-coloured beauty, saying that it's better for the sun. We head off on the coastal roads accompanied not by the manly, Guevaran chug of an Enfield or the even-handed moan of a scooter, but by the two stroke tuk-tuk of the tuk-tuk and its chunking gears. I give it up after a few days, though, since they are dull to drive and I have scraped the caramel on an electricity pole.

Time and the journey are running out. We are in a train back from Kandy to Colombo, a high line though tea plantations and hill fortresses. It goes through many tunnels, and as soon as it does, diesel fumes fill our carriage. No view, no beach, no surf break without its petrochemical underpinning wafting into your face: the trip has been a fossil fuel education, a doctorate in diesel. After a while, some kids in another carriage begin screaming in the tunnels, playing with the echo. It creates an effect that is not easy to reproduce on a page of two dimensions. And that's what these sounds, these memories of sound, are often doing: trying to create secret burrows and geometries behind the page, tapping the wall for hollows and backstories, probing the world with sonar like the bats hanging upside down all through the Royal Botanic Gardens at Peradeniya, where we whiled away our last full day in Sri Lanka, feeling done with it all and a little homesick.

An auto is taking us to an airport hotel. It speeds past a Pure Veg restaurant just in time for us to hear the riff, strings maybe, that comes after the verse in Billie Jean, just that perfect slice of pop and no more.

Hotel Paradise is not, we decide, really an airport hotel. It has mauve mosquito nets and a bathtub with signs asking guests not to stain it with hair dye. It is a place for furtive sex by the hour and adulterous assignations in the no-man's land on the far side of the runways, far away from the real airport hotels. It is permeated with a strong, musky fragrance. It is flown over by five aircraft in the night, droning upwards or downwards, dragging their counterpane of sound over our horizontal bodies.

The screaming in the train tunnels had already set me on edge. It was done in jest but sounded like a hurricane wind, tearing down the world. In Trivandrum airport there was a man brushing his teeth after landing. Good practice – but he was making himself retch and gag. We all do this sometimes, I guess, trying to get to the back of the tongue. But he was doing it with furious intent, like penance, or as if he was addicted to the gag reflex, retching and choking himself right there in the middle of the bathroom at baggage reclaim.

On the flight to Dubai there is a baby crying. There is often a baby crying on flights; their ears take in so much more sound than those of an adult. They are rightfully terrified by the roaring and rushing, the painful changes in air pressure. They realise that they are in hell. But this infant screamed like no other I have ever heard. He screamed himself into exhaustion, into hoarseness, into a state of bewilderment and tiredness where the end of each wail seemed to lose its way and wonder what it was doing, and where it had come from; but then it was time for the next building wave of pain and panic, crashing against our eardrums and the moulded plastic of the cabin. My Kindle was stocked up with stories about the Trump administration's tax bills, sexual predators, paedophile Congressmen, Sri Lankan cricketers choking and vomiting in Delhi smog, children who couldn't go out and play six days out of seven, the selling of men into slavery in Libya, the wildfires engulfing California, the energy demands of Bitcoin, the genocidal Buddhists of Myanmar, the legacy of Robert Gabriel Mugabe, the threats of Hindu nationalists to behead Bollywood actors, the normalisation of American Nazis, the sixth extinction, the dying corals and ceremonies of mourning held for vanished species – and I realised that this child was screaming on our behalf. Crying for all the newsreaders who never cried, for the fish that couldn't make a sound, letting out a kind of primeval, end times, furiously sorrowful and exhausted roar that we crave, that would do us a lot of good, a kind of sonic retching to expel some of the poison, a flight-time wail of superhuman strength and endurance, out-screaming the engines in the cold dark air.

I was being poisoned by the in-flight meal but I didn't know that yet, so I clicked through the entertainment channels. There was an episode of the animated show *Rick and Morty* where Earth is menaced by huge alien heads who hover in orbit and intone: 'SHOW ME WHAT YOU GOT!' The Pentagon is beaming them string theory and Da Vinci's drawings but Rick tells the president that what they are actually asking for is music. Planet Earth wins out in a kind of intergalactic *Idols* (the other planets/contestants are all destroyed by a death ray) with Rick, Morty and Ice-T working together to create some tunes. I watched it twice in a row – partly because I liked Rick's song 'Get Shwifty', which saved Earth from annihilation, but also because the episode seemed to access some deep truth: that the only thing a superior form of extraterrestrial life might ask of us would be music. That we might be at the beginning of the end of democracy, climate stability and possibly the human race, but didn't we make some astonishing sounds in the one second of evolutionary time allotted to us.

Afterwards, I found a documentary on the Estonian conductor Paavo Järvi – nothing special as a documentary but by the end I found my throat closing up over Sibelius and Scandinavian folk music. Thirty-six million people are studying classical piano in China, we learnt, and then saw footage of the young guy with spiky hair who had been placed top in the country, smashing his way through Prokofiev, unleashing torrents of musical energy. Then it was the finale from the *The Firebird* with its suspended, shimmering, otherworldly chords and (you know how it is on planes: the thin air, the wine, the compulsory reflection) I was crying into my refresher towel, thinking of humankind and all the gorgeous noise we made, once upon a time, at the end of the day.

Five by three

I

There was a phone box upslope from the youth hostel. It stood out on the hillside, a dab of red against the greens and greys. It was the same colour as the bike panniers, waxy red and waterproof, that had carried everything I'd needed over the past weeks, through the wind and rain.

That was a good feeling. Striking camp, slotting the panniers back on the bike, being on your way. And so was rolling on and off the ferries ahead of the cars.

You watched an island approach, like this one with its terracotta cliffs and a rock pillar rising from the waves. The shoreline slowly resolved: a boatyard, a hotel on the pier. White and grey pebbledash houses with laundry lines outside, clothes snapping in the wind.

The ferry bumped against the tyres of the pier, the ramp clunked down. The line of wet tarmac stretched out ahead, glowing when some light came through the clouds. Just a single lane with some passing places for cars, but there were none. This island was wilder and emptier than the others.

So I didn't expect the phone box to be in use, but could see someone, two people, through the glass slats. I waited outside on a track streaming with water.

Can you help me?

She had an old-fashioned raincoat and hair with a stripe of white.

It doesn't take my money.

He had dreadlocks and glasses that weren't in good shape: taped up, beaded with rain.

I realised the problem. It was one of these payphones where the coin only dropped once the call had been answered. She dialled and waited, then got through and the 50p chunked down into the box.

She was Rafa, from Italy; he was Steve, from Belgium. They told me not to check into the hostel: it was full of rules and stinky, drying boots. I should come with them to the beach down there. There was a stone building, a bothy, where you could stay for free, or pitch a tent in the paddock outside.

They liked it so much here that Rafa had been trying to change her ticket back, but kept getting cut off. This had resulted in some tension, since Steve clearly did not enjoy fishing coins out of their fabric purse and dropping them into the Telecom box.

We walked down the track to the sea, me wheeling my bike alongside. She said that Steve didn't fly. He was like – she didn't know the English word – but like a Taliban with these things. Steve said he liked to get high, but not with fucking easyJet. He was going to hitch back to Italy, ride with truckers through the Channel Tunnel – he'd done it before. Not budget airlines, that wasn't travelling.

Fancy, he said, fiddling with my panniers, looking inside.

Steve was a bit younger than me, Rafa a bit older. I was twenty-something. No need to pin things down too exactly, but it was before Obama, it was Bush and Blair. It was a time before smartphones – just. My photos from the trip were taken on a disposable camera.

Most are just of the bike (with the Revolution Cycles logo: a red cog) posed against various things – a cliff, cove, a standing stone – with no one in frame. But then Steve and Rafa appear, sitting at the bothy fireplace, leaning back over armchairs to look at the camera.

Steve is pale with an orange tint in his dreads, holding the camera's gaze. Rafa is darker, more Mediterranean. Though she didn't like the sun, she said, and loved how overcast it was here all the time. She has the Susan Sontag stripe in her hair and a book in her hand.

Rafa was reading the Brontë sisters and loved how they'd never really gone outside, making up all those stories without leaving their cottage. She also loved Keats and Italo Calvino (he was from Liguria, like her). And Robert Louis Stevenson and Melville, Borges, GK Chesterton and Robert Walser. You didn't often get a list like that. She seemed from a slightly different era.

I wondered how she could concentrate on all that nineteenth-century prose, given how much they smoked. It started over morning coffee and went on all through the day. Steve carefully lighting and then stubbing out his thin joints, storing them in a matchbox. Rationing out the tobacco, burning the lump of hash, crumbling it in.

Steve mostly read the bothy visitor's book, reciting bits out loud to us. There was a long-running battle between those who wanted to keep the locations of these stone shelters secret, and those who wanted a more democratic approach. Someone crossed out the GPS coordinates of another shelter; someone else hit back a few weeks later: *Which meanspirited pedant did this? Shame on you elitist curmudgeon!* What was a curmudgeon? I tried to explain. It's you Steve, Rafa said. Actually it's you.

The photo also shows horns, skulls and whalebones above the fireplace that they tended all day when it rained, stoking it with folded pine twigs, boiling the blackened kettle and talking about the village where they lived. A place high up in the Apennine mountains, a very old settlement, but almost deserted now – I must visit.

Rafa drew the horns and skulls. She was always drawing things in her journal. Not bad, but stoner doodles and dreamcatcher patterns tended to encroach from the margins.

In the corner of the room is Steve's didgeridoo. He would sometimes take it out in the evenings, giving an impromptu performance, complete with huffy circular breathing, for whoever happened to be there.

So what do you do in this village then? asked one of the 'Gore-Tex people' (Steve's phrase) who would pass through for a night or two with their hi-tech gear. Steve responded that they did nothing, they tried to be as lazy and unproductive as possible to subvert the capitalistic economy.

The hiking party from Norwich or Norway looked a little bemused.

We look after the plants, Rafa said. Tomato, *rucola, amarena*. We get in wood for winter. Sometimes Steve snowboard to town for flour and we make a cake.

The village was called Tonno, which sounded like Tuna, but actually it was related to *tun*, an old Celtic word that meant settlement. Steve and Rafa were into ancient European sites, standing stones and sacred places – that's why they'd come here. And me?

I was homeless. No, that was an exaggeration. But I had moved out of one place and could only afford another after the summer, when the festival was over and the rents came down. So I was cycling through the islands for three weeks, killing time, using these pages from a road atlas photocopied in the library.

Killing time? Steve turned the phrase over.

The copies came out a bit light, so I'd been tracing the outlines of the islands in pen as I went. The crinkly inlets, islets, the skerries – it was an endless embroidery. The roads were clear enough, but what my maps didn't have were contours or any sense of gradient.

You've been using this? Steve laughed. I like you, man.

They weren't like the beautiful Ordnance Survey maps that the climbers brought, and which we pored over in the firelight. All those stacked contour lines, crimping at streams or watersheds, getting the famous ranges down in two dimensions. Here Steve found common ground with the Gore-Tex people – a love for heights and being in the mountains. He would take himself off into the Alps for weeks at a time, Rafa said – it worried her.

The climbers could read these stacked brown lines so intimately. Here was an exposed scramble, a famous step, a knife-edge ridge. It was like returning to a favourite line in a book, the way they spoke about them, the words they used. This route was 'thoughtful', that one was 'burly' or 'thuggish'. There was an exposed dome of granite nearby here: Open Secret that was called, since some climber had seen the sun shining on it one afternoon, hiding in plain sight.

This was the thing with bothies: there was a changing cast of characters from day to day. Climbers and hillwalkers came and went, even some kayakers who pulled up on the boulder beach. They had fresh mackerel caught on hand lines and some peat-smoked whiskey, offering us a dram.

A sip of the white man's firewater, said Steve after a long pause. Why not?

He was someone, it became clear, who thought very carefully about what he put in his mouth – the first hardline vegan I'd ever spent time with. He and Rafa mainly ate from a pot filled with a ceaselessly evolving risotto. A gunked-up pot that was never really cleaned, but just had more rice and stock and veg churned into it as needed. We would just scoop out the rice with hunks of bread.

I'm also trying to be vegetarian, said a local joiner who'd arrived with his white van and teenage daughter. He talked about his love for growing vegetables, for eating broccoli raw, just like that. He listened respectfully to the didge performance (which Steve had insisted on doing in pitch darkness, to feel better the vibrations) and was trying to enter into the spirit of the thing.

I just cannae get enough of it. Isn't that right Claire?

Dunno, she said, hiding behind a packet of Walker's crisps all evening. But then next day she and Steve were hula-hooping on the beach: where had those come from? She was swivelling her hips, he was shouting instructions, telling her what she was doing wrong.

We invented pastimes. You balanced an egg-shaped beach pebble on a boulder, then threw other pebbles until it fell. Rafa said it was too aggressive, too male, but Steve and I played Egg on Coast for hours. Whole sequences of different pebbles were balanced at various levels, each to be picked off until the dusk came down and the rocks would begin sparking off each other.

Steve had a minidisc player with battery life that he was carefully conserving. At a certain point each day he would allow himself a few minutes with headphones on. I had a brief listen: it was dance music, techno and trippy psychedelic stuff.

Poor boy, said Rafa as we watched him dance in the paddock, jabbing the air, hamming it up for us. Such terrible music he likes.

The sun came out strongly for the first time. We warmed up by running along the shore, then charged the clear green swell. Because of the Gulf Stream the beaches and bays could look turquoise, tropical – even when right next to peat bogs and marsh.

Steve, there is little children on the beach, said Rafa as he embarked on a nude salute to the sun. He replied that they were naked all day, and anyway his penis was so small in the cold.

He was very white, one of the palest people I had ever seen: limbs the colour of milk. And he had an unusually shaped body: something about the elongated, pear-shaped backside that ended in a high, narrow waist, more like a woman's physique. But he was totally unselfconscious, all for public nudity and unashamed ablutions, pissing against a dry-stone wall at a moment's notice. He wasn't an artistic one like Rafa, he didn't need to leave any trace of his existence behind. Just a little fart, now and then.

Each day the 2 p.m. ferry rounded the headland, drawing its long wake towards the mainland. With phones long dead, it became the only way of telling the time. The bay was cupped by red-brown sandstone cliffs on each side; a grey helmet of cloud sat halfway up the slopes of the glen – these marked the edges of our world, portrait and landscape.

A place walled off from the world with its demands, schedules and its fees just to exist – we had found a kind of idyll. There was no owner or manager, no overseer. There was no rent. The whole place was wild camping, *campeggio libero*, 'savage camping' as they called it in France. Steve and Rafa switched between French and Italian among themselves – I felt bad consigning them to English in my presence.

The pine smoke hung under the slate roof, warding off the biting flies. The midges kept these islands less visited than they otherwise might be. Some of the Gore-Tex people had whole anti-bug ensembles, donning hoods and veils in the evenings, walking around like beekeepers or some kind of priesthood.

Most days we tramped to and from the post office that sold UHT milk, chocolate and a single postcard. All Steve ever bought was crisps for 20p: a vegan treat. They only had cheese and onion flavour but that was okay because it didn't contain real cheese. There were just a few houses along the road and each garden seemed the same: a small flower bed, that line of wind-tormented laundry and often a trampoline, all tiny under the grey, leaky ceiling of the north Atlantic.

They both wore raincoats that were old and well used. Worn down around the collar and hood until they had gone shiny where they should have been matt, or matt where they should have been shiny. Something about those worn-in jackets gave me such a good feeling. The *tic-tic-tic* of rain against an anorak and I am back there, picking my way between tussocks, watching oiliness run out of the peat bog and pool on water in the path.

Idylls are good to remember but hard to write about: there is not much conflict or drama. Though Steve, I sensed, was always ready for some, and made the most of things when it arrived.

One afternoon we came back from a walk and there were people all over the paddock. They were unloading cars and carrying boxes of booze in wheelbarrows. It was a group of teenagers from the main island to the north. They had come for an eighteenth birthday party.

Eighteen years my God, said Rafa. The most fascistic age.

They were hooking up CD players to car batteries and lighting disposable barbecues, those foil trays filled with coals and a little grid to burn Value burgers and 'plastic sausages' – Steve was looking on in disgust – while scorching the grass below. All afternoon he glared through the bothy window, watching the alcopops take effect. When boy band ballads began playing early the next morning he stormed out and confronted them.

You come to a place like this – with *a car battery?*

All right pal, all right, said the ringleader, while some of the women laughed nervously.

Don't smile at me girl, Steve shouted, I'll fucking break your battery!

But on the other hand, he was out of tobacco. And so he asked if I could go and parley with these people, smooth things over and maybe get a handful of Golden Virginia – which I did, while hearing them out.

To just come steamin' in like that, said the birthday boy, I mean it's our island.

Yes, yes of course. But they were from Europe, you know? Passionate types.

When the partygoers left we surveyed the mess of bottles, blackened foil, scorched grass, crushed lager tins.

I'm surprised you could speak anything to them that morning, Rafa said. When I get angry my English is not good. I will only shout *Stupid! Stupid! Stupid!*

Steve was sniffing. That fucking plastic sausage smoke was still in the air.

The teenagers left and the idyll returned. No signal, nothing to do in the evenings but sit around the fire and talk. The kind of talking and telling that must once have been all we did as humans, Rafa said. When memories and stories come up and can be related in their fullness, in their own sweet time.

Steve spoke about his years in squats and protest camps: Amsterdam and Athens, Thessaloniki. He'd worked on construction sites in Belgium, then in an auto parts warehouse. Packing pallets, wrapping them with industrial cling film and then using a flamethrower to shrink it on – good times in the belly of the beast!

Rafa had been studying at university, social development. But she hated it and dropped out to care for an old woman in the mountain village, someone with special powers – a witch! Also, Rafa had a problem with her ears: a perpetual ringing that was made worse by loud noise, so the quietness of the village suited her.

I told them about the big, draughty concert hall where I worked in the box office. The sound of the orchestras tuning up and singers sound checking. The ageing clientele who came to see the symphonies on Thursday evenings, fewer and fewer each week. The database, my boss called them – they were expiring too. Sometimes an old woman would come and beg me to take her husband's name off the mailing list: he'd been gone for years.

They asked about my cycle trip and I said it was great on the small islands but tough on the bigger ones or the mainland where there was more traffic. How much it made me resent cars and petrol engines – and the *aggression* of that noise. The drivers, the white vans and lorries that just barrelled past on an incline with *no idea* how many calories it was costing you. No one had any idea of what the real cost of anything was any more. And why did people think they *deserved* big Land Rovers and Jeep Cherokees anyway? Why did they take it as their due, as the most natural thing in the world?

I'd been to all the anti-war marches, but the cyclist–driver encounter was the only thing that made me well and truly furious, that made me talk in angry political italics. This kind of talk endeared me to Steve, this and my anger at privatised rail services. The whole way north I'd argued with a conductor, since two companies ran on the same line and I'd boarded the wrong train, just a few minutes later, but run by a different operator. Up and down the carriages we went: him telling me to pay a full open fare (plus extra for the bike berth); me telling him that yes, sometimes people arrived too late to be let into the concert hall where I worked, but did I turn them away? No, I took them up to the balcony, let them in between movements, showed a bit of human feeling – and this was *exactly the same situation.*

No, the conductor shot back. It's like someone arriving with a ticket to a different concert.

Ah he got you, Steve laughed. That capitalist pig got you!

When the cloud ceiling lifted we did longer hikes. Up along the cliffs to look at the famous sea stack, leaning out the water like a slanted *I*. Or to a colony of gulls and gannets on ledges of the cliffs. The birds would hang on the wind, eye-level with us having our lunch, then hinge their wings and dive while others rose up again. A raucous, swirling commotion that we watched and watched, until a Walker's packet was whipped out of our hands. Steve gave an anguished cry. It flew up, then was rammed by a downdraft, joining the lip of the ocean far below.

To make up for it we picked litter off the beach on our way back: hundreds of ear bud axles, big hunks of fishermen's polystyrene. There was a washed-up dolphin, grinning horribly. Maroon and basalt rocks with swirling strata that got half-submerged by sand and looked like planets.

But I think it's now part of the ocean, this? Rafa wondered as I tugged at a rope encrusted in seaweed.

Thank you! said a passing walker.

Somebody's got do it, Steve shot back.

Rafa and I shared a look, and then again when he walked behind me, methodically picking up citrus peels that I had scattered along a path. They weren't from this ecosystem: look, there was a label. They were from South Africa and could hurt a bird's stomach.

At least not from Israel, said Rafa.

Bizarrely, there was an Israeli flag draped from one of the isolated cottages in the glen. Steve kept threatening to take action. What the fuck was a *Zionist flag* doing on a Scottish island?

Steve *per favore*, Rafa said. We're on holiday.

And then told me about a march in Genoa when he had spent all morning making a banner, only to find that it read FREE PLASTINE.

Go make it on the hills with rocks Steve. FREE PLASTINE!

She laughed and laughed.

Yes it's very funny, he said. The situation here in the Middle East.

The Middle East was the local nickname for our part of the island, just right of centre on the map. Beyond that was the Far East, where we visited the remains of a Neolithic village.

The glaciers carved out this valley, giving it the characteristic, broad-bottomed U-shape. Steve was reading the information panel next to the excavated ruins. When the ice age retreated, the soil was fertile. People had been living here 5 000 years ago. It was older than Stonehenge, older than the Pyramids. Steve pointed to the artist's impression of the Neolithic villagers.

Rafa there's you. My broad-bottomed Neanderthal.

I could see what he meant: the big forehead and jaw. It gave her a slightly androgynous look. But then there was the delicate cut of her lips and eyes.

We visited a blackhouse too, a stone-walled hut bunkered down in the dunes and sea grass, covered in turf and reed. As we sat in the darkness under the corbelled roof, a memory surfaced of another time and place. A childhood scene, a school trip in the great southern escarpment. A beehive hut with a floor of polished dung. That sense of a fundamental human shelter, rounded, curved over you like an eggshell, like the dome of a dark night sky.

As the days went by, we began to run out of food. The hillwalkers often left provisions behind: apples and oatcakes (which were to our liking), pot noodles and instant soups (which were not). You could live like this, Rafa said, you wouldn't believe what supermarkets dumped in skips.

But as the days grew shorter, there were fewer visitors and supplies eventually ran down. I was broke, but those two seemed to exist almost completely outside the economy. Counting out coins from their fabric purse seemed like agony to Steve.

I offered to ride to the convenience store right at the southern tip of the island – it was marked on my road atlas. But because the map lacked any topography, I badly underestimated the trip.

The road 'sneaked' through a range of hills in the middle of the island – one of Rafa's mistakes that you'd never want to hear corrected. Hairpinning up and down, sneaking the long way around sea lochs that reached their watery fingers far inland.

Riding back, my red panniers were loaded with fruit and potatoes, rice and lentils. Every ounce of it had to be paid for in calories expended, drawn out through the cogs, gears, the thick, knobbly tyres of my mountain bike – and now the wind was against me. It was the most physically taxing day of my trip, of my life maybe. My legs and lungs burned. But the provisions felt earned, valuable, sacred even. All this would nourish us in the days ahead.

I freewheeled down the glen, arriving back just as it was getting dark. Rafa and Steve had been worried, and when they saw me, they began waving something. It was a bit of tarp tied to a washed-up pole. They had made a flag out of beach flotsam and were waving it in the paddock, encouraging me, shouting:

The Revolution is coming!

I let my bike fall and staggered across the grass. They ran towards me with arms outstretched.

The Revolution is here!

II

There were five of us, all lined up and facing a red velvet curtain. We'd been told to report to the hotel lobby at 6 p.m. It was one of those smart, bland business hotels in a part of town known for its lap-dancing bars and stag nights – locals called it the pubic triangle.

Petros was in the line-up too, a big man looking unconvinced in his black beard and thick-framed glasses – even his balding head seemed to radiate scepticism – and then three strangers. There were only five audience members per performance, but I had comps through the box office where I worked. This theatre company was known for its site-specific productions. One year the back of an Audi as gangsters drove it through the city at night. The next something about body snatchers amid the dripping urinals of a public toilet. So these were hot tickets, I told Petros, cutting-edge theatre.

It was hard to impress the man or get him involved in anything I suggested. Theatre is shit – he would say things like that as we sat in the small kitchen of the flat, with laundry hoisted up above us on its rack and pulley. It's a fucking boring, dying art form – let's just admit it. He was dismissive of the festival in general: all those people clogging up the pavements, dirty hippies and street musicians – that's why he cleared out at this time of year and went back to Greece.

I'd been sub-letting his room while he was gone, a tiny upstairs garret in a shared tenement flat on Leith Walk. From here I could climb out onto the roof, smoke and look towards the Forth Bridge through a gap between the grand buildings of the New Town. There it was, so satisfyingly geometric, so honest about its structure.

Petros would call from Athens or some Greek island, call the phone on a little table at the bottom of the stairs.

Was I having sex in his bed? Had I been fucking girls on his mattress – or boys, or both, he didn't judge – had I found the sex toys in the second drawer down?

Why not? he would shout down the phone: *Why the hell not?* or

The curtain rose and there were five actors facing us, looking into our eyes, right up close. There was a man in front of me, but after a minute or so, the performers shuffled around. A woman came and stood opposite, looking down on me slightly. She was tall like a model, her body strong and statuesque like a dancer. Way out of my league was my first thought, a total goddess.

The lights dimmed, taverna music played and our partners led us to candle-lit tables. I could hear everyone else begin talking, but my partner remained silent. Petros was chatting away, laughing. The sound of flirtation filled the hotel bar, but this severely beautiful woman with her long Modigliani face only looked at me, and in a way that I'd never been looked at before. She wore an asymmetrical dress with a single strap. I tried some small talk, but she just took my hand, smiled and looked still more meaningfully into my eyes. As if to say: let's dispense with words for this evening, we both know what's what.

The music changed, the scenes changed. We danced a waltz with each other, my hand resting on the thin strap across her shoulder. We gathered in a circle and were told to ask any last questions. She spoke for the first time, untying her dress so that it fell away from her breasts.

Is this what you wanted to see?

By the time we left the hotel, Petros was in a state of high excitement. He said he needed a whiskey to calm down. We should meet Mara in one of the bars and explain to her what a ridiculous and cynical experience we'd been through, what a fool I'd made of myself and what a goddamn whore his 'date' was – look, there were already five new audience members waiting in the lobby.

At one point, we'd been asked to write our names and addresses on a postcard. On leaving the performance, we were ushered through a room papered in cards and letters written to previous audience members. Previous victims, Petros said.

I believed in what we had, he told Mara, who was absorbing it all in her wry, unruffled way, through her grey eyes.

There was a connection there. He'd felt it. And now she was with another man, the bitch. The performance of romance, how the mind deceived itself, what we were so ready to believe, and so quickly – brilliant really.

He gripped my head in his arms and thanked me for the tickets, then told Mara what I'd said when my date had showed me her breasts — which were, let's admit, incredible — and asked: is this what you want to see? And I had replied — tell her what you said!

I'd be lying if I said that I didn't.

Which was too much for Petros. He put his head down on the table — *I'd be lying if I said that I didn't!* — and howled with laughter.

It was me trying to enter into the spirit of the thing, I told Mara, role playing and all that. What was I supposed to do in that situation?

She shrugged as if to say either sure, understandable or what do I care either way. I should get her a ticket and she would check it out for herself.

The three of us paid for our drinks and walked home through the city.

A theatre, a concert hall, a cinema — they were clustered together on a busy road that ran below the black rock of the Castle. Over the years I had worked in each, slipping into back rows and balconies as the house lights went down. In the theatre I clipped reviews from the press; in the concert hall I typed out credit card expiry dates; in the cinema I tore tickets and ushered people to their seats.

Which is where I'd met Mara, also dressed in our uniform of black jeans and black long-sleeved top. The idea was to be invisible, which suited us fine. We agreed that this was the perfect way to absorb film: no payment, no expectation, no anxiety about whether the person next to you was enjoying it. There was no person next to you. You were alone, dressed in black, a mere technicality. The only thing you had to do was alert the projectionist if something went wrong with the sound.

It only happened once, during the premier of *Grizzly Man*, Werner Herzog's documentary about Timothy Treadwell, a man who was in love with wild bears in Alaska and then got eaten by one. I adored the film. The ecstasies that Treadwell had experienced — the lumbering grizzlies, the icy rivers, the little bee that he thinks is dead but isn't really (*A little bee!* he croons), the way he marvels at the warmth of a bear's dung, sinking his hands into it: *This came from inside her!* — to me it all seemed to outweigh Herzog's chiding Germanic voice, droning on about the brute indifference of nature.

But Mara didn't know: Treadwell pretended to be alone out there, but he wasn't really. He'd cut his girlfriend out of shot in all the footage, and she'd been eaten too. She'd attacked the bear with a frying pan – there was an audio recording of it, but no visuals, since Treadwell didn't have time to take off the lens cap. Herzog didn't even let us hear that: we had to watch him listening through headphones to their fate. Their grizzly fate.

Such things we discussed over lunch, often spent in a nearby cemetery where Thomas De Quincey was buried, the opium eater. Maybe it was a soggy meal deal sandwich, a baked potato or a baguette from one of the shops on Lothian Road, terrible Scottish baguettes that, we complained, scratched the roof of your mouth.

The bees and the bears and the summer melt of Alaska merged into the images that flowed and flickered through the long winters, like a magic lantern show of stages and screens thrown up in the darkness. Post-rock bands from Glasgow or desert blues from Mali, youth orchestras from Colombia or Ukraine, a Wagner Ring Cycle where people camped out on the pavement, hoping for cheap tickets, a comedy guitar duo from New Zealand that everyone raved about. But mainly the films, flickering on through the darkness: this week a love story from Korea, next week a reverse love story from France. You meet a couple just as they are disintegrating and in five scenes track back to their first meeting, *5x2*. An anti-romance, said Mara, not a romcom but a romtrag – what a wonderfully cynical idea. And don't worry, she said, turning to me: the world finds a way of looking after damaged hearts.

Six, seven, eight years but now it was over. Seven years in that steep old city with its vaults and bridges, viaducts and tenements. The sloping cobbled streets that gave bachelorettes in high heels such trouble – sometimes there were National Health Service workers handing out flip-flops on Saturday nights, when the scenes of revelry got medieval, when club basslines boomed through the Cowgate and long lines of punters came out of the chippies, maybe one of them ordering that mythic Scottish delicacy: the deep-fried Mars bar. Dark and Gothic

Old Town, with its bony churches and sooty war memorials. Fancy New Town with its kings and colonists on their plinths and tall columns, all encrusted with history. But it wasn't mine, thank God, it was another country: of curved terraces, locked gardens and long cycle paths through the greenbelts. Up the river, past the modern art gallery, allotments, past Her Majesty's prison and up into the hills; or down to the docks, then coast along the shoreline, down past housing estates and breakwaters and hardscrabble promenades, work back upslope on the long Leith Walk, joust with the buses, cut through the echoey rail station with the bike workshop in its basement – the workshop where the Revolution was made from second-hand parts – then up again to the palace and the parliament with turf on its roof. Lock up the bike but keep going, up through the valley of gorse and grass, trace the lip of the Crags, that rock diagonal scored beyond the towers and spires, tempting you out of the daily routine, into the heavenly kingdom that was close at hand (*A little bee!*), that was just up there on the cliff paths with the day-trippers, joggers and dog-walkers. Smoke a little in a sunny nook and piece the city together, matching where you'd been to what you were seeing now, now that summer was here, now that the northern latitudes were spinning into the light and a single day could contain multitudes, could have a lifetime's worth compressed and concentrated into it – that fairground feeling, I thought to myself (mainly just myself), that sense of the turning world, the carousel, the whole human production wheeling about you.

Petros, Mara and I had PhDs to finish. We sat around a big dining room table in the flat and wrote them up together. Hers was in literature, like mine, so we tended to form an alliance at the table, trying and (and failing) to suggest what music should be listened to while working. Petros had carefully assembled work-appropriate playlists: mixes of drone artists and ambient electronica, Scarlatti and Bach. He had strong musical opinions. I should never, for instance, touch my guitar in his presence. Though sometimes he would pick it up and play us a tango or a sarabande in the evenings, as the sun went down over the Forth. On his door, us flatmates had stuck a Far Side cartoon. We are in hell and the devil is ushering a large, distinguished looking man into a flaming cavern of grinning banjo and ukulele players: *Here is your room, maestro.*

The flat had a shifting cast of southern Europeans (who tended to be scientists) and Scots (architects or art college grads). There was a performance artist, Beth, who made work with foodstuffs. She put parsnips on a string and wore them as a nose; or she painted sausages as they gradually turned green in jars. It was hard to understand but she always seemed to be getting new grants and residencies. There was a painter-decorator, Handsome Stuart, who had a slick gaming set-up in his room and let us use it for first-person shooters like Call of Duty, which was like having crystal meth next door.

Mara didn't actually live there but was always coming around. She and Petros got together after he broke up with Beth, with whom he was still friendly and rudely affectionate. You see, Petros would tell me. It's not the end of the world, people switch and shuffle – life goes on.

The person I'd moved to this city to live with five, six, seven years ago – she'd met someone else, a woman, at the Revolution Co-op, the cycle workshop under the station where everyone seemed to be tattooed, bisexual and into something called polyamory (the first time I'd heard the word).

So I was now single, Petros continually reminded me. I was a good-looking guy, not bad-looking anyway. And the city was *full* of tourists, actors, students, even contortionists – he'd seen one on the Royal Mile yesterday, cramming herself into a glass box, like this. And I should be taking advantage, not moving back into my ex's place, hiding away from the world.

I know, I said, I knew – I was just going back for a short while, just until a room became available in the flat again, just to pack up and stuff. She was gone anyway. She and the bike mechanic were driving through the Highlands in a converted Ford Transit.

So, Petros said, I would be house-sitting her bourgeois little house and watering her plants while those lesbians, and their dogs, were having a fine old time in the van? Maybe I was beyond help.

In the pub across the road, he like to expound a sexual philosophy that he believed to be enlightened. Because he had the ability to find almost any woman, of almost any age, sexually attractive. It was true – even our weekly cleaner, the Estonian. He loved a big woman. Why not? Once you'd come over to this way of thinking, the world was a fascinating place. I looked at Mara as he spoke, but her grey eyes didn't give much away.

The pub was Swedish, which meant it served pear ciders and meatballs, and had beautiful bar staff – the eyes of whomever you were talking to tended to flick away over your shoulder. We ended up there most days, some part of the extended crew of architects and artists, physicists, painter-decorators and grad students. Not in any organised way: it was just a place for social gathering and gossip, a local. Which woman behind the bar was Handsome Stuart sleeping with now? And which one had given him chlamydia?

But mainly we sat in the small kitchen of the flat. It was almost as if, in a place with such generous rooms and high ceilings, we all liked to cluster in the smallest nook, where you could barely get to the fridge around someone else's chair. We cooked, we brewed espresso after dinner and went out dancing: a late-twenties second wind, much nicer than any other clubbing I'd done. The dancefloor was where Petros relinquished all judgement and became pure joyfulness, pure benevolence: a dancing bear of a man, doing the most mincing and ridiculous moves, locking eyes with you all the while – it could be hard to extricate yourself.

Yes, Mara said, he needs a lot of affirmation on the dancefloor. It's good you're here to take a shift.

Petros kept on probing about my love life, but since the break-up there wasn't much to tell. I'd kissed someone outside a hotel on one of the islands during my cycle trip, a redhead. Which sounded promising? But then we'd gone in for a meal of Cullen skink, and that smoked haddock chowder had somehow killed the mood. Fucking Scottish food! Petros said, shouting over the noise of the club. We needed to go to Greece, where people knew how to eat, where even the vegetables were pure aphrodisiacs, where just a single aubergine could make you hard. Next summer.

I didn't mention Rafa, whom I found myself thinking of quite often. Did I find her attractive, with her strong brow and toothy teeth, some lightly stained by tobacco? Rafa in her enchanted old raincoat and her long hair with the white stripe, pinned up with clips or falling down over her pale shoulders. Where were Steve and Rafa now, I wondered. Had they left the island?

As the days got shorter again, I had to run or cycle often to keep away the seasonal blues. Mara swam lengths at some far-away pool. Sometimes Petros played basketball, but most of his free time was spent online: a big man hunched over a tiny laptop or stroking a newly released device called an iPhone in the middle of dinner.

You have a wound in your hand, Mara would say.

It's my addiction, he would reply. We all have one.

Petros was the first internet-addicted person I knew. Which meant that he introduced us to the new strains of humour that were evolving there: viral clips, famously bad music videos. Among our favourites were two English teenagers, Ginger Kev and his sidekick, rapping about their DaySaver bus pass while switching their hands from V-sign to peace sign: *Fuck! Peace!* And then Speak, the Hungarian rapper, who couldn't really seem to think of much to say – except *Yeah, c'mon!* and *Stop the war!* – while tinny piano riffs played and his pale backing singers sang, very out of tune, in the background. It all became part of our shared lingo, our family lexicon. As if, even today, I could call up Petros (wherever he may be) and simply say: Fuck peace. Stop the war.

If it was sunny, Mara and I would walk up a nearby hill and look down at the city (Petros didn't do walks): the Athens of the North. We sat on a bench, fitted the city together and wondered why he was such a musical fascist. If it was rainy, we played Special Ops missions in Handsome Stuart's room, blasting away at helicopters and trucks and weapons bases in snowy landscapes. A whole December we spent doing that – an orphans' Christmas for those who couldn't go home, or didn't have one to go to.

Duty calls? Mara would say, standing up from the table in her boots and black leggings.

Nice piece of ass huh? Petros would say, giving it a squeeze.

I couldn't work them out. He liked to talk about anarchist friends back in Athens but wouldn't be caught dead spouting anything that might appear in *The Guardian* or left-wing papers. He loved getting a rise out of liberals and hated my suggestions about going to Gleneagles for Bush, Blair and the G8. This protest carnival stuff was just feel-good nonsense, a pantomime. People giving flowers to the police, feather dusting fences and blockades – what the fuck was that? And that cycle protest that I took part in each Friday, which took over the roads and blocked rush hour traffic – we're not blocking traffic, I corrected him with the Critical Mass slogan: We *are* traffic! – nothing, he went on, *nothing* could be more guaranteed to piss off the public and make them hate cyclists even more than they did already.

Mara had been to the Sorbonne, spoke five languages and seemed to be operating under a continental feminism so advanced that it was unfazed by Petros's deliberate boorishness – as if to say, see me take the crassness of male desire in my stride. But mainly she was kind, amused, watchful, wary of sentiment, slightly aloof. Someone who didn't have much to prove and didn't confide – so it took longer to get to know her. She had a brother back in Athens who, I gathered, was not well.

Mara broached things close to her heart, I came to realise, in cryptic or coded ways, often by talking about the writers and artists she loved – Italo Calvino (who she was writing her thesis on), Rabelais, the crackpot utopian Charles Fourier. She also had the whole of Greek mythology in her head, and naturally assumed that I got all the references, but in fact I felt embarrassingly ignorant and monolingual around her. How was it that she spoke so many languages?

She explained (as we reloaded bazookas, executed hostages, called in air strikes) that she was born to Greek parents and had a French education. Her family had moved around a lot when she was young – her father had worked for the ministry of foreign affairs. Age two, she was taken to Czechoslovakia, where she had a Russian nanny. There were family recordings of her speaking Czech, but she no longer understood what she was saying. She wanted to get back to that, to learn the language again. The important thing, the right thing, she felt, was simply to go on learning about the world. Writing about it, having ideas about it, was secondary.

She did have something of the Eastern Bloc about her, I thought. Exactly what was hard to say – maybe a deliberate unstylishness, an unconcern with how her hair fell. But then this Warsaw Pact uncoolness (which was cool anyway) had been overlaid and combined with Parisian chic: people were complex mixtures after all. After Prague they had moved to Italy, where she learnt Italian and so now: Calvino. Our study break was over.

We sat around the table and tapped away at our dissertations. Above us was a framed picture of the Forth Bridge that I'd found at a charity shop, a sepia photograph of it under construction.

Its three arched cantilevers were still reaching across to each other in space, their geometries not yet linked up. So on each plinth rested three lattices of steel girders, struts and supports – like industrial haystacks or Cubist bird's nests, like three unfinished sketches. One day they would all be joined, and one day we would be done with our theses.

III

There was a small sign, *Tempio Buddista*, pointing us up through the pines on a dusty track. We passed figurines of the Buddha and offerings under the trees, the air warm and resinous; but something else too – a derelict structure of broken glass and toilet paper. We were in hills above the sea, with sounds of summer holidays filtering up from the town below.

The monk was standing in the shade halfway up, waiting for us. He was bald with thick glasses and a glum, disapproving face that made me think of Philip Larkin, the English poet. The monk led us to the corrugated iron dorms where we would stay: Steve and me in one, Rafa in the other. Bathroom in the main house where he lived, and a communal kitchen where we gathered for meals.

After hours of silent meditation, eating took on a profound intensity. In the centre of the table was a big revolving disc. The monk wheeled it around and around, helping himself to seconds, thirds – he had a major appetite. How did that square, I wondered, with the path of asceticism? With the non-attachment to sensory pleasures about which his little pamphlets had so much to say?

But there was another aspect to this: the food had been left by previous visitors to the centre (a group of Sri Lankan monks) and it was our duty not to waste anything they had bestowed – so Rafa explained to me. This was on the first evening, when we could still communicate. The retreat proper began the next morning, and from then on it was not a word for five days: not only no speaking but also no reading or writing.

That I had not expected. I thought I was going on holiday, but no sooner had we arrived in the mountain village where Steve and Rafa lived and we were off again: to a Buddhist temple in the hills above Lerici. We could see the Cinque Terre on the way back, and the Golfo dei Poeti – the Bay of Poets where Lord Byron and Romantics used to come, Rafa said, where poor Shelley drowned with a copy of Keats's poems in his pocket.

I should have been down there, bursting joy's grape against my palate. But here I was getting leg pains in a corrugated iron mindfulness centre. Or doing hours of 'working meditation' (the monk's household and garden chores) in the hills above a coastal riviera that was so tantalisingly near.

Scooters quacked as they rounded blind corners, powerboats droned from the bay. Construction noise, shrieks and laughter, amplified music drifted up the valley to where we sat around the table in silence. There was no asking anyone to pass the pepper. We wheeled the Lazy Susan this way and that, spooning out jackfruit and coconut milk curries, peaches and cheeses, fried zucchini and tomatoes. At the end, Steve and the monk would rinse out their bowls, sluicing all the left-over morsels, both sweet and savoury, into a small glass, and then drink the concoction down. They seemed to be looking at me as they did it, implying that I should join the ritual – but something in me resisted.

There's always a little Hitler in there somewhere – I remembered Petros's words about hippie communes, ashrams. He made fun of me for wanting to hang out with these types: eco-warriors, do-gooders and dreadlocked crusties, those bike workshop activists who'd stolen my girlfriend – no ethics.

After dinner I found myself letting the dishwater out the sink instead of pouring it (as instructed) onto the vegetable patch. I secretly put peels in the trash rather than the *rifuti biologico* bin. All kinds of contrary feelings were surfacing: regret, exasperation, resentment at the monk who I was sure didn't like me, oddly petulant desires coursing through my stilled mind. To not follow the rules pinned up in the bathroom, to not cut all the paper napkins in half in an effort to save on paper, to violate the four Noble Precepts more generally.

Let thoughts come and go like clouds, allow your mind to empty (we had been told), detach from past and future. How overbearing it all was – trying to regulate what was going on in that one last, tiny rampart of privacy: the few square inches of your cranium. I resolved to flood mine with memory and thought, to fill the long, silent hours by replaying the chain of events that had brought me here.

I was house-sitting my ex's place when a text message arrived: *in edimburgo for protest camp in forest ... come join!* It was on the outskirts of the city, a long bus ride out into an area of ring roads and office parks. You passed IKEA, then an ancient chapel rumoured to have something to do with the Holy Grail.

Welcome to the Technopole, said Steve, pointing to the name of the bus stop. He said we were near the biotechnology institute where Dolly the sheep had been cloned. Welcome to techno-dystopia, more like.

We picked our way through roadside bushes full of lager cans and then into a pine forest ravine wedged between a housing estate and an industrial park.

The camp had been here since the anti-G8 protests, Steve explained, when he'd come over to march against Bush and Blair. This had been a moment of connection for us back on the island: that we had both converged on the fancy hotel in the Highlands where the leaders of the free world were deciding our fates. I caught a bus to Gleneagles on my own and basically milled around – the protest site was miles from the actual hotel. But Steve had been part of the Black Bloc, the mask-wearing anarchists who'd tried to scale the fences and then been dispersed by horse-mounted riot police. I remembered that, like some nineteenth-century cavalry charge – and the helicopters landing behind with their double rotors, the Chinooks!

Back then this forest camp been their base near the city, and he'd met such interesting, committed people. But now it turned out most of the crew were away in Iceland, campaigning against an aluminium smelter with Björk. And he and Rafa weren't so sure about the ones left behind.

Under the trees, sitting round a grubby fireplace of half-burned wooden pallets, there was a man in a waistcoat and pleather pants. He was tapping on a small tabla drum and singing – *shanti, shanti* – while a woman with a baby tried to get his attention, which he was clearly finding annoying. When the woman heard that I lived here, she came up to me and asked where she could find 'a free medicine' since she had a problem with her leg. Her thigh was covered in a crude fabric bandage, and underneath that was an awful boil. It had just burst in the shower, she said, and all this stuff just came out and out, it didn't stop! She looked frightened.

I gave her directions to the Royal Infirmary, and she went off in a battered car, taking the baby with her. The man kept tapping on his drum and talking to another, younger, woman round the fire: they were agreeing that they didn't trust hospitals and wouldn't go near them. This other woman was drinking tea from half a coconut shell and being a real know-all, going on about her advanced homeopathic training and herbal remedies for the boil – but she'd winced in disgust when the bandage was removed.

Steve, Rafa and I wandered across the peri-urban fields to the back of IKEA. Steve had seen a big wooden spindle, one used to wind cables on. We should wheel it back to the camp: it would make a good table maybe, for when the others got back? I noticed that he always liked to be busy, doing some manual labour, visibly contributing to the collective and setting himself apart from the freeloaders round the fire.

I know everything! I am homeopathic genius! I am Jesus Christ!

Rafa was trying to do a Scottish accent as she impersonated our new enemy. It was important to have them, we reckoned, and recalled the car battery barbarians back on the island.

I figured it was hard for Rafa and Steve to be as quick and witty as they really were when speaking in their third language. This meant that our conversation sometimes existed on a rather basic, pen pal level. But that was fine by me: to smoke one of Steve's tiny joints and cease from mental fight for a while, to take a break from the cerebral jousting with Petros and Mara around the dining table. Walking back from IKEA, I had a vague sense that keeping these two couples apart might be for the best.

In the middle of a field stood an old stone tower. Entering at the bottom, you could see the traces of a spiral staircase along the inner walls, then the blue summer sky where the roof should have been.

Didn't it seem ancient, Rafa said. Like something from Raperonzolo, the woman with the long hair?

We rolled the spindle back to the ravine and they showed me the damp treehouse where they were sleeping. The tabla man and coconut shell woman were smoking hash and now clearly flirting round the fire, which was giving off horrible fumes from the painted wood. You could feel rain coming.

Don't you want to come and stay with me? I asked Rafa and Steve.

I could tell they were feeling a little downcast about this forest camp, a little embarrassed maybe. They'd wanted to show me something but it had turned out grotty. They kept talking about places they would take me back home, the mountains and the sea.

I told them I was looking after someone else's cottage, house sitting for … one of my professors. There was plenty of room, really, and a bath. Steve was uncertain but Rafa said she would love that: a bath. So, we bundled up their things, walked back to the Technopole and rode into town.

The main issue with six or seven hours of meditation, I found, was sheer physical pain. For most of my life I'd avoided sitting on the ground. But now here I was, cross-legged in some pants provided by the retreat, stiff hips and leg bones crunched under me. The corrugated iron temple ticked as the sun heated it up. Within minutes it was unpleasant, and as the hours dragged on each session became a kind of torture.

Try to sit with the discomfort, read one of the monk's pamphlets. Breathe into the spaces of resistance. It was the only reading matter permitted, and even this (he left me in no doubt) was a special concession on my behalf. Not able to sit still, not able to empty my mind, not particularly interested in focusing on the breath going in and out my nostrils, not swabbing the bathroom to the monk's standards – I wasn't very good at any of this, and maybe it was beginning to annoy Steve.

Maybe you can *ordinate* your stuff, he had said even before the silence began, pointing to the clothes and toiletries spilling out of my rucksack, the pile of contraband books on the floor. And clearly things were getting heavy for him too as the days progressed. Is everything okay? I asked (gestured) after a working meditation in which he had been sniffing, flaring his eyes, snapping at insects which he normally he would have tolerated or even celebrated. He mimed a huge wave swelling and breaking on his head, then went off to sleep in the forest.

The other issue with meditation was that my emptying mind would immediately default to my now former girlfriend, who couldn't help letting me know (whenever we were in touch) about how she was experiencing what the polyamory community called NRE, or New

Relationship Energy. She was exploring a whole new aspect of her sexuality, after all, and wanted me to hear that, since didn't I know her better than almost anyone? Hadn't we grown up together really? Meeting just after school and then with each other all of university, even though we were at opposite ends of the country: a long-distance relationship that (when combined with soaring fares due to rail privatisation) had made our undergraduate days quite celibate. She was catching up for lost time in a way – surely I could understand that?

Her father was a surgeon who'd been buying each of his children property in a bid to avoid inheritance tax, in her case a semi-detached stone cottage along a river near the botanical gardens. As Steve, Rafa and I walked down from the bus station, he looked uneasy amid the fancy tenements and food shops, the big vehicles parked outside on the cobbles. These rows had once been for nineteenth-century workers, I said, for the masons and artisans who built the much grander houses and crescents of the New Town all around.

But I don't think any more, Steve said. Didn't the chief of the Royal Bank of Scotland live around here? We should pay him a little visit. Others might forget what had happened in the financial crash, Steve said, but not him, oh no.

I showed them round the cottage. That must be the professor's daughter with the short hair, and maybe her dog, a greyhound lurcher cross. Beautiful, Rafa said, picking out Italo Calvino's *Difficult Loves* from the bookshelves. She loved dogs.

I made a vegan stew as they took a bath together, which was long and ended in consternation. Since when the water drained out there was black ring around the tub. Not to worry about that, I said, ushering them into the kitchen. Though I never could quite scrub it out.

On a paper napkin, Rafa drew a map of how to get to Tonno, their village in in the mountains above Genoa. Though probably I would fly to Milan Malpensa and then get a train. Now they had visited me, I had to visit them.

Are you sure there's no butter in here? Steve asked. Such a rich flavour.

No butter, I said, even though there was. And I felt bad about that as I sat on an Italian hillside in these oddly constrictive meditation pants, picking over all the lies I had told.

The vegan issue created constant friction in Italy. Steve would cross-examine bakers as to whether their focaccia contained rennet. Or ask deli owners if it was *really* so difficult to make a pesto without cheese? And why were the olives so expensive anyway? This was local produce.

Olive oil and bread, salt and pepper, tomatoes and rocket. This was our diet in Tonno, the earthly paradise that I was so regretting leaving.

I followed the map Rafa drew, and which I still have with me now: tissue-paper thin between the pages of an old journal. Malpensa to Milano, Casella, Busalla, where they picked me up in a tiny Fiat and raced up the bends of a forested valley.

Piano Steve! And you change a gear! said Rafa, showing me a CD of Paul Simon and then putting it in.

She was teaching Steve to drive, which didn't seem wise on roads like this, where corners were so blind and drops so sheer – but who was I to blow against the wind? He was opposed to the fossil fuel industry; she was opposed to giving him lifts everywhere – that seemed to be the gist of their conversation. Like all couples, they needed witnesses from the external world, now and then.

I closed my eyes and put my face in the window, feeling the sun as we sneaked up into the mountains. Travelling like this, single but not alone, meant a glorious relinquishing of control.

No quibble country! – that was the tagline of some tyre dealership where I grew up. It promised that with you our valued customer there would be no time-wasting, no hassle, no more sweating the small stuff. No more deliberations or negotiations, none of the endless decisions that had sometimes made travel seem like one long argument strung across three continents. No more desire to see this temple or eat in this restaurant, her not wanting to, me insisting; or me not wanting to and her insisting – none of that, just the implacable unfolding of the universe as seen through the back window of a Fiat Uno. I was lighting out for No Quibble Country. I was bouncing into Graceland.

At the end of the road was Tonno: just a few old stone houses, half of them abandoned. There were runnels of water alongside the flagstone paths, a mountain stream guided through the hamlet. It pooled in basins for drinking near the top and washing down below. Tonno with its derelict mill down by the river proper, the millstones overtaken by the immense greenness that was everywhere, the deciduous green of sun filtered through a million north Italian leaves: chestnuts and beech, wild cherry. There were fireflies at dusk and vegetable patches that Steve and I ran a hosepipe to after the stunning heat, him rubbing a stem between his fingers and saying smell that.

What was it, that mysterious, cool and mineral smell?

It was tomatoes of course. Didn't I know what tomato plants smelled like?

I didn't. And I never knew *rucola* grew like a weed, a peppery weed which you could just mash into a paste with a mortar and pestle, along with some nuts and garlic and salt and oil – and that was a meal (every meal) on enzyme-free bread, followed by a handful of dark, slightly bitter cherries from the *amarena* trees. When you see fruit grow like this, Rafa said, you don't again want to buy in the supermarket.

We hiked above the treeline to find still greener meadows, the paths running onward across spurs and ridgelines, north to the maritime Alps, gateway to France and Germany and the whole of Europe. A patchwork of linked paths and *rifugios* and campsites – an infinity, Steve said, a paradise of wandering.

But no sooner had we arrived in Tonno than we were off again. The Fiat was hurtling back down the curves, a scent of lavender coming in through the window as the car grazed roadside bushes. To Genova Piazza Principe and then we were on clanking trains down the coastline, in and out of tunnel after tunnel so that the eyes kept having to readjust to the vividness. A world of coves and beaches, fields and steep towns – all in a series of quick exposures.

The summer was just coming into its own, with people on the move, people going on adventures and pilgrimages. *Bella gioventù* – the beautiful youth of this (it struck me now) big, diverse continent, a pan-European, non-aircon carriage full of people who fell easily into conversation, people with big hair exchanging numbers and addresses, no one bothering with the fare.

Once upon a time an old woman had said that to us – she and I, her and me – when we were fighting our way through the tourist-industrial complex of Venice or Tuscany. An old woman who had reached her bent hands towards our faces and whispered, with no malice or envy that I could discern, only intergenerational goodwill and sheer human feeling: *Bella gioventù*.

After three days I couldn't take it any more. Through a series of handwritten notes I made it plain to the monk that I really would have to leave now, but that I was happy to wait out the week in the town below – no hurry. Rafa said fine but Steve insisted that he would come with me. And so now here we are walking away from *Tempio Buddista*, down the track towards the sea, past the figurines and the derelict buildings. I'm wondering how long the silent Vipassana forcefield will last, when we'll be out of its reach, or if I've disappointed him terribly.

Eventually he broke the silence:

You were wearing your yoga pants backwards the whole time.

We looked at each other, two thin men on a dusty track, then burst into laughter.

It was too complicated to explain.

We laughed for a long time, then we chuckled, then we sighed. Then we gave each other a hug.

Now there were days of walking ahead of us. Nothing to do but make our way back along the coastline that I had seen in a series of bright flashes from the train. Up and down hills and bays, north to the resort town where Rafa would meet us again, her soul washed clean and calm.

What are days for? Where can we live but days? What was that beautiful Larkin poem? It had been at the edge of memory since I met the monk, whose face was not disapproving after all. Just a little disappointed, like everyone's, eventually.

Days are to be happy in – it was something like that. And where else can we live but days? But oh, solving that question brings the doctor and the priest, in their long coats, running over the fields …

Since the idea of handing over money for a piece of ground to lay our bodies on was never going to be possible, ideologically speaking, for

Steve, we will sleep in fields above the overpriced coastal towns called the Cinque Terre, the Five Lands, and chew basil leaves to clean our mouths out at the end of the day. Steve will insult a good number of tourists – once shouting: I'm sorry, but I can't answer that question, that is such an *American* question! – and keep up the fight for animal-free bread and vegan ice cream. But will also confide, one evening on a warm hillside, after we've put down our packs and unrolled sleeping mats in the dusty vegetation, how all this had put strain on his relationship with Rafa. Who was so much more accepting of the world as it was, and who'd said to him something that he couldn't shake off, something which kept crowding into his brain during the retreat. She said that fighting over all these small things could make you into a small person.

And to be honest, they were going to separate after this summer. Rafa would stay in the village, he would go back to Belgium, or maybe Amsterdam. Maybe he would walk there, get up onto those paths above Tonno and just go. They didn't want to mention it, they hadn't wanted to spoil my holiday, but there it was. And it was okay, really it was okay.

IV

It felt like a city in the wake of something, Athens. Something world-historical but complex and painful, something everyone was sick to death of talking and thinking about. Every block and building seemed ringed by a low tide of graffiti. Slogans and spiky black tags grew out the asphalt and up the walls. It was clearly angry and political, though I couldn't read the script.

Back in the Scottish Swedish pub, Mara and Petros would sometimes fall into discussions with friends from back home, intense conversations in Greek. They huddled in an alcove with another, smaller Petros (we called him Baby Petros), speaking fast and with an earnestness that I never saw in English. They never explained it to me – the crisis, the protests, the disappointment – and I never asked. When you come from somewhere in the aftermath, you don't always want to talk about it, not to outsiders. You might try to explain, but then not like what you find yourself saying, or the sound of your own voice. You might just want to be elsewhere for a little while, if only in memory.

They'd never asked me about the situation back home, and I was happy to return the favour. More than happy to tag along as a tourist, day-tripper, island hopper. First Athens, then we would drive down to the Peloponnese and take a ferry, stopping en route at some ancient theatre where Petros's friend had done sound design for a performance of Aristophanes. The play where the women withhold sex from their men, trying to stop the Peloponnesian war – surely I could relate?

Around the kitchen table in the weeks before our trip, there was a big debate about which Greek island we should visit. Mara and Petros argued over the merits and pitfalls of shortlisted candidates, Baby Petros chipping in. Which island group, for starters? Length of boat trip, and was there free camping? Wild beaches or beach infrastructure? All these matters were carefully considered. Discussing your island of choice: that was a nice national pastime. Such a dearth of islands where I came from, actually, except for the famous one. You could only go there on a tour with ex-political prisoners.

I'd been to Samothraki once – to which Petros he could only roll his eyes. The island where they held trance parties and built ovens out of mud? Could I never get enough of those dirty hippies? And Lesbos – I'd been there. Of course I had.

Did I fancy Rafa? Was that it? Did I like girls with matted hair? Did I like hanging around with people who left a dirty scum in the bath?

I wasn't quite sure myself. Was she beautiful, or more like – striking? During meditations I'd snatched glances at her side profile through half-closed eyes: Neolithic brow, proud Genoese nose, neck and cheeks so pale a brown that the blue of veins showed through. Both she and Steve had quite bony faces with accentuated features, the kind you might see in old Dutch paintings. Faces from a time when there was a more varied, more forgiving sense of what people should or could look like. Though sometimes I did wish (a little guiltily) that she, that both of them, were a little better looking.

In Athens we stayed in Mara's family apartment. People here lived out their European lives in rented apartments, perfectly comfortable – that was good to know. Her grandmother was mostly cutting vegetables in the kitchen, not feeling the need to acknowledge her guests much. In the adjoining apartment was her aunt, who I only saw through a crack in the door. She was suffering from Huntington's disease. Mara said it haunted the genes of her family. Her brother was also unwell and had gone into a psychiatric clinic for a while.

The apartment was dimmed by blinds in the summer heat. Petros stayed in the bedroom with aircon, pawing at his laptop in the gloom while Mara showed me the city. He'd never been to the Acropolis, and he wasn't going to break that perfect record on my account. So she took me, then to her favourite cafes and bookshops, leading me through narrow streets near the city centre.

Look there was still some white powder on the pavement. Could I smell that? The lingering scent of tear gas. The sounds of protest would sometimes echo in the distance, as if important things were happening just off-stage.

No police were allowed on the campus nearby, Mara said, the Athens Polytechnic. Because in the 1970s the regime had sent a tank through the gates, killing many people. Ever since, no police were allowed on university property in Greece. So this neighbourhood became a state within a state, a haven for anarchists and left-wing dreamers. Or drug dealers and organised crime – depending on your politics. Petros would say criminals, though actually he loved hanging out here, ogling the students and drinking iced coffees.

It was bewildering, I said, not being able to read general signage and the slogans on the walls. But there were some English phrases here and there: Smash G20 and Right to Laziness. The hostile Tourists Out! was offset by Chill Bro. Fuck the Police came round often, once in beautiful calligraphy, high as a whole building. There was even a Fuck Street Art, scrawled over some mural of a manga teddy bear in a gas mask or a bug-eyed alien, a wizard or a lizard. Every building, every steel shutter and bus stop was covered in the stuff, like an infestation, like a kitsch and gaudy dream rising out of the asphalt, climbing up the walls.

I thought of Steve and how much he would like it here. This, I imagined, was his natural habitat. And I remembered his definition of an anarchist, as explained to the local tradesman who'd arrived on the island with his daughter and white van, who'd said he was confused, because didn't anarchy mean chaos and violence?

Steve replied (the most lucid speech I even heard him give) that the word had been twisted from its real meaning. Because most people secretly resented being told what to do, but they also loved it, and they feared real freedom. And so they resented those who raised things that touched them close, who questioned the idea of authority – they pushed them away, twisting their ideas into something else.

But that was getting too abstract, rather put it like this. If you were in a public toilet and you cleaned up your own mess rather than leaving it for someone else to do, if you took hold of that toilet brush without being forced or noticed, then you were an anarchist. And those were the kind of people he wanted on his island.

Fair enough, said the local dad.

Mara and I walked and walked in the heat, through the narrow streets, hours of walking, looking, talking. We climbed a hill, passing old fires, beer cans, toilet paper, burnt plastic and broken chairs. We saw the Acropolis from a distance and the entire bowl of the city, its white buildings spread in all directions.

Petros's mother lived in a smaller apartment across the city, where we arrived to find her deep-frying octopus. He immediately began arguing with her over the finer points of the whitebait or artichoke prep. She took us into the lounge to show us photo albums of her only child. Mara and I had to stifle our laughter. What are you doing, he was shouting from the kitchen, what are you showing them? When Petros's mother went back to arguing with her son in the kitchen, Mara carefully peeled a photo out of the album and placed it in a book in her bag.

Next day we struck out from the city in a small red Nissan. By evening we were sitting in the dusk at the great open-air theatre of Epidaurus. The shallow rake of the stone seats made the trees and hills behind seem part of the staging, a diorama stretching even up to the blue mountains in the distance. Mara said that was typical of ancient Greek theatres, though not Roman ones. Petros said the acoustics were miraculous: if you whispered down at the bottom, people could hear it right at the back of a 14 000-seat amphitheatre.

Look there was a Petros Papapetropoulos in the orchestra, said Mara. Viola player.

Petros yanked up his hoodie and began waving his arms like Ginger Kev.

Notorious Petropoulos, poppin' off the top of this acropolis!

It was a joke we had about how long it would take a Greek rapper to spell his own name (like the Notorious B.I.G.), what with all the I's and O's and U's.

Fuck peace, stop the war!

You're such a dickhead, said Mara, laughing.

Just before the play began there was a commotion in the audience. A couple began arguing a few rows in front of us, first in low voices but gradually more heated. They were glamorous, beautifully dressed – and neither of them were backing down. Other audience members were now getting involved, shushing them, beginning to shout and scold.

But at a certain moment, a very delicious moment, the fight tipped into something so overblown and theatrical that we realised: it *was* theatre. The Aristophanes had begun, a play all about discord between the worlds of men and women, with two actors planted in the crowd to kick things off.

As darkness fell, Mara and Petros translated dialogue from either side, filling me in on the plot. But it was okay, I told them as another man capered around the stage in anguish, begging for sex, humping the scooters, lamp posts and other street furniture of this modern adaptation – I got the gist.

At a restaurant afterwards we met Stavros, the long-haired man who did the score and was now holding court at a big outside table. People didn't appreciate how much work it was to compose electronically, Stavros said, so he'd been putting down extra names on the programme, names of his friends. When producers saw a whole ensemble of real musicians listed, they were inclined to pay better – they didn't understand contemporary sound design. All the tour guides went on about the fabled acoustics of the theatre, Stavros said, but that was a bit of a myth. He'd even set up sensitive recording equipment at various points in the stone seats to see if they could pick up whispers, or paper being torn on stage, or the proverbial pin being dropped. But no – so the actors wore concealed mics, taped to their cheeks and painted skin colour. People complained otherwise.

I liked seeing Petros being a little subverted like this, a little wrong-footed on home ground, especially by the only person he'd ever confessed any admiration for. Stavros, Stavros, Stavros – you should rather stay with your boyfriend, Mara said, squeezing my arm. Us two can carry on to the island.

It happened again when he miscalculated the drive to the ferry port and now we were rushing along the coastal roads, looking at the boat in the distance, even beginning to hear its horn sound. Would we make the ferry to Kythera? It suddenly seemed like everything rested on that, on the vessel we were rushing for in the late afternoon – though in a rare idiomatic blip, they said 'running for'. Eventually just a dark shape against a sea of golden light, us running for it madly, tiny car slamming round the curves like this was our last chance of leaving for another world.

On the island, Petros regained the upper hand a little. He did this mainly by starving us, not allowing us to eat breakfast, then making us swim and snorkel all morning, holding off lunch until the last possible moment, not allowing us to place the order – he would see to all that.

So that when the food arrived, it was momentous. The feta came in one dry, crumbly slab at the top of the salad, sprinkled with oregano. The red onion tasted sweet.

Fish is fruit, Petros would say, ordering a grilled catch of the day. A table of food that was either raw or cooked very quickly, simply. Charred red peppers in oil, smoky aubergine, bread and water as standard. One meal, one long meal a day.

We stayed in a small house in the middle of the island. From there it was an easy drive to various beaches, and the village was one of the few places with running water. The name gave that away. Millopotamus: place of mills and potable water.

My companions were going very brown – they seemed almost in competition. With his balding head and heavy, ironic eyes, Petros was beginning to look a bit (I said) like Salman Rushdie.

Little white racist, he said. Worried about his sunburn! Careful now, don't forget your knees.

He drove us to beaches in the middle of the day, turned us loose in the tremendous heat, as if in a kind of sociological experiment. Then made us rank the sunbathers around us – like this woman hiring an umbrella. Gold, silver or bronze medal?

Maybe not a medallist, said Mara, but special mention.

Fucking orange medallist, said Petros. Too much self-tan.

I wasn't sure whether I could ask Mara to rub sunscreen into my back. Especially after that walk in Athens with her, in that tangle of narrow streets. So I asked Petros.

Fuck no, he said. Would you rub it into mine? He turned his back towards me, vast and hairy. I imagined trying to work the cream through all of that.

Exactly.

Now he began packing up our things, glaring across the beach. Some kids had arrived with guitars and djembe drums, and it was crucial that we leave before sunset. He could already smell the stink of weed. Maybe I wanted to go and join them for some Kum ba yah (whenever I picked up a guitar, Petros would sing Kum ba yah, loudly and tonelessly, until I put it down again).

I kept wondering when Mara was going to slip that photograph out of the book and confront him with it, the picture taken from his mother's album. It showed a younger Petros with long hair and a headband that made him look like a tennis player, sitting cross legged around a campfire and playing campfire guitar. Could it be? The maestro? With a joint in his mouth and playing guitar for people in patchwork pants, people wearing shoulder bags decorated with beads and those little bits of mirror. On the back was written *New Year's Eve 1999, Σαμοθράκη*. Samothraki, said Mara, land of the lotus eaters.

I came to realise she'd kept the photo less as ammunition than memento. A reminder, she said, that we should all be a little kinder to our younger selves. Else we could be a little cruel when we saw them reappear in other people, not so? She didn't think that she and Petros would spend another summer together.

We drove back to Athens the way we'd come, through Epidaurus and Sparta. Dropping me off at the airport, there was a problem. I wanted to fly to Heathrow and pick up my long-haul flight home – or back to where I'd come from, anyway.

But that flight didn't start in Heathrow, the man at the desk told me. It started in Edinburgh. He was late middle-aged with a moustache and greying hair, a veteran of check-in.

Yes, I knew there was a connecting flight prior, Edinburgh-Heathrow. But I wouldn't be taking that one, I just wanted to pick up the longer flight. So Athens-London, London-Cape Town.

Petros was incredulous: What the fuck? It's not like changing a bus!

Mara stepped forward, looked the man in the eye and asked: How can we resolve this? Please tell us sir, what do you advise? And then spoke to him in Greek.

Eventually he tapped at his keyboard, phoned his supervisor, made a plan.

Lucky she is your girlfriend.

The baggage disappeared on its little conveyor.

V

The ferry to Eigg was small and carless. It pulled out backwards from the mainland, then threaded the islets and skerries. The west coast receded, along with the pale grey strands of rain that clung to it, leaving us in the clear. It would be two or three days of holy sunshine.

On the ferry to a small island, Mara said, you could scope out the cast of characters who would be part of your trip. The locals sat inside; they'd done this journey many times before. But on the outside deck we had two guys drinking mid-morning beers and a woman wearing big headphones – maybe she was trying to avoid their attentions.

There was only one taxi on the island, driven by a man named Charlie. There was only one road, which led from the ferry port in the south to the cabin where we were staying, with views north. The cliffs of Rum, wild and austere, then Skye beyond and the Cuillin ridge.

Mara had written to say that she was about to leave Scotland. It was three, four, five years after she talked me onto a flight back home. She was tired of contract lecturing and was going to be a schoolteacher in Paris. But she would do one more trip before she left, to the isle of Eigg, and did I want to come?

Rum, Eigg and Muck – I remembered those names, the Small Isles. I remembered my mother smiling about them. We had visited Skye together when I was about four years old, so it must be close to my earliest memory: my mother pronouncing those names with delight. And then another, Camasunary, which was somewhere we had stayed. It sounded magical to me, like an incantation: Camasunary.

Charlie was at the pier to meet us, a big man with red beard and an old Merc full of dog hair. We hadn't booked a taxi, he was just there. He seemed to know all the places to wait for visitors: outside the minimarket or at the bottom of the Sgùrr, a giant chunk of granite that loomed over the southern part of the island. Just when we were tired of walking, there Charlie would be, with radio on and car door open, holding out a flask of whiskey.

He pointed out the wind turbines and the solar panels, telling us that Eigg was all renewables and off-grid: solar, wind, tides. The local community had clubbed together and bought the island from the landowner, so it was one of the few that was communally owned – most of the others were lairds and absentee landlords and all that. He said there were about a hundred islanders, and when there was a great sunset, everyone posted it on Facebook, each from their different angle. And you had to be sure to like each one, it being a small community and all.

We re-encountered the ferry passengers at our log cabins. The owner Mick showed us all around, and said he wanted to sell up, by the way, in case anyone was interested. Beautiful views, beach with famous singing sands, more cabins than he knew what to do with – and a whole fleet of vehicles thrown in too. He pointed to a line of rusted caravans, tractors, a Land Rover. No pub on the island so he'd built one, The Whale's Head, in an old bothy. Come inside.

We bent down to enter the old stone building. Inside was a darts board, a picture of Marilyn Monroe with tinsel round her neck and a mummified cat that had been found when redoing the dry-stone walls – this was propped on the mantel. The centrepiece of The Whale's Head was a round pool table: a disc of green felt about a meter in diameter, with a single pocket in the centre. It was hooked up to a motor powered by a golf buggy battery, and by flicking a switch you could make the disc revolve. The pub was tiny and you didn't have space to play the shot from the wall or the corner – so then you hit the switch and it came round to you.

The two beer-drinkers were a journalist and photographer doing a story on the upcoming referendum, when the Scots would vote on being independent from England. They were talking to 100 people throughout the land and had pitched Eigg to the editor because it was 100 per cent renewable energy. But when they got here they were told it was only 85 per cent renewables. And where was the story in that? Didn't matter, they'd decided to just have a good time.

The woman with the headphones was a noise artist from Madrid. She was here on a residency, to record the sound of the beaches that sang and squeaked when you walked on them. Also the bubbles and insects of the peat bogs, trying to understand these natural cycles through sound. Here was a picture of a treble clef she had drawn in the sand, and then walked on.

That sounded like fun, I said to Mara in our cabin, which had thin red curtains and a view north. A wooden stile led you over the fence and to the sea.

Sounded like too much EU funding, she said, pouring a grappa. Like Beth, Petros's ex, who made art out of food and put the sausages in jars – remember? She knew they'd carried on sleeping together, Mara said. But what did it matter now.

When we weren't in the red cabin we were walking. Up the Sgùrr, or along the ridgeline behind us, up to the Finger of God – the rock spire that, Charlie said, all islanders were expected to stand on at some point. We walked for hours in the holy weather.

On top of the ridge, I checked the OS maps and realised that we were looking due north, over the sea to Skye, right into the bay of Camasunary. I told Mara about my childhood memory of it, or the name anyway. And then how I had made a pilgrimage back there, on that long, lonely cycle trip years ago. Rolling on and off ferries with my bike, stashing my red panniers in the bracken and hiking onwards where the road ended.

I wanted to go back to that enchanted place, Camasunary, which I remembered my mother saying so clearly. I could remember her tone of voice as she said it, even after I had forgotten so much about her, and after she had forgotten everything.

But when I arrived, the pebble beach was choked with litter, plastic waste from fishing boats and the salmon farms, the trash thrown overboard by shipping, which the currents gathered and brought there. Bits of synthetic rope, tangled netting, plastic drums, crates, bottles, earbuds, flipflops, the corner hunks of polystyrene trays. The whole beach was caked in it, a metre deep, clotted with it. A cow was chewing, choking on a plastic rope. I almost gave up right there, but fortunately I didn't, since it was the journey when I ended up meeting Steve and Rafa, in a place almost as idyllic as this one. But mid-way, there was this terrible beach that had made me retch with misery, world sadness and private sadness all mixed up.

And then to look back at it from here, Camasunary, across the water and across time, like an open secret. As if it was the light echo of a star, or a world that no longer existed but still emitted so much love – I couldn't really explain. Maybe the place I was looking for could only be in the past, not the future. Not the past, in memory rather; but then only if it was barely remembered, almost unscathed by memory.

After Skye, I crossed to Mull, cycled to Iona and lit a candle for my mother in the abbey there, thinking that, when I was four and travelling through these islands with her, an idea of beauty was imprinted, deposited in my young head, and that twenty or thirty years later I was still redeeming it. The glens streamed with waterfalls and a following wind whistled through them, whipping me back to the ferry in no time at all.

A few years after our trip to Eigg, Mara wrote to say she'd met a man while teaching in Paris, a Tunisian, and fallen pregnant – unexpectedly. It meant that she'd finally taken the genetic test for Huntington's disease, one she'd avoided all her life, and it had come back negative. She loved being a mother. Petros had three kids, by the way, despite always saying how much he hated children. She sent pictures of forest fires in Greece, the glow of flames behind the Acropolis. I should come and visit before there was nothing left, here or anywhere. Also, there were regular beach clean-ups in Camasunary, by local volunteers – she sent a link.

Steve and I never spoke again after our walk above the Cinque Terre – there was no falling out, life just went that way. When we'd talked and talked with all the pent-up speech from the Buddhist retreat, and he'd been wrestling with two opposing, equally true truths. One was that you should accept the world just as it was, without bitterness or resentment (like Rafa did, still meditating away back there, washing her soul clean). The other was that you could *never* accept the world as it was. Because it was such a mess, and there was so much injustice. And so you had to fight, make a noise, ask about ingredients, be otherwise.

Rafa and I wrote to each other for a few years, not emails but actual letters that followed me even when I moved back home, or to the city that slowly became one, where I sit now with some old photos on the walls. A man and woman at a fireplace, staring back over armchairs at the camera. A rock pillar rising out of the sea. A bike with red panniers, a bridge under construction.

Rafa had left Tonno, the village in the mountains, to become a carer, looking after old people mainly. She'd also gone back to university: much better now that she was older and knew who she was. She told me Steve had lost a toe from frostbite after getting caught in the Alps, but otherwise he was doing well – the toe didn't affect his ability to cycle everywhere. He was in Copenhagen now, in that part of town where the squatters and anarchists lived – it was even a kind of tourist attraction.

She still had the number of that red callbox on the island, the one where we'd met, remember? And sometimes she would dial the number, just to think of it there, alone on a hillside under the grey skies, just to hear it ring.

Notes and sources

v   *A journey is a gesture inscribed in space* ... Damon Galgut, *In a Strange Room* (2010). Reproduced with permission.

6   *wreathe waves in glory* ... William Finnegan, *Barbarian Days: A Surfing Life* (2016).

21   *'segregated lavatories' of the Company's Garden* ... Alex La Guma, *In the Fog of the Seasons' End* (1974).

23   *with a touch of Nuremberg* ... Paul Maylam, *The Cult of Rhodes: Remembering an Imperialist in Africa* (2005).

24   *almost as significant an organ as Cleopatra's nose* ... William Plomer, *Cecil Rhodes* (1933).

27   *he would immediately be sent to a psychiatric institution* ... Lynette Johns, 'Mental asylum is full of prophets, court told', Independent Online, 4 September 2001.

48   *the more rarefied category of fiasco* ... *This American Life* podcast 699: Fiasco! 'What happens when fumble leads to error leads to mishap and before you know it you have left the realm of ordinary mistake and chaos, and you have entered into the more ethereal, specialized realm of fiasco?'

61   *A subterranean pollen-scent of chemicals* ... Nadine Gordimer (with David Goldblatt), *On the Mines* (1973).

69   *the familiar shrink-wrapped equivalents in a supermarket meat case* ... Jonathan Franzen, 'My Father's Brain', in *How to Be Alone* (2002).

69   *a line of light under a locked door* ... From Patricia Lockwood's *No One Is Talking About This* (2021).

72   *a fully equipped moral self* ... These ideas draw on Dasha Kiper's *Travellers to Unimaginable Lands: Stories of Dementia, the Caregiver, and the Human Brain* (2023).

84   *The telephone book of most cities* ... From a review by Michael Jackson in *Utopian Studies* 11: 1 (2000).

86   *But scratch the surface a little* ... Margaret Atwood, *In Other Worlds: SF and the Human Imagination* (2012).

86 *Once the dream of paradise starts to turn into reality, however* ... Milan Kundera, *The Book of Laughter and Forgetting* (1979).

87 *a defining, constitutive feature of humanity* ... Zygmunt Bauman, 'Utopia with no Topos', *History of the Human Sciences*, 16(1) (2003).

91 *wonderful places to be a child and terrible places to be a teenager* ... Lyman Tower Sargent, *Utopianism: A Very Short Introduction* (2010).

91 *Beetles everywhere, spiders, ants in the milk* ... A letter from Millie Polak to her sister-in-law in England, trying to convince the latter not to leave her life behind and travel to Gandhi's Phoenix ashram. It appears in Ramachandra Guha's *Gandhi Before India* (2013).

92 *every fruit-juice drinker, nudist, sandal-wearer, sex-maniac* ... George Orwell, *The Road to Wigan Pier* (1937).

94 *the most beautiful eye of any living creature* ... George Orwell, 'Some Thoughts on the Common Toad' (1946).

103 *its nonexistence combined with a* topos ... Gregory Claeys and Lyman Tower Sargent, *The Utopia Reader* (1999).

103 *A map of the world that does not include Utopia* ... Oscar Wilde, *The Soul of a Man Under Socialism* (1891).

104 *As more and more of the earth's surface is mapped* ... This section draws on Margaret Atwood's essay 'Dire Cartographies' from her 2012 collection *In Other Worlds*.

104 *As soon as you, the writer, have said* ... Ursula K. Le Guin, *The Language of the Night: Essays on Fantasy and Science Fiction* (1979).

106 *The trouble is that we have a bad habit* ... Ursula K. Le Guin, 'The Ones Who Walk Away from Omelas' (1973). Republished in *The Wind's Twelve Quarters* (1975).

109 *But, knowing only that I didn't want to study war no more* ... Ursula K. Le Guin, Introduction, *Hainish Novels & Stories*, Volume One (2017).

110 *I'm interested in anthropology because I'm interested in human possibilities* ... David Graeber, Charlie Rose Conversations, https://charlierose.com/videos/10730 (2006).

111 *and the strongest, in the existence of any social species* ... Ursula K. Le Guin, *The Dispossessed: An Ambiguous Utopia* (1974).

112 *no embroidered uniforms, but much goodwill* ... Peter Kropotkin, *The Conquest of Bread* (1892).

112 *it would strip the world bare like locusts* ... Mahatma Gandhi, *Young India* (1928).

113 *The divine man has no right to waste money* ... Reece is quoting Frederick Evans, an elder of the Shaker settlement New Lebanon in New York. Erik Reece, *Utopia Drive* (2016).

115 *if God were to put our planet around another star* ... Margaret Turnbull, addressing the 2006 AAAS Annual Meeting.

115 *an island apparently so fundamentally hostile to human flourishing* ... Judah Bierman, 'Ambiguity in Utopia: *The Dispossessed*', *Science Fiction Studies* 2(3) (1975).

119 *levels of human perturbation of the Earth System* ... Will Steffen et al., 'Planetary boundaries: Guiding human development on a changing planet', *Science* 347(6223) (2015).

120 *before the genre was reinvented* ... Jill Lepore explores the relation between SF, X-capitalism and 'Muskism' in her podcast 'The Evening Rocket' (Pushkin, 2021).

120 *some fiction that might actually come to pass* ... Kim Stanley Robinson, 'Dystopias Now', *Commune* 5 (2020).

121 *a non-human-centred and perhaps impossible love* ... Stephanie LeMenager, 'Climate Change and the Struggle for Genre' in *Anthropocene Reading: Literary History in Geologic Times*, ed. Tobias Menely and Jesse Oak Taylor (2017).

146 Utopiensium Alphabetum (Utopian Alphabet) from the 1516 Louvain edition of Thomas More's *Utopia*.

147 *numberless projects of social reform* ... Ralph Waldo Emerson to Thomas Carlyle, 30 October 1840.

147 *a salve against the broken materialism of the West* ... Akash Kapur, *Better to Have Gone: Love, Death, and the Quest for Utopia* (2022).

155 *an expensive but rather vulgar gift from another galaxy* ... Ian Jack, 'You can find utopia in India – if you're willing to close your eyes', *The Guardian*, 5 May 2018.

156 *take your eyes off something for five minutes* ... David Wickenden, 'A Pottery for Auroville' (1982). Reprinted in *Auroville: Dream and Reality*, ed. Akash Kapur (2018).

156 *before the seeds could sprout* ... Excerpt from 'Amrith' by R. Meenakshi, translated from the Tamil by the author. First published in *Seeds of Flame* (1983) in Auroville. Reproduced with permission from the author.

156 *this particular area wants to remain wilderness* ... Alan Herbert, 'A Living Being' (2009). This also appears in Kapur's anthology (see above).

160 *an eco-village where a visitor can get a good cappuccino* ... Emily Schmall, 'Build a New City or New Humans? A Utopia in India Fights Over Future', *The New York Times*, 5 March 2022.

161 *smacks of spiritual authoritarianism* ... Hannah Ellis-Petersen, 'Bulldozers, violence and politics crack an Indian dream of utopia', *The Guardian*, 16 January 2022.

161 *a referendum on human nature* ... Chris Jennings, *Paradise Now: The Story of American Utopianism* (2016).

164 *a significant leakage in both directions is allowed* ... Amit Chaudhuri, *Finding the Raga: An Improvisation on Indian Music* (2021).

165 *music subjected to a kind of 'jet lag'* ... Menon is quoted in Chaudhuri, *Finding the Raga*.

165 *improvisation is deferral* ... Chaudhuri, *Finding the Raga*.

171 *a huge black mountain of water* ... Richard Lloyd Parry, *Ghosts of the Tsunami* (2017).

208 *Like all couples, they needed witnesses from the external world* ...Pankaj Mishra, *The Romantics* (1999).

Acknowledgements

My thanks to everyone who read and commented on drafts. Thank you to my editors and publishers: Angela, Caren and Jeremy. Above all, thank you Anna.

This book is dedicated to my mother, Carola Margaret Rose Seath.

www.ingramcontent.com/pod-product-compliance
Lightning Source LLC
Chambersburg PA
CBHW070142100426
42743CB00013B/2794